ABE QCF Study Manuals

People Planning and Resourcing

Diploma Level 5
Human Resource Management

In this December 2011 first edition:

- Full and comprehensive coverage of the key topics within the subject
- Activities, examples and quizzes
- Discussion points
- Practical illustrations and case studies
- Index
- Fully up to date as at December 2011

BPP Learning Media

First edition December 2011

Published ISBN 9781 4453 7942 5

British Library Cataloguing-in-Publication Data
A catalogue record for this book is available from the British Library

Published by
BPP Learning Media Ltd
BPP House, Aldine Place
London W12 8AA

www.bpp.com/learningmedia

Printed in the United Kingdom

Your learning materials, published by BPP Learning Media Ltd, are printed on paper sourced from sustainable, managed forests.

We are grateful to the Association of Business Executives for permission to reproduce the Learning Outcomes.

Contents

Introduction

Welcome to the first edition of the BPP Learning Media Study Manual for the ABE HRM Level 5 Diploma unit, People Planning and Resourcing.

Business qualifications are traditionally very demanding. Students therefore need learning resources which go to the heart of the topics involved, yet are user-friendly and sufficiently interactive to retain the student's attention and interest. This book achieves exactly that.

This book has been specifically designed to cover the syllabus content and learning outcomes issued by the ABE for this unit, and has been reviewed and approved by the ABE.

Features include:

- An introduction to each chapter and a list of specific study objectives
- Concise yet comprehensive coverage of syllabus topics
- Activities and discussion topics to ensure student participation and ensure progress
- Chapter round-ups and quizzes to consolidate knowledge.

Features in this Study Manual

Definitions of important concepts. You really need to know and understand these before the exam.

Ideas and topics which are designed to be thought-provoking, or possibly controversial. If you are attending a college, you will be able to discuss the topics with your lecturer and classmates. If you are studying alone, you can use the discussion topics as a stimulus for thought and brainstorming of ideas, or raise the issues with a friend or workmate and see what perspective they can add.

Where you may find it helpful or interesting to carry out further research, we include references to websites that you may like to visit.

ACTIVITY — Activities give you a chance to test the knowledge that you have acquired and think more widely around the subject. In some cases suggested answers are supplied, and you should refer to these once you have had a good attempt at the activity. In other cases, the activity involves you considering your own experience, so there may not be a formal answer supplied.

An illustration of a particular technique or concept, generally with a solution or outcome that demonstrates a particular point.

A practical example or illustration, usually involving a real-world scenario, intended to stimulate thought.

Chapter Roundup — Reviews the key areas covered in the chapter

Quick Quiz — A set of short, sharp questions testing your knowledge of the topics in the chapter.

Syllabus and Learning outcomes

Learning Outcome 1

The learner will: Understand the principles behind the design, implementation and review of people (human resources) plans.

Assessment criteria	Indicative content	Chapter where covered
The learner can:		
1.1 Explain the purposes and potential benefits of people planning.	1.1.1 The purposes and goals of people planning, with special reference to the links between people planning and an organisation's strategic goals, vision, mission, values and 'Big Idea'. 1.1.2 The benefits of systematic people planning, especially for organisations relatively untouched by turbulence, uncertainty and discontinuous change.	1
1.2 Assess the disadvantages and dangers of people planning in a turbulent, highly competitive and fast-moving world.	1.2.1 The continuing debate about the value and relevance of people planning in today's world of work and organisations, characterised by constant uncertainties, turbulence, discontinuous change, political disturbance (in some regions), and globalised competition.	1
1.3 Design a cost-effective people plan for a specified corporate scenario.	1.3.1 The development of people plans appropriate for specified corporate scenarios, incorporating the organisation's high-level strategy, its people demand requirements and supply forecasts, plus proposed action plans to address any significant discrepancies.	1
1.4 Create mechanisms for measuring and monitoring the effectiveness of a people plan during its implementation, and where necessary devise remedial processes to ensure its continued relevance and value.	1.4.1 Mechanisms and techniques for measuring and monitoring the effectiveness of a given people plan. 1.4.2 The creation of risk assessments and contingency plans within people plans, plus remedial programmes for implementation where necessary in order to ensure that the people plan remains relevant and worthwhile.	1

Learning Outcome 2

The learner will: Know how to identify and take account of all the relevant internal factors when designing the people plan.

Assessment criteria	Indicative content	Chapter where covered
The learner can:		
2.1 Describe systematic methods for analysing the strengths and weaknesses of a workforce.	2.1.1 Systematic methods for analysing the strengths and weaknesses of an organisation's current workforce in relation to the organisation's future human resource requirements.	2

Assessment criteria	Indicative content	Chapter where covered
2.2 Identify methods for calculating key indices of organisational performance through people and show how the results may be interpreted in order to undertake remedial action if appropriate.	2.2.1 Principal techniques for assessing and quantifying various indices of people performance and contribution, plus a range of courses of action to resolve difficulties where necessary.	1, 2
2.3 Explain the corporate benefits to be gained from securing high levels of employee commitment and engagement.	2.3.1 The commercial, competitive and strategic benefits to be gained from creating a workforce characterised by high levels of employee commitment and engagement.	8, 10
2.4 Explain how to construct commercially-defensible plans for promoting employee commitment and engagement throughout a given workforce.	2.4.1 The methods and techniques typically used by organisations seeking to secure high levels of commitment and engagement from their employees.	2, 8
2.5 Apply the above knowledge and skills to specified organisational scenarios.	2.5.1 The application of the above models, tools and principles to broadly-defined corporate scenarios.	2, 8

Learning Outcome 3

The learner will: Know how to identify and take account of all the relevant external factors when designing the people plan.

Assessment criteria	Indicative content	Chapter where covered
The learner can:		
3.1 Describe the features of any given labour market (local, national, international or global) and their application in corporate people planning.	3.1.1 The principal features of any given labour market: geographic (local, national, international or global), demographic, political, psychological (whether work is viewed as a central life interest or merely a financial necessity) and cultural features.	3
3.2 Construct a well-informed set of predictions concerning the future labour market, generally and in relation to particular locations, regions or types of labour.	3.2.1 The future of any given labour market both generally in relation to the above features, but also in relation to specified categories or 'segments' within the working population, e.g. skilled/unskilled manual workers, the service sector, IT, management etc.	3
3.3 Evaluate the significance of key external variables – principally political, economic, social and technological factors – for the design of people plans.	3.3.1 The significance of all relevant external variables (PESTLE: political, economic, social, technological, legal and environmental) so far as the development of labour markets is concerned.	3

Assessment criteria	Indicative content	Chapter where covered
3.4 Apply the above knowledge and skills to specified organisational and business-sector scenarios.	3.4.1 The analysis and application of the above principles, models and techniques to particular organisational scenarios.	3

Learning Outcome 4

The learner will: Understand the major approaches to people resourcing used by organisations in the modern world.

Assessment criteria	Indicative content	Chapter where covered
The learner can:		
4.1 Describe the high-level purposes for people resourcing, especially related to an organisation's vision and strategic goals.	4.1.1 The goals and objectives for an effective, business-focused people resourcing strategy.	4
4.2 Identify the principal routes through which people resourcing may be undertaken, and the contingencies that may affect approaches to people resourcing in a variety of contexts.	4.2.1 The range of people resourcing routes, processes and systems (including traditional/systematic models and techniques, and transformational visions for employee engagement) identified and evaluated according to their generic suitability as well as their specific relevance to any given set of corporate and resourcing strategies (especially for organisations pursuing a transformational vision for employee engagement).	
4.3 Explain the legal, ethical and professional background to people resourcing.	4.3.1 The legal, ethical and professional criteria which govern the strategies and operational systems for people resourcing.	4, 5, 9

Learning Outcome 5

The learner will: Understand what is involved in recruitment and selection, including all relevant ethical/legal and professional aspects and methods for evaluating the effectiveness of recruitment and selection systems.

Assessment criteria	Indicative content	Chapter where covered
The learner can:		
5.1 Explain how to design and embed cost-effective recruitment/selection strategies, procedures and systems, both in general and also when catering for specified contingenices.	5.1.1 The development and design of recruitment and selection strategies/practices targeted towards specific resourcing scenarios and functioning within appropriate legal/ethical/professional criteria and standards.	5

Assessment criteria	Indicative content	Chapter where covered
5.2 Explain how to design recruitment/selection processes which do not unfairly discriminate on grounds of gender, ethnic differences, age, religion, sexual orientation or disability.	5.2.1 The basic establishment of recruitment and selection systems which do not discriminate on any grounds: religious, ethnic, gender, sexual orientation, age or disability.	5
5.3 Describe the specific recruitment and selection processes used by organisations when resourcing across national borders.	5.3.1 The development and implementation of recruitment and selection processes used by organisations when recruiting across national borders.	4
5.4 Explain the necessity for systematically measuring the effectiveness of recruitment and selection and identify the problems of accurate measurement.	5.4.1 Methods for analysing and measuring effectiveness (the 'validity' and 'reliability') of recruitment and selection. 5.4.2 The complexities involved in calculating the effectiveness of people resourcing strategies and practices, including the problem of defining cause/effect relationships, the potential impact of intervening factors or variables and the selection of meaningful criteria.	6, 7

Learning Outcome 6

The learner will: Understand the processes and activities which together comprise systematic, cost-effective recruitment and selection.

Assessment criteria	Indicative content	Chapter where covered
The learner can:		
6.1 Explain the various methods of recruitment available to organisations and identify relevant criteria for choosing appropriate methods.	6.1.1 The various methods of recruitment available to organisations and their characteristics, applications, cost-effectiveness (both generically and in specific recruitment scenarios), benefits and disadvantages. 6.1.2 The development of defensible criteria to be used as the basis of recruitment plans for resolving previously-defined requirements.	6
6.2 Describe and explain the growing use of technology within recruitment, with special reference to e-recruitment.	6.2.1 The applications of technology to recruitment, with special reference to the scope, advantages and disadvantages of e-recruitment.	6
6.3 Evaluate the use of different tools to underpin an effective recruitment process.	6.3.1 The design, use and evaluation of job descriptions (accountability profiles) and person specifications (competency frameworks).	6

6.4 Identify and evaluate the various methods of selection available to organisations and devise and justify appropriate methods of selection to be used when selecting for specific vacancies.	6.4.1 The principle methods of selection available to organisations and their characteristics, applications, cost-effectiveness (both generically and in specific selection scenarios), benefits and disadvantages, concentrating on selection interview, psychometric testing, assessment centres, application forms and references/testimonials. 6.4.2 Methods for evaluating the effectiveness of the selection interview, psychometric tests, assessment centres, application forms and references/testimonials. 6.4.3 The construction of defensible selection plans to cater for specified selection scenarios. 6.4.4 The design and application of selection techniques which cater cost-effectively for special-case scenarios e.g. transient organisations.	5, 7
6.5 Assess the circumstances in which organisations may outsource parts of their people resourcing activities to recruitment agencies and/or other outsourcing providers and specialists.	6.5.1 The application of outsourcing in people resourcing, including the use of recruitment agencies and/or other outsourcing providers and specialists.	4, 5

Learning Outcome 7

The learner will: Understand the systematic and businesslike methods for encouraging employee retention and managing employee departures (through voluntary turnover, retirement, redundancy or dismissal).

Assessment criteria	Indicative content	Chapter where covered
The learner can:		
7.1 Describe both the benefits and risks associated with strategies and practices specifically intended to improve employee retention.	7.1.1 A review of the benefits and risks associated with employee retention and employee 'loyalty'.	2
7.2 Identify the standard methods for measuring and analysing labour turnover.	7.2.1 Definitions for labour turnover and the principal methods for measuring the incidence of turnover.	2
7.3 Explain how to implement the various mechanisms available to organisations in order to manage employee retirements and redundancy programmes in ways that are legally and ethically compliant yet are also businesslike and cost-effective.	7.3.1 Procedures for the systematic, legally-compliant, ethically-appropriate and cost-effective management of employee retirements and redundancy programmes.	2, 4, 9

Assessment criteria	Indicative content	Chapter where covered
7.4 Outline the principles and objectives that should govern the design and application of an organisation's discipline and dismissal procedure.	7.4.1 The design and implementation of a legally- and ethically-compliant discipline and dismissal procedure.	9
7.5 Identify a range of standard techniques for measuring employee absence, and cost-effective routes for reducing employee absence when absenteeism has reached the point where concerted action is required.	7.5.1 Methods for measuring employee absence. 7.5.2 Cost-effective routes to reduce (or eliminate) unnecessary employee absence on the part of individual employees, groups of employees, or throughout the organisation as a whole.	9

Learning Outcome 8

The learner will: Know how to create and apply an 'employer of choice' or 'employer brand' strategy and process platform.

Assessment criteria	Indicative content	Chapter where covered
The learner can:		
8.1 Describe what is meant by the 'employer of choice' or 'employer brand' attribution and identify the defining features.	8.1.1 The concepts of 'employer of choice' and 'employer brand' defined and explained. 8.1.2 The key ingredients found in an 'employer of choice' or 'employer brand' organisation, so far as the personnel/HR function and people-management strategies and practices are concerned.	10
8.2 Outline and explain the benefits of becoming an 'employer of choice' or an 'employer brand'.	8.2.1 A review of the benefits to be gained by the organisation (and by its workforce) from securing an 'employer of choice' or 'employer brand' status.	10
8.3 Identify and justify the actions to be taken by an employer when seeking to become an 'employer of choice' or an 'employer brand'.	8.3.1 The construction of action plans intended to transform an organisation into an 'employer of choice' or 'employer brand'.	10

Assessment

- Assessment method: written examination (unless otherwise stated).
- Written examinations are of three hours' duration.
- All learning outcomes will be assessed.

Recommended reading

Please refer to the Tuition Resources section of the Members' Area of the ABE website (www.abeuk.com) for the recommended reading for this subject.

Chapter 1

People planning

Throughout this study text the term People Planning will be used to describe the activities outlined in the next paragraph. Historically these activities were described as 'manpower planning', a later term that is often used is Human Resource Planning. As part of your studies you may find these terms used in other books and texts, essentially they are all referring to the same type of people related planning activities.

Human beings are one of the resources that an organisation must obtain and manage in pursuit of its objectives. People Planning is the task of assessing and anticipating the skill, knowledge and labour time requirements of the organisation, and initiating action to fulfil or 'source' those requirements. If the organisation (or a particular area of its activity) is declining, it may need to plan a reduction or redeployment of the labour force. If it is growing, or moving into new areas of activity, it will need to find and tap into a source of suitably skilled labour.

It is widely considered that People Planning has fallen out of favour, the reason often cited is that the rapidly changing economic situation makes such exercises futile. However the highly changeable environment is one of the primary reasons for introducing some level of planning. Without some level of prediction as to future staffing levels and skill requirements, the organisation is simply leaving too much to chance and consequently cannot expect to achieve its strategic goals.

People Planning has however evolved from the original 'manpower planning', today it is far less mechanistic, it is open to a far greater range of factors to consider. CIPD research shows that many organisations interpret the activity in a variety of ways:

- succession planning (62%)
- flexible working (53%)
- demand supply forecasting (53%)
- skills audit/gap analysis (49%)
- talent management (42%)
- multi-skilling (36%)
- role design (35%)
- risk management (34%)
- outsourcing (29%)
- career planning (28%)
- scenario planning (20%).

The primary focus of this study is on a systematic approach to planning and resourcing an organisation, this approach will include the discussion of all the above subjects, albeit some in greater detail than others.

This first chapter provides an introduction to People Planning and the various concepts and challenges associated with the topic

- scenario planning (20%).

The primary focus of this study is on a systematic approach to planning and resourcing an organisation, this approach will include the discussion of all the above subjects, albeit some in greater detail than others.

This first chapter provides an introduction to People Planning and the various concepts and challenges associated with the topic.

TOPIC LIST		LEARNING OUTCOMES
1	People Planning	1.1, 1.2
2	The process of People Planning	1.3
3	Evaluating People Planning	1.4, 2.2
4	The People Plan	1.4
5	People Planning in action	1.4

1 People Planning

1.1 Reasons for People Planning

1 **Creates a link between business and HR plans**. Much is written about the link between business and HR plans in the strategic planning of organisations. People planning ensures that the strategic plan has to be understood in order that the people plan can fit; and demonstrates to the organisation that the people planning needs to considered and incorporated.

2 **Better control over staffing costs and numbers employed.** Whatever the future prospects may be for an organisation, whether they be growth or reduction in headcount, an organisation needs a plan. If the future is unknown, it may be prudent to recruit temporary or agency workers and so design flexibility into the organisation and so in turn partition off the permanent workforce from the turbulent period.

3 **More informed judgements about the skills and attitude mix in the organisation.** Whilst headcount numbers will always be a concern, attention also needs to be given to the skills mix within the workforce. Does the current workforce have the skills and attitudes that will ensure organisational success in the future?

4 **Maintain a profile of current staff.** If HR does not know what resources it has currently, how can it plan for the future? To enhance planning, the organisation would benefit from not only knowing the numbers, position, grade etc but this would be greatly enhanced by knowledge of skills, experience etc. Marchington and Wilkinson (2008)

1.2 The historical development of People Planning

People Planning originally came into existence as 'manpower planning'. Manpower planning was heavily focused on workforce headcount predictions with particular focus on age profiles, expected leavers and growth in future positions. Whilst these factors are important is came to be realised that the heavy emphasis on headcount was overlooking other important considerations. These were factors such as cultural fit, ability to communicate with customers and personal drive and motivation. The emphasis is now on looking at a 'bigger picture' and how the People Plans support the achievement of the organisation's objectives.

UNION OIL

A review of how Union Oil conducted its People Planning in the mid-1970s gives an interesting historical insight into how people planning was conducted. As can be seen, the focus is weighted towards management positions. From this it can be seen how the practice has developed over time.

The organisation identified four key elements to people planning:

(a) Accumulating the necessary information
(b) Using an organisational change model
(c) Forecasting recruitment needs
(d) Planning managerial succession and career development

The process began with HR asking:

- Will the organisation have the mix of talents, skills, maturity, and drive required to compete in the economic environment in five years
- How many openings will occur in the top five tiers of the organisation in the next few years? How do those identified for succession compare to the current incumbents
- Are there places in the organisation where capable managers are hard to find; and yet other places that are bottlenecks of capable managers and nowhere for them to progress

- When related to financial and operating planning and outside economic events, what do productivity trends tell the organisation about manpower needs
- Does most recruitment occur in high profit years when the level of starting salaries is high and competition for good candidates the highest
- Are attrition costs under control, what are the future prospects
- Are the best-performing managers being retained, and marginal performers being managed out, or do the HR policies, including salaries and benefits, appeal to employees who prefer security to the risks of growth and innovation

The plan that was identified comprised five programmes:

- Before the process could begin a comprehensive data bank had to be created that would store the employee demographics and skills information
- A simulation model was created to provide some insight into the future
- Having suffered erratic recruitment practices, forecast the organisational recruitment needs for a five-year period
- Establish a succession planning system to enable the filling of managerial positions
- Develop a method to relate the output per employee to a range of operating goals

To simulate the impact of change on the organisation, a model was created that analysed age, function, geographical distribution, status and skill, new starters and leavers, and recognised the operational relationships and the aging process.

The model made three assumptions:

(a) In a career-orientated organisation, the age distribution of employees was roughly related to their years of service; employees were categorised under five age groups

(b) The hiring rate for each age group is fairly constant

(c) The attrition rate for each age group is fairly constant

The modelling also needed to take account of:

- The output per employee in key areas of the business
- Depending upon the size of the income generating parts of the business, the administrative support could be determined
- Changes in consumer demand
- Changes in the organisation's strategy and/or policy
- Changes in government legislation.

There were a number of observations made about the approach to people planning:

- The people planning process did not achieve optimal impact until it came to be thought of as another dimension of corporate planning
- Maintaining a reliable inventory of employee skills presented many problems
- Managers make only token adjustments as to how they see the future evolving environmental trends. Consequently HR made a number of assumptions. However, the managers were then sceptical as to the confidence that could be given to the qualitative output from the model.

The search for talent errs in favour of the currently effective managers and those who have already had any rough edges smoothed off; where is there space for the new entrepreneurs or rough diamonds? Adapated from William E Bright (Harvard Business Review 1976)

As part of the move away from the historical 'manpower planning' Liff (2000) notes that 'there has been a shift from reconciling numbers of employees available with predictable, stable jobs, towards a greater concern with skills, their development and deployment'.

(a) **Recruiting** the required number and type/quality of staff

(b) **Retaining** the required number and type/quality of staff – and therefore letting go those who are not required (by natural labour turnover and/or by planned downsizing)

(c) **Utilising** staff in the most efficient and effective manner: increasing productivity, introducing multi-skilling and other forms of flexibility and so on

(d) **Improving** the skills, capabilities and motivation of staff, so that they become a more flexible resource, capable of fulfilling emerging requirements

It is arguable that forecasting staff and skill requirements has become more *difficult* in recent times because of the increasing uncertainty and rate of change in the business environment. However, it has also arguably become more *necessary*, because the risks of 'getting it wrong' (particularly in an era of global economic recession) are correspondingly greater.

Taylor (2010) supports this thinking and explains why organisations should not be quick to dismiss its value:

(a) **People plans should be regarded as adaptable**. The perception of plans as 'set in stone' has been allowed to dominate too much of the thinking on the subject. They should be regarded as evolving and adaptable to changes in the environment. Events do not evolve so quickly that the plan cannot be updated and adapted as required. Additionally, to do so only maintains the value and relevance they can bring.

(b) **Turbulence requires more attention to planning**. In periods of high turbulence the organisational manager faces two options

    (i) Abandon any formal planning and rely entirely on intuition and being able to quickly and correctly respond when the picture becomes more clear.

    (ii) Continue to plan, however adapting the process to allow for a variety of responses and focusing on flexibility.

    If the organisation adopts the second option it will be in a position to respond even more quickly than the organisation that has adopted option a.

People planning is a form of **risk management**. It involves realistically appraising the present and anticipating the future (as far as possible) in order to get the **right people** into the **right jobs** at the **right time** *and* managing employee behaviour, organisational culture and systems in order to **maximise the human resource** in response to anticipated opportunities and threats.

1.3 People Planning and corporate planning

People Planning may be defined as a process that anticipates and maps out the consequences of business strategy on an organisation's human resources requirements. This is reflected in planning of skill and competence needs as well as headcount.

Corporate strategy is dependent upon the input from human resources, and the two are mutually interdependent. If the corporate plan envisages a cut in output, for example, or the closure of a particular plant, then the human resource plan will need to consider redeployment of staff, redundancies and so on. If the corporate plan specifies a move into a new product market, the human resource plan will have to source the required labour from outside or within the organisation, through recruitment, training or sub-contracting.

In turn, the availability of labour resources can act as a constraint on, or spur to, the achievement of corporate goals. If there are skills shortages and employees cannot be recruited or developed cost-effectively, plans for expansion or diversification may have to be curtailed. The availability of multi-skilled or expert teams, on the other hand, may inspire innovative strategies for growth and change.

Lam and Schaubroeck (cited in Torrington et al, 2002) argue that HR planning is critical to organisation strategy, because it is able to identify:

(a) **Shortfalls in organisational capability** (skills, knowledge, people) which would *prevent* the corporate plan from being implemented successfully

(b) **Surpluses in organisational capability** which might *shape* the corporate plan by suggesting opportunities to capitalise on currently under-utilised resources

(c) **Poor utilisation of people** in the organisation, which would highlight the need to add value through *revised HR practices*.

The strategic impact of HRM in general and People Planning in particular is such that we should expect to see a senior HR manager at the organisation's strategic apex, alongside the heads of other major functions such as finance and marketing.

> ***Some people might still argue that proactive forward planning to meet human resource requirements is a waste of time, especially for small to medium-sized businesses. Why does it have to be so complicated? Surely, if you are short of staff, you hire some – or train or promote some of your existing staff? And if business declines and you find yourself with superfluous staff, you make some redundancies? In fact, it is not quite so simple. We will suggest why.***

1.4 Why is People Planning necessary?

An attempt to look beyond the present and short-term future, and to prepare for contingencies, is increasingly important. Some manifestations of this are outlined below.

> [Human resource] planning has maintained its imperatives for several reasons: (i) a growing awareness of the need to look into the future, (ii) a desire to exercise control over as many variables as possible which influence business success or failure, (iii) the development of techniques which make such planning possible. Livy (1988)

(a) Jobs in innovative and fast-changing contexts may require experience and skills which cannot easily be bought in the market place, and the more complex the organisation, the more difficult it will be to supply or replace highly specialised staff quickly. The need will have to be anticipated in time to initiate the required development programmes. The decline of the 'job for life' and the common desire to gain wide and rounded experience have contributed to higher rates of employee attrition. Leavers must be replaced with suitable staff. At senior levels, succession planning should identify potential replacements, internal or external, for those expected to retire or simply move on.

(b) Employment protection legislation and increasing public demand for corporate social responsibility make downsizing, redeploying and relocating staff (e.g. in response to economic recession) a slow and costly process.

(c) Rapid technological change is leading to a requirement for human resources that are both more highly skilled and more adaptable. Labour flexibility is a major issue, and means that the career development and retraining **potential** of staff is at least as important as their actual qualifications and skills. Thus, 'trainability' is now a major criterion for selection.

(d) Organisations that differentiate themselves in the market through superior customer service or other people related activities, need to place people as the centre of their corporate strategy. If their people are to be the difference they need to invest time and effort in finding and developing the right people.

(e) The scope and variety of markets, competition and labour resources are continually increased by environmental factors such as the expansion of the European Union, the globalisation of business and the explosive growth of e-commerce.

(f) Information and Communication Technology (ICT) has made available techniques which facilitate the monitoring and planning of human resources over fairly long time spans: accessing of demographic and employment statistics, trend analysis, 'modelling' of different scenarios and variables, and so on.

(g) Labour costs are a major proportion of total costs in many industries and must be carefully controlled. Cost control action will involve carefully planned remuneration schemes, strict control of headcount and avoidance of waste in such forms as over-staffing and unnecessary activity. Business process reengineering and the deskilling of jobs may lead to redundancies, especially among over-qualified staff.

Armstrong (2009) sums up the aims of People Planning as follows:

(a) To attract and retain the number of people required, with the skills, expertise and competences required.

(b) To anticipate potential surpluses or shortfalls which will need to be adjusted.

(c) To develop a well-trained and flexible workforce which will support organisational adaptation to external changes and demands.

(d) To reduce dependence on external recruitment to meet key skill shortages (by formulating retention and development strategies).

(e) To improve the utilisation of people (most notably by developing flexible working systems).

1.5 A contingency approach to People Planning

It has been suggested that **long-range, detailed people planning** is a necessary form of risk management, preparing businesses for foreseeable contingencies. However, there has been some disillusionment about the feasibility and value of such planning, given the rapidly evolving and uncertain business environment and the kinds of highly flexible organisational structures and cultures that have been designed to respond to it.

(a) The trend in **organisation and job design** is towards functional feasibility (multi-skilling), team working, decentralisation (or empowerment) and flexibly-structured workforces to facilitate flexible deployment of labour. Peters (1994) cites successful US businesses like management consultancy - McKinsey, news corporation CNN, and manufacturer - Titeflex as examples of 'unglued' structures made up of small, functionally versatile units that come together and disband constantly, according to task requirements; that find their own customers, set up their own networks and generate their own projects; that continuously re-educate themselves to meet new demands. Such structures are entirely flat, output/customer-focused, business-generating, information-seeking, continuously learning and shifting. Indeed Peters can be credited with the idea of de-layering organisations and specifically delayering the management levels. Such organisations sweep aside traditional barriers to innovation, customer service and creative problem-solving – but also effectively abolish 'jobs' and predictability of labour utilisation.

(b) Within flexible structures and markets, where manipulating information – not making things – is the primary business activity, the traditional concepts of 'job' and 'career' are being eroded. Bridges (1995), for example, foresaw a workforce made up of **'vendor workers'** who sell their services to a variety of clients and work for them on a project basis. This fundamentally changes the nature of 'job vacancies' and of the labour pool.

(c) With emphasis on continuous improvement, customer service and product innovation, organisations are striving to be more adaptive, visionary, fluid in their structures and holistic in their thinking. The **'learning organisation'** embraces learning at all levels and in all areas, focusing on the process of learning and adapting to what is learned: People Planning is thus seen as an opportunity to explore different scenarios, without pre-conceived requirements or solutions.

In such environments, a different, less prescriptive approach to People Planning may be required. Kane and Stanton (1994) suggest three broad approaches that respond to these uncertainties:

(a) **The staff replacement approach**. Staff are recruited or promoted to fill a vacancy as and when it occurs – if it is still required – with little formal planning. While this is essentially reactive, and does not provide for much change in the knowledge and skill base of the organisation, it allows a degree of flexibility on an *ad hoc* basis. Organisations or units with relatively stable environments may have little difficulty filling vacancies as they arise, while in volatile environments and organisations with high staff mobility and turnover, it may be recognised that longer-range projections of labour requirements are in any case meaningless.

(b) **Short-term Human Resource Strategy.** In environments where long-term forecasting of future requirements is quickly rendered obsolete by change and uncertainty, yet the ability to adapt the skills and knowledge of the workforce is required, a short-term strategic model may be more suitable. This approach has a 'key issues' orientation: HR and line managers collaborate to determine what the organisation's **key HR issues** are in the short term, emphasising flexibility and speed of response to emerging threats and opportunities. HR plans are thus more likely to be:

- Focused on short-term action planning and implementation
- Based on simpler data analysis
- Owned by line managers.

(c) **Vision-driven Human Resource Development.** This approach is long term in its orientation and is appropriate when the nature of the future environment is uncertain. It is driven by organisational vision, mission and core values, rather than detailed staffing forecasts and targets. Such an approach is often employed where a major cultural shift is required, calling for corresponding shifts in employee attitudes, skills and behaviours.

When the future environment can be described with some certainty, traditional long-range People Planning remains a useable approach.

The process of choosing the appropriate approach may be shown as follows (adapted from Kane and Stanton (1994):

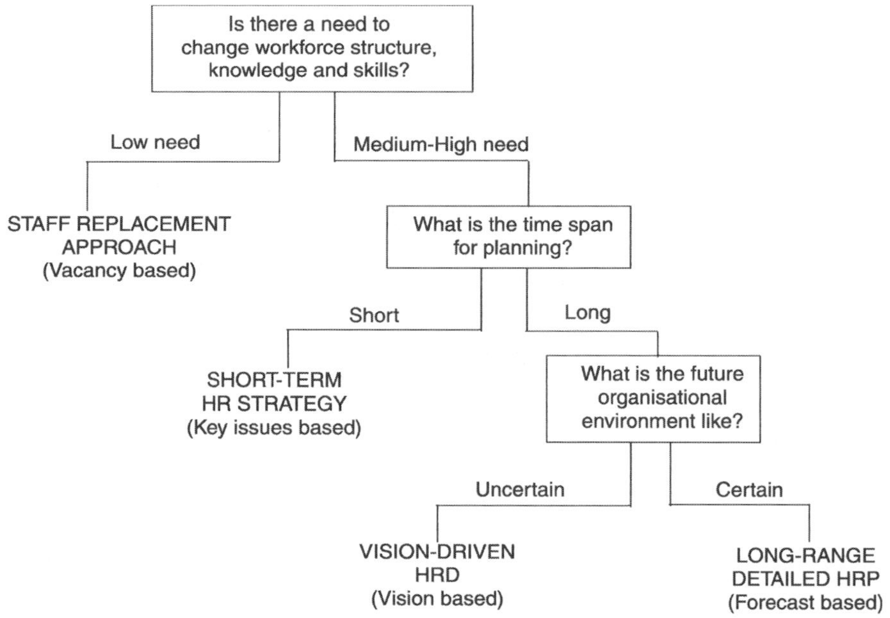

Figure 1.1: Approaches to human resource planning

Note that an alternative (and possibly confusing) terminology emphasising time scale would be to use 'short-term', 'medium-term' and 'long-term' as equivalent to the three possibilities outlined above. Confusion might arise from the contrasting uses of the phrase 'short-term'. The terminology equivalents are tabulated below.

Kane & Stanton terminology	Alternative terminology
Staff replacement approach	Short-term HRM
Short-term HR strategy	Medium-term HRM
Vision-driven HRD (and long-range HRP)	Long-term HRM

It is variously argued that Human Resource Planning is a necessity of modern management, and that rapidly evolving situations and uncertain future events are not a valid reason to not plan. Think of an organisation you are familiar with; does that organisation have a People Plan, and if not, why not?

If it does, how does it manage the unpredictable future?

Let us now look at the HR planning process. We will look at these processes in greater detail in subsequent chapters. The purpose of this section is to introduce the concepts and terminology.

2 The process of People Planning

As Taylor (2010) describes, People Planning is essentially a four-stage cycle:

1 Forecasting future demand for human resources.
2 Forecasting future internal supply of human resources.
3 Forecasting future external supply of human resources.
4 Formulating responses to the forecasts – closing the gap.

2.1 Forecasting future demand

Forecasts of the **demand** for labour, competences and productivity levels will be affected by both internal and external factors.

Internal factors

(a) **Organisational objectives**. Organisational objectives will drive requirements for resources and the long and short-term plans in operation to achieve them. Where plans are changed, the effect of the changes must be estimated: proposed expansion, contraction, innovation or diversification of the organisation's activities will affect the demand for labour in general or for particular skills.

(b) **Staff characteristics and utilisation**. Labour requirements will depend in part on the expected productivity or work rate of different types of employee and the expected volume of business activity. Productivity in turn will depend on a range of factors, such as capital expenditure, technology, work organisation, employee motivation, management style and negotiated productivity deals.

(c) **The cost of labour** – including overtime, training, benefits and so on – and therefore what financial constraints there are on the organisation's labour or skill levels.

External factors

(a) **Demand in the relevant labour markets**. In recent years, economic recession and computerisation have encouraged downsizing and delayering, thus reducing demand for labour generally in advanced economies. At the same time, the growth in the service sector has created new markets, products and business processes creating demand for new skills.

(b) **Government policy**. Government economic policy can have a significant influence on the demand for labour, both by influencing the availability of credit and by the expansion or reduction of staff numbers in government departments and related bodies.

(c) **The changing nature of work**. Advanced nations are seeing a continuing decline in manufacturing industry and significant growth in service industries of all kinds. These changes have obvious effects on the demand for a range of categories of labour. Demand is falling for manufacturing production labour of all grades, but particularly for unskilled and semi-skilled workers.

(d) **Technological developments**. Quite apart from the impact of computerisation, technological developments are likely to continue to have significant effect in a number of areas.

Think of an organisation you are familiar with; what is the greatest factor influencing their People Plans? Is it internal factors such as unclear organisational objectives, unsuitable or expensive employees or it is external factors such as shortage of skills, reduced government funding or new technology replacing the previous production method?.

2.2 Forecasting future supply

The available **supply** of labour, competences and productivity levels may be forecast by considering internal and external factors.

Internal factors

(a) The competences, skills, trainability, flexibility and current productivity level of the existing work force.

(b) The structure of the existing workforce in terms of age distribution, skills, hours of work, rates of pay and so on.

(c) The likelihood of changes to the productivity, size and structure of the workforce.

External factors

The present and potential future supply of relevant skilled labour in the **external labour market** will be influenced by a range of factors. These certainly include economic conditions generally, government policy and actions and the changing nature of work. In addition, the HR planner will have to assess and monitor factors such as those given below:

(a) **Skill availability**: locally, nationally and also internationally: labour mobility within the EU has had a major influence on the UK work force, for example.

(b) **Changes in skill availability**, due to education and training trends, resources and initiatives (or lack of these), and rising unemployment (worker availability) due to economic recession.

(c) **Competitor activity**, which may absorb more (or less) of the available skill pool.

(d) **Demographic changes**: areas of population growth and decline, the proportion of younger or older people in the workforce in a particular region, the number of women in the workforce and so on.

(e) **Wage and salary rates** in the market for particular jobs. ('Supply' implies *availability:* labour resources may become more or less affordable by the organisation).

2.3 Formulating responses - closing the gap between demand and supply

Shortfalls or surpluses of labour/skills/productivity which emerge may be dealt with in various ways, in accordance with the organisation's specific HR and business objectives and policies (for example, equal opportunities), cultural values (for example about encouraging commitment, quality focus or developing people within the organisation) and available structures and technologies. Detailed action programmes may be drawn up for the following strategies.

Bear in mind that there are also **external constraints** on HR planners in considering any or all of the above: UK legislation and EU directives, regulations and court rulings, the organisation's employer brand (reputation in the labour market) and other factors must be taken into account when planning to hire, 'fire', or alter working terms and conditions.

The following flow chart helps determine the order in which the process can be followed.

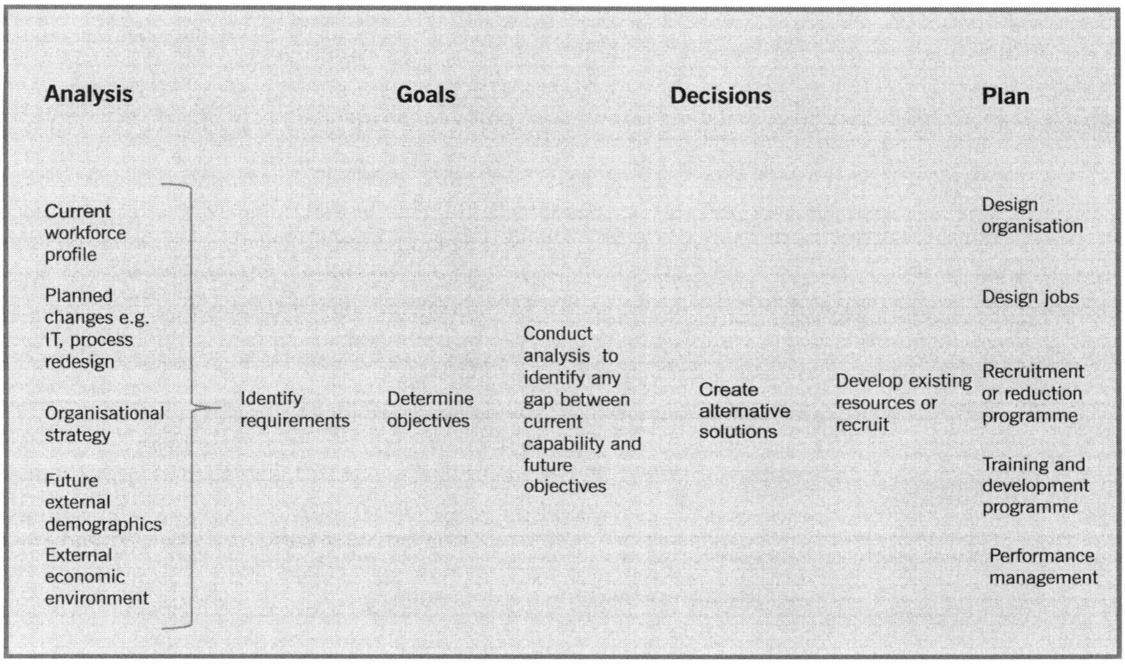

TESCO

Tesco is a company that has seen continuous growth for a number of years and needs to recruit on a regular basis for both the food and non-food parts of the business. For example in 2008/09 4,000 new managers were required to support business growth. Tesco regards workforce planning as vital for the company.

Tesco identifies three main causes for vacancy creation:

- opening new stores in the UK and internationally
- retirement, resignation and internal promotion
- the creation of new types of jobs due to changes in its processes and developments in technology

Tesco uses a workforce planning table to establish the likely demand for new staff. This considers both managerial and non-managerial positions.

This planning process runs each year from the last week in February. There are quarterly reviews in May, August and November, so Tesco can adjust staffing levels and recruit where necessary. This allows Tesco sufficient time and flexibility to meet its demands for staff and allows the company to meet its strategic objectives, for example, to open new stores and maintain customer service standards.

Tesco seeks to fill many vacancies from within the company. It recognises the importance of motivating its staff to progress their careers with the company. Tesco practises what it calls "talent planning". This encourages people to work their way through and up the organisation. Through an annual appraisal scheme, individuals can apply for "bigger" jobs. Employees identify roles in which they would like to develop their careers with Tesco. Their manager sets out the technical skills, competencies and behaviours necessary for these roles, what training this will require and how long it will take the person to be ready to do the job. This helps Tesco to achieve its business objectives and employees to achieve their personal and career objectives.

ACTIVITY 1

15 mins

To what extent would People Planning be possible and desirable for:

(a) A company designing, manufacturing and selling personal computers?

(b) A large local government authority?

(c) An international airline?

2.4 Beginning the Planning Process

Plan development is typically based on an assumptive model; often the main assumption is that the past is a good indicator of the future e.g. employee attrition. However, as has been experienced since 2008, assumptions about demand, future growth and employee attrition can be difficult to rely upon. This is not an argument for not planning, simply to approach with caution. It is important therefore to fully consider the external factors and how these could change.

Graham and Bennett (1992) devised a process that can be followed when people planning

step 1

Create a planning group.

The group should consist of line managers within the organisation in addition to HR professionals

step 2

Identify the organisation's HR objectives

Within the context of the overall organisational objectives and taking into consideration:

- Capital equipment plans
- Reorganisation plans
- Changes in products or output
- Marketing plans
- Financial limitations

step 3

Audit present utilisation of Human Resources

Conduct internal audit

- Number of employees by category
- Employee attrition by level, grade or job type
- Amount of overtime worked
- Assessment of performance and potential of current employees
- Comparison of remuneration to local market

step 4

Assess the external environment

Place the organisation in the context of:

- The recruitment position
- Population trends
- Local housing and transport plans
- National agreements
- Government policies on education, retirement, subsidies etc

step 5

Assess the potential supply of labour

- Local population movements
- Recruitment and redundancy by local organisations
- Employing new worker categories e.g. part-time workers
- Productivity improvements, working hours and practices

Given the inherent risk in trying to predict an uncertain future, the organisation can employ a technique of scenario modeling. This will create a variety of different models of what the future may look like. Some of the predictions will have a greater probability of coming to fruition and so the probability can be weighted. However more importantly this approach helps identify the core drivers concerning the human resources and does provide a range of options.

Torrington et al 2011 argue that planning is enhanced if:

- Plans are flexible and regularly reviewed, the creation of a plan is not seen as the completion of the requirement
- All stakeholders in the organisation are involved
- Planning is owned and driven by senior management and not HR who need to facilitate the process
- Plans are linked to organisational and HR strategy
- Plans are simple to understand and interpret
- Plans are acceptable if limited to issues rather than having to be all-encompassing and organisation-wide.

2.5 Systematic techniques

Mathematical method: time series or ratio-trend analysis look at past organisational performance and the numbers of people employed in different roles to make informed judgements about how many will be required in the future. This method is highly reliant upon stable environments and most obviously lends itself to public sector organisations planning to provide services based on population demographics.

This method can also be applied to seasonally affected organisations such as hotels planning occupancy during the summer, or retail businesses anticipating Christmas demand.

Work study: this method focuses on the tasks and processes conducted by the organisation. The numbers required are modeled on the requirements of the tasks and processes to run efficiently and effectively. This method most lends itself to production line types of activities that can be broken down into discrete tasks.

This method can be modified by introducing into the equation the expected productivity improvements that will be gained over time (this rate of improvement is based on the rate of improvement gained over previous years of conducting the activity)

Working back from costs: this approach ignores the implications of past or anticipated future demand and focuses on the budget available. The process begins with the amount of money available and from that position calculates how many positions, at what salaries, can be afforded. The service or output that will be achieved will be determined by the resources available or what is referred to as 'resource-based provision'. In the current economic climate with many public sector organisations finding themselves under severe financial restraint, an option available to them is to provide services up to the level that can be afforded, rather than according to need.

Managerial judgement: this method is not system-based but therefore benefits from being able to incorporate an element of subjectivity into the analysis, which can be especially useful during highly turbulent times. Stainer (1971) identified three major benefits to the approach:

- it can be quick and requires little if any data
- intangible factors such taste, fashion can be taken into account
- opinions of managers in other organisations, as well as experts, can be taken into account

Whilst managerial judgement has its benefits, it can also be considered little more than guesswork and so often the process is enhanced if complemented with some form of mathematical approach.

While managerial judgement can simply be asked for as part of the people planning process, certain situations often catalyse the relevance.

- **Budget projection**. During the organisation's annual budget development round, departments will be predicting growth, contraction or no change. Certain departments, such as HR, may argue that the development of their budget and consequent resourcing requirements are dependent upon the plans of the other functions ie if the overall organisation headcount is expected to increase, HR may need to increase to support the growth. As the respective departments plan their budgets, they will have a headcount in mind and most likely at what points during the budget year the headcount will change. These changes in headcount can then be used to inform the required numbers.

- **Change.** For many organisations the plan often becomes pertinent when a major change is to occur. Whether the change to be made is a reduction in headcount due to redundancies, the introduction of a new product or service, the introduction of new technology or process redesign, they may all require a full evaluation of the staffing requirements and skills required. These occasions can make it easier to engage management in the planning process as the requirement is clear to see and all those affected by the change can see the value in the process.

ACTIVITY 2 15 mins

People planners are human beings, and so are the human resources or staff themselves: what might be the major limitations on the reliability or objectivity of statistical methods in people planning?

3 Evaluating People Planning

3.1 How reliable is People Planning?

People planning can be regarded as a scientific, statistical exercise, but it is important to remember that statistics in themselves are limited in value.

Forecasting is not an exact science. Few exponents of even the most sophisticated techniques would claim that they are wholly accurate, although:

(a) The element of guesswork has been substantially reduced by the use of computer models to test various assumptions and to indicate trends

(b) The general principles can still be applied to indicate problems and stimulate control action.

Mathematical methods can be used to create a more accurate model of the future than simple subjective estimates. Computerisation has greatly enhanced the speed, ease and accuracy with which they can be applied, and many PC-based HR software packages are now available. Even so, there are a number of assumptions involved, and the results are purely **quantitative** – for example, numbers of staff required – where **qualitative** information may be required for meaningful decision making: the effects of change, re-staffing or management style on the culture of the organisation and individual/group behaviour and so on.

HR SOFTWARE.
If you are curious about PC-based HR software, you might like to check out Software Source, a site established by the CIPD to provide information on HR software suppliers and products.

http://softwaresource.co.uk

Where end products are measurable, **work-study techniques** can offer a reasonably accurate forecast of staffing requirements. In service sectors and 'knowledge work', however, end products and output may not be easily subject to standard-setting. For example, the number of telephone calls, interviews, customers served, or ideas generated is likely to fluctuate widely with the flow of business and the nature of particular transactions.

Managerial judgement forms the simplest and cheapest method of assessment. As such, it may be the most appropriate – and most common – method for small organisations. At the best of times, however, this method has the disadvantage of a high degree of subjectivity, and although this can be controlled to an extent (by requiring managers to support their estimates with reasons and to reconcile their estimates with those of senior management), it is a source of potential risk.

A measure of flexibility will need to be built into any HR plan, so that it can be adapted to suit likely or unforeseen contingencies. Above all, it should not be seen or communicated as an inflexible plan, as if it were based on certainty.

> 'Clearly, the more precise the information available, the greater the probability that HR plans will be accurate. But, in practice, they are subject to many imponderable factors, some completely outside an organisation's control... international trade, general technological advances, population movements, the human acceptance of or resistance to change, and the quality of leadership and its impact on morale. The environment, then, is uncertain, and so are the people whose activities are being planned. HR plans must therefore be accepted as being continuous, under constant review, and ever-changing. Since they concern people, they must also be negotiable.'
>
> Cuming (1993)

3.2 Is People Planning working?

A **human resource audit** is an investigation designed to:

(a) Give a picture of the current structure, size and productivity of the organisation's labour force

(b) Check that HR plans, systems, policies and procedures have been and are being carried out

The best test of the accuracy and effectiveness of People Planning is to check whether the reality has, in fact, conformed to the forecasts and plans: a basic system of control.

(a) **Actual staffing levels and trends** should be checked against budgets.

  (i) If people planners have allowed for reductions in staffing levels through natural wastage, it is important to ensure that such wastage is allowed to happen. (It is a natural tendency for managers to seek replacements for any staff losses, even those which have been budgeted for.)

  (ii) The budgets themselves may be (or may have become) inappropriate. The people plan must constantly be reviewed and revised in the light of changes and actual (unanticipated) events.

(b) **HR records** should be checked to identify that any change (promotion, transfer, redundancy, recruitment, etc) has been properly approved, in line with the HR plan.

This process may uncover:

(i) Inadequate authorisation of particular types of change; for example, it may be common to transfer employees within the same department without proper approval or reference to the overall staffing plan.

(ii) Unauthorised or unnecessary use of agency or temporary personnel.

(c) **Staff utilisation** should be reviewed: how efficiently is the human resource employed? This process may uncover a need for fundamental change (such as a complete restructure or automation of work). Under-utilisation of a skill category is an inefficient use of the organisation's resources, as well as a common source of personal dissatisfaction among staff.

3.3 Is People Planning cost-effective?

Although labour costs in many manufacturing companies are falling as a proportion of total costs, as processes are increasingly automated, HR costs are still significant and may form a large proportion of total costs in labour-intensive sectors such as services.

An organisation should therefore assess the **cost** effect of any people plan – recruitment drive, training initiative or downsizing exercise – in proportion to the **expected benefits** to be derived from it.

A **cost-benefit analysis** is a comparison of the cost of an actual or proposed measure with an evaluation or estimate of the benefits gained from it. This will indicate whether the measure has been, or is likely to be, cost-effective – or 'worthwhile'.

There are a number of reasons why a cost-benefit analysis of the people plan might be useful.

(a) It emphasises the **total cost** of the plan, including wages and related costs, in relation to gains in efficiency or effectiveness.

(b) It allows costs of the plan to be **compared** with other options. For example, once the cost of recruitment has been evaluated, the organisation can assess the merits of alternative plans such as:

(i) Outsourcing the activity

(ii) Developing and multi-skilling existing staff

(iii) Buying capital equipment or altering work processes in other ways to enhance productivity.

(c) It emphasises that **cost-effectiveness** – not cost-minimisation – is the aim. For example, temporary or part-time workers may be 'cheaper' for the organisation – but if long-term gains in stability, expertise, management succession, business relationships, knowledge preservation and motivated output are lost (compared with employing full-time, permanent staff), this would be a false economy.

It should be clear that the People Plan, at the stage of closing the gap between supply and demand, actually involves planning in a number of areas of HRM. We will end this chapter with a summary of the People Plan.

4 The People Plan

Once the analysis of human resource requirements has been carried out, and the various options for fulfilling them considered, the **people plan** will be drawn up. This may be done at a strategic level. It will also involve tactical plans and action plans for various measures, according to the strategy that has been chosen. Typical elements might include the following.

(a) **The resourcing plan**: approaches to obtaining skills/people within the organisation, and by external recruitment.

(b) **The internal resource plan**: availability of skills within the organisation; plans to promote/redeploy/develop.

(c) **The recruitment plan:** numbers and types of people, and when required; sources of candidates; the recruitment programme; desired 'employer brand' and/or recruitment incentives.

(d) **The training plan:** numbers of trainees required and/or existing staff who need training; training programme.

(e) **The re-development plan:** programmes for transferring or retraining employees.

(f) **The flexibility plan**: plans to use part-time workers, jobsharing, homeworking, outsourcing, flexible hour arrangements and so on.

(g) **The productivity plan:** programmes for improving productivity, or reducing manpower costs; setting productivity targets.

(h) **The downsizing plan:** natural wastage forecasts; where and when redundancies are to occur; policies for selection and declaration of redundancies; redevelopment, retraining or relocation of employees; policy on redundancy payments, union consultation and so on.

(i) **The retention plan:** actions to reduce avoidable labour wastage.

The plan should include budgets, targets and standards. It should allocate responsibilities for implementation and control (reporting, monitoring achievement against plan).

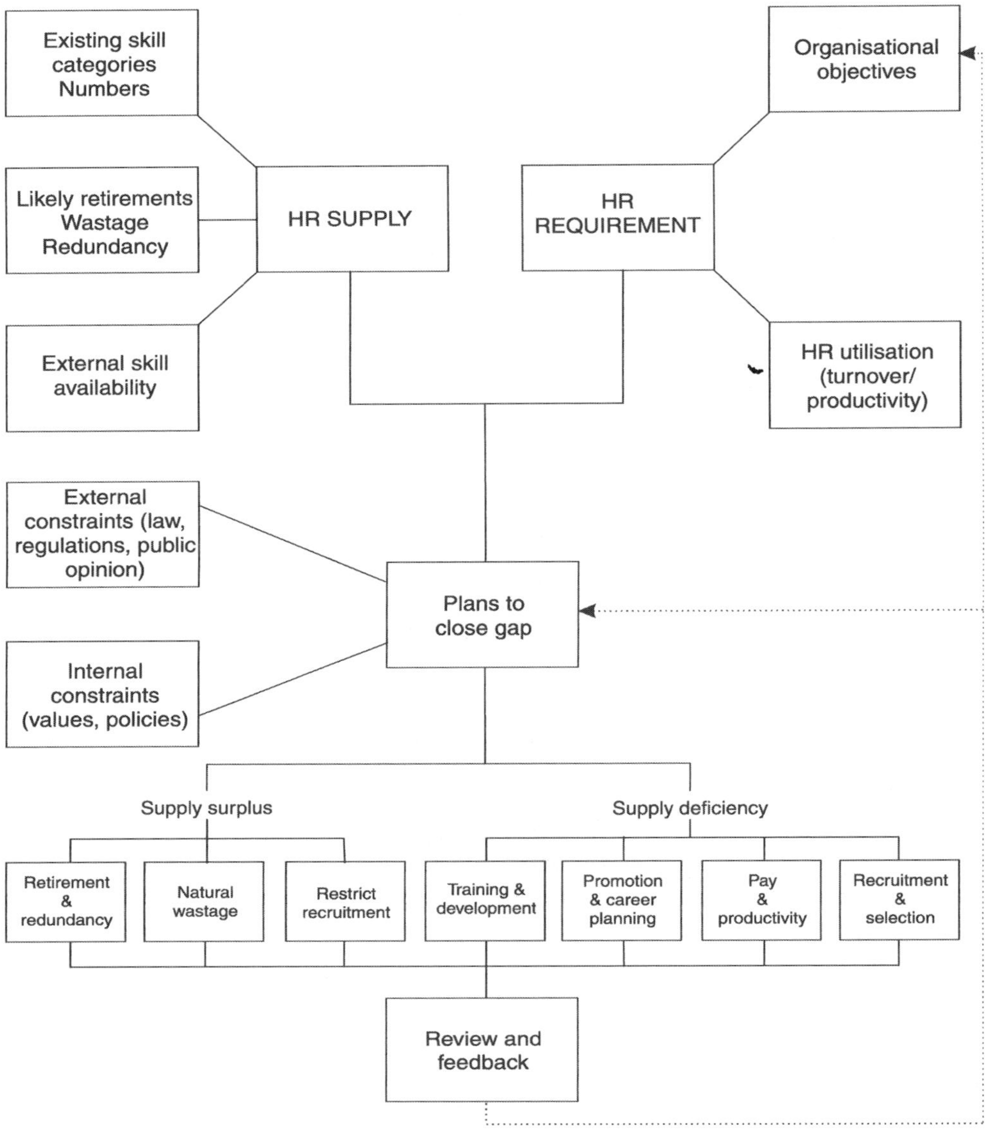

Figure 1.2: The People Plan

These components will be considered further as we progress through the study manual.

We will now look at what People Planning can look like when put into action.

5 People Planning in action

5.1 Singapore Airlines

Corporate Strategy

Singapore Airlines (SIA) is generally regarded as a brand leader in the aviation industry, and has managed to maintain this status for over 20 years. It is considered to have three main aspects to its strategy:

(a) Excellent service

(b) Continuous innovation

(c) Technology superiority

The first aspect, service excellence, is the one that is of particular interest to Human Resources professionals. The market differentiator that SIA aims to achieve is the passenger service delivered by the cabin crew, the topic this section will mostly focus on.

The second aspect is continuous innovation. SIA were the first airlines to introduce the personal entertainment system and video-on-demand for every seat.

The third aspect is the use of new airplanes. By using newer planes SIA is able to have both lower operational costs and lower maintenance costs.

> Singapore Airlines since its creation has sought to differentiate itself in the market, this has traditionally been represented through the Singapore Girl figure.
>
> Singapore Airlines' customer service standards are symbolised by the gracious "Singapore Girl". In her distinctive uniform, a sarong kebaya in batik material designed by Parisian couturier Pierre Balmain, she epitomises Singapore Airlines' tradition of friendly service and Asian hospitality.
>
> The Singapore Girl was created in 1972, when Singapore Airlines was formed following the division of the former Malaysia-Singapore Airlines into two carriers -- Malaysian Airline System and Singapore Airlines. She has been a leading figure in Singapore Airlines' international marketing and advertising campaigns ever since the airline's creation.
>
> A Global Icon
>
> The Singapore Girl is a global marketing icon, one of the airline industry's most instantly-recognised figures. This recognition factor gives the airline a great advantage over its competitors.
>
> Singapore Airlines Website 2011

The use of the Singapore Girl continues and she fronts the recruitment site for the airline. The symbol of the Singapore Girl also reinforces how the airline seeks to differentiate itself through its Human Capital. By differentiating itself through its Human Capital the airline seeks to achieve sustainable competitive advantage. Duplicating Human Capital is the hardest corporate resource to copy and so by adopting this strategy SIA makes it harder for competitors to copy its formula for success.

Human Resources Plan

Singapore Airlines' approach to Human Resources has five elements:

(a) Rigorous selection and recruitment processes
(b) Extensive training and retraining of employees
(c) Cohorts of successful service delivery teams
(d) Empowerment of front-line staff
(e) Motivation of employees

(a) Rigorous selection and recruitment processes

More than 80% of all Singapore Girls are either Singaporean or Malaysian. The rest are from countries including China, India, Indonesia, Japan, Korea, Taiwan and Hong Kong. Cabin crew applicants are required to meet a multitude of criteria starting with an initial screening looking at age ranges, academic qualifications and physical attributes.

When reviewing these criteria from a European perspective the emphasis on gender and nationality look somewhat alien. From the 16,000 applications received annually, only some 500 to 600 new cabin crew are hired to cover turnover rates of 10 per cent, including both voluntary and involuntary attrition. After the initial training, new crew are carefully monitored for the first six months of flying, through monthly reports from the in-flight supervisor during this probationary period. Usually around 75 percent are confirmed for an initial five-year contract, some 20 percent have their probation extended, and the rest leave the company.

In a later chapter we will look at the development of selection criteria, and the importance this can have for getting the right people into the organisation.

(b) Extensive training and retraining of employees

Whilst many service provider organisations focus on training as a key element of success, SIA remains the airline with the highest emphasis on this aspect. Newly recruited cabin crew are required to undertake intensive four-month training courses – the longest and most comprehensive in the industry. The syllabus includes:

- Product knowledge including food & beverage
- Service procedures
- Passenger handling
- Deportment & grooming
- Language & communication skills
- Safety equipment procedures
- First aid

Flight crew are also required to embark on 29 months of comprehensive "on-line" training before any promotion to first officer.

Singapore Airlines has seven training schools for the seven core functional areas of cabin crew, flight operations, commercial training, information technology, security, airport services training and engineering.

They not only train on job-related skills but they also believe in a programme of continuous training and retraining. The approach of continual training ensures that SIA staff are familiar with continuous change and development and so are able to deliver the new services SIA introduces regularly.

In addition to delivered training, SIA managers often assume the role of mentors and coaches to guide new employees rather than just being managers and superiors.

In addition, SIA also adopts a job rotation approach to allow management to obtain a more holistic picture of the organisation. Rotating to other departments every few years enables managers to develop a deeper understanding of operations at other areas of the organisation; this promotes a corporate outlook, reduces the likelihood of inter-department conflicts and facilitates change and innovation as people bring fresh perspectives and approaches to their new roles.

In later chapters we will see that investment by the employer in training and development, and long-term career development, are key aspects to employee retention and motivation.

(c) Cohorts of successful service delivery teams

Effective teams are often a pre-requisite to service excellence. In view of this, SIA aims to create "*esprit de corps*" among its cabin crew. The 6,600 crew members are formed into teams of 13 where team members are rostered to fly together as much as possible, allowing them to build camaraderie and better understand each other's personalities and capabilities.

In later chapters we consider the role that the supervisor plays in retaining and motivating the employee.

(d) Empowerment of front-line staff

Employees need to feel empowered in order to expend discretionary effort. It is pertinent that employees are able to make decisions independently, as front-line staff frequently have to handle customers on their own since it is not feasible or even desirable for managers to constantly monitor employees' actions. At SIA, senior management emphasise that staff must have a clear concept of the boundaries of their authority and that it is the responsibility of management to communicate and explain the empowerment limits.

In a later chapter we will see that empowerment and freedom to act are powerful factors in engaging employees and contributing towards long-term retention.

(e) Motivation of employees

Rewards and recognition are key levers that any organisation can use to encourage appropriate behaviour, recognise excellence and emphasise both positive as well as undesirable practices. SIA employs various forms of reward and recognition including interesting and varied job content, symbolic actions, performance-based share options and a significant percentage of variable pay components linked to individual staff contributions and company's financial performance.

SIA's reward and evaluation system is highly aligned with the desired behaviours. The key element is "on-board assessment", which encompasses image (grooming and uniform turnout), service orientation (crew's interaction and passenger-handling capabilities), product knowledge and job skills, safety and security knowledge and adherence to procedures, work relationship (team-working spirit), and for the crew member in charge, additional factors of people management skills and pre-flight briefing session.

Whilst this study text does not focus on reward, it is important to recognise that SIA reinforce the training and messages provided to employees through a reward system.

Based on "Strategy and organization at Singapore Airlines: Achieving sustainable advantage through dual strategy". Loizos Heracleous, Jochen Wirtz. Journal of Air Transport Management. 2009.

Chapter Roundup

- Organisations are better prepared for the future with a People Plan. Whilst there are criticisms of plans being unadaptable and too time consuming, organisations will at some point need to consider how to respond to the external environment; it is better to have done that in advance than react at the time.
- Planning creates a link between business and people plans; provides better control over staffing costs and numbers employed; provides a more informed judgements about the skills and attitude mix in the organisation.
- People Planning is a form of risk management.
- Manpower planning is considered the first version of People Planning; it was high numerically driven and required a stable environment, its legacy however is valuable.
- For People Plans to be successful they must be linked to the organisation's strategic objectives
- People Planning is essentially a four-stage cycle: Forecasting future demand for human resources; Forecasting future internal supply of human resources; Forecasting future external supply of human resources; Formulating responses to the forecasts – closing the gap
- Demand for labour, competences and productivity levels is affected by both internal and external factors.
- Scenario modeling creates a variety of different models of what the future may look like; this enables an organisation to think through the resourcing implications if faced with the scenario in reality
- Different methods of planning can be used, however the models have to balance the aspiration for clear numerical output with flexibility and an accurate reflection of the current situation.
- Human Resource audit considers actual staffing levels and trends; HR records; staff utilisation.
- The People Plan should involve tactical and action plans.

Quick Quiz

1 According to the CIPD what percentage of respondents consider People Planning to be 'risk management'?

- 53%
- 49%
- 34%
- 20%

2 Liff noted that there had been a shift from reconciling numbers of employees available with predictable, stable jobs - to what?

3 According to Armstrong, name two aims of People Planning

4 What is alternative terminology to Kane and Stanton's Staff Replacement Approach?

5 Identify two of the internal factors when forecasting future demand

6 Identify two external factors when forecasting future supply

7 According to Graham and Bennett how many steps are included in the People Planning process?

8 Why is 'Managerial judgement' not considered to be a fully systematic planning technique?

9 What is a cost-benefit analysis?

10 How many elements may a typical People Plan include?

Answers to Quick Quiz

1 34% (Introduction)

2 A greater concern with skills, their development and deployment (para 1.2)

3 You could have included:

(a) To attract and retain the number of people required, with the skills, expertise and competences required.

(b) To anticipate potential surpluses or shortfalls which will need to be adjusted.

(c) To develop a well-trained and flexible workforce which will support organisational adaptation to external changes and demands.

(d) To reduce dependence on external recruitment to meet key skill shortages (by formulating retention and development strategies).

(e) To improve the utilisation of people (most notably by developing flexible working systems). (para 1.4)

4 Short-term HRM (para 1.5)

5 You could have chosen from the following three choices: Organisational objectives; Staff characteristics and utilisation; The cost of labour (para 2.1)

6 You could have chosen from the following five choices: skill availability; changes in skill availability; competitor activity; demographic changes; wage and salary rates (para 2.2)

7 Five (1. Create a Planning group; 2. Identify the organisation's HR objectives; 3. Audit present utilisation of Human Resources; 4. Assess the external environment; 5. Assess the potential supply of labour) (para 2.4)

8 Because it incorporates an element of subjectivity into the analysis i.e. the manager's judgement (para 2.5)

9 A cost-benefit analysis is a comparison of the cost of an actual or proposed measure with an evaluation or estimate of the benefits gained from it. (para 3.3)

10 Nine (1.The resourcing plan 2.The internal resource plan 3.The recruitment plan 4.The training plan 5.The re-development plan 6.The flexibility plan 7.The productivity plan 8.The downsizing plan 9.The retention plan) (para 4)

Answers to Activities

Activity 1

(a) The computer company is operating in an extremely volatile and changing market, which will present People Planning difficulties. The technology, and associated skills, are constantly changing, along with competitive pressures: an innovative competitor could 'steal' the market. This is also a highly-skilled business, however, with skill shortages in the labour market, and long training times: despite the difficulties, long-term planning will be important.

(b) Some years ago, the local authority would have represented a fairly stable (not to say 'ponderous') bureaucratic structure, with fairly rigid, predictable HR plans. Reductions in funding, and the contracting out of services, have made People Planning more difficult and desirable: workforce reduction and flexibility, and the use of People Planning to change organisational culture, will be key issues.

(c) The airline is a business which is potentially volatile, and sensitive to barely controllable factors such as price wars, political/terrorist action, industrial action, airspace restrictions, crashes affecting image, global recession affecting travel, and so on. At the same time it is dependent on several categories of employees (airline pilots, aerospace engineers) who are scarce and have long training cycles: planning ahead for selection and retention will be crucial.

Activity 2

(a) Statistics are not the only element of the planning process, and are subject to interpretation and managerial judgements that are largely qualitative and even highly speculative (involving future growth, say, or potential for innovation).

(b) Trends in statistics are the product of social processes, which are not readily quantifiable or predictable. Staff leave for various social reasons in (unpredictable) individual cases, to get married, relocate or whatever. The growth of the temporary and freelance workforce is a social trend, as are the buying patterns which dictate demand for goods and services.

Chapter 2

Internal analysis

In the first chapter we were introduced to the idea of People Planning relating to the strategic objectives of the organisation. It was highlighted that to be effective it has to ensure active participation of line managers; it could be argued that it is best *led* by line managers and *facilitated by* HR. Anyone who is conducting a People Plan needs to be able to partner and consult with the business. To ensure this process is effective this chapter begins with discussing the People Planning stakeholders in the organisation.

In the first chapter we considered the objective numerical approach typified in 'manpower planning' and can be referred to as 'hard' planning, there is also what maybe referred to 'soft' planning. Part of the perception of 'manpower planning' being out dated is the reliance on numbers which potentially fails to be responsive enough to the rapidly changing environment of today. 'Soft' planning departs from the numerical considerations and looks at employee attitudes and commitment, and so whilst more subjective is seen to be responsive. In this chapter we will consider both but with a biased towards 'soft' planning.

TOPIC LIST		LEARNING OUTCOMES
1	The stakeholders in People Planning	
2	The process of Internal Analysis	2.1
3	Labour turnover and retention	7.1, 7.2, 7.3
4	Employee retention in action	2.4
5	Organisational performance	2.2
6	Summarising and evaluating the current situation	2.5

1 The stakeholders in People Planning

1.1 Introduction

Stakeholders 'Any group or individual who can affect or [be] affected by the achievement of an organisation's objectives'. (Freeman, 1984).

Conducting a People Planning exercise may not automatically have the buy-in and backing of the organisation, it maybe seen as time consuming, irrelevant or ill timed. One method to ensure greater organisational buy-in is to understand who are the primary people of influence, who needs to support the initiative and who will champion it. With support of key influencers in the business, the exercise will enjoy greater endorsement and increased probability of success.

1.2 The management of stakeholders

While an organisation can have many stakeholders, there are certain key stakeholders who have a **direct interest** and have **direct influence** over the organisation, for example the Managing Director, Chief Executive or Managing Partner. Stakeholders in this position needed to be treated with respect and it is important that they are fully bought into, and supportive of, the People Plan and the proposed actions.

For example, as the People Planning process commences it needs to consider who to consult. The list could include:

The Chief Executive	Trade Unions	Recruitment agencies
Board members	Employee consultation committee	Local schools
Divisional directors	Employees	Higher Education institutions
Heads of Department		Competitors

It may be surprising to see to see competitors in the list above, however in certain situations such action is necessary. For example there maybe a national shortage for certain skills. The required solution is to increase the availability of this this of skilled workers by allowing more immigration, however the government limits the number of such skilled workers into the country. To persuade the government to increase the number allowed into the country it is necessary for the whole industry unite and lobby the government.

The list above includes a group simply described as 'Heads of Departments', however some departments will be bigger than others, some may be more profitable or deliver key services. Some departments may have more complex issues than others e.g. national skills shortage or simply have a Head who is enthusiastic about the value of the process and so a useful ally to engage with. Consequently, stakeholders will sometimes need to be subdivided and prioritised.

Once identified, stakeholders need to:

- Be informed of the People Planning process and intended outcomes
- Be consulted with, to gain their requirement, insights, issues and opinions
- Kept up to date with progress
- See that their contribution, issues etc are reflected in the output and design
- Be kept informed of the proposals and 'onboard' with the plans

ACTIVITY 1 — 20 mins

Identify the stakeholders at the college you attend for your course of study

The management of stakeholders is important in any process that requires resources to be engaged in a process. We will now turn our attention to the process of gathering internal information.

2 The process of Internal Analysis

2.1 Identifying future requirements

Forecasts of the demand for labour, competences and productivity levels will be affected by many internal factors. This process can be a **'bottom up'** or **'top down'** approach.

The **'bottom up'** approach focuses on the operational requirements that face managers. The discussions will focus both on the numbers required and the skills and competencies. The outcome could therefore be skewed towards headcount or needing a programme of skills development.

The **'top down'** takes the organisation's strategy and maps the human resources requirements necessary to meet the goals. The discussions could involve far more complex thinking as to whether entire functions could be outsourced or even offshored. The discussions therefore will be more focused on managing major change programmes and their achievement than designing training interventions.

Both these approaches can be considered 'soft' planning as they rely upon the value judgements of managers. The 'bottom up' approach relies on departmental managers to give best estimates as to the requirements based on their judgement and experience. The risk with this approach, as with opinion-based information, the manager in question may be overly optimistic, may be inflating the figures in anticipation of a future reduction by more senior management, or may simply not be 'on message'.

The 'top down' approach is opinion of senior managers as to the requirements. Hopefully, having been intimately involved in developing the organisation's strategy, they will be able to articulate the requirements. However this group does not always have consensus, and the managers are susceptible to their own egos and aspirations skewing the information. The issue of stakeholder management is a key skill to achieving the balance of reflecting the various opinions with the right outcome for the organisation.

Blending both sources of information may result in a more accurate forecast.

2.2 Factors to consider

(a) **Organisational objectives**. Organisational objectives will drive requirements for resources and the long and short-term plans in operation to achieve them. Typical changes include the following.

- Changed levels of demand
- Introduction of new products and services
- Entry into new markets
- Technological change of all kinds
- Changes to geographical locations
- Decision to outsource or offshore a service or production

The probable extent of change may be estimated by market research, competitive analysis, trends in technological advances and so on (although sudden changes in market conditions complicate the process: the effect of global terrorism on defence spending, for example, or the 2008 collapse of global financial markets).

(b) **Staff characteristics and utilisation.**

Labour requirements will depend in part on the expected productivity or work rate of different types of employee and the expected volume of business activity. Productivity in turn will depend on a range of factors, such as capital expenditure, technology, work organisation, employee motivation, management style and negotiated productivity deals.

Workforce data:

- Numbers in current workforce, expressed as full time equivalents
- Skills and capabilities
- Level and/or status within the organisation
- Performance ratings
- Talent pipeline, potential for promotion or skill development
- Predicted sickness levels
- Predicted attrition levels, voluntary and involuntary
- Likely retirements

Employee characteristics to be considered include the following:

- Age
- Sex
- Ethnicity

Ethical and legal considerations relating to discrimination must be respected.

(c) **The cost of labour** – including overtime, training, benefits and so on – and therefore what financial constraints there are on the organisation's labour or skill levels.

TESCO

Tesco takes a rather different approach to analysing its internal workforce. They use the skills they have developed in understanding their customers and apply these to understanding their own employees. They conduct qualitative and quantitative research and categorise five 'identities' within their own workforce.

(a) Work-life balancers: mainly older women who value most highly part-time employment or flexible hours. They are not seeking challenging work or responsibility.

(b) Want it all: degree holders aged between 25-34 who work in head office. This category is prepared to embrace the company values and work hard. In return they want a career, high pay and challenging work. However, if they do not receive this they will seek employment elsewhere.

(c) Pleasure seekers: this group is part-time students and single males but with service of five years. They are prepared to work long hours but their commitment is to enjoying themselves and travel rather than the company. This group is not loyal and will leave for higher pay.

(d) Live to work: typically young married men or older managers with long service (+ 10 years) and working in Head Office or distribution. This category is committed and ambitious and prepared to sacrifice home life for the office. Consequently they are prepared to work long hours and seek challenging assignments and promotion.

(e) Work to live: mainly women over 35, with or without children, with service of 10 years or more. Their primary focus is to be able to work close to home. This group is not interested in working long hours, nor any challenge but is however willing to do repetitive tasks.

Using this information Tesco tailor their employee benefits programmes in order that they appeal to the various segments, and so create a greater level of employee loyalty and commitment, without spending money on providing benefits to segments that do not value them

ACTIVITY 2 — 30 mins

Bratton and Gold (2007) note that many HR departments practise 'e-HR': using the Internet and related ICT systems (including internal networks or intranets) to support their activities.

(a) How might e-HR be used in HR planning?

(b) What other sources of information can you think of, that might be used in supply and demand forecasting for HRP?

2.3 Forecasting internal supply

The available **supply** of labour, competences and productivity levels may be forecast by considering:

(a) The competences, skills, trainability, flexibility and current productivity level of the existing work force.

(b) The structure of the existing workforce in terms of age distribution, skills, hours of work, rates of pay and so on.

(c) The likelihood of changes to the productivity, size and structure of the workforce. Such changes may come through:

(i) Wastage (turnover through resignations and retirements), promotions and transfers, absenteeism and other staff movements. This will require information on:

- The age structure of staff (forthcoming retirement or family start-up)
- Labour turnover for a comparable period
- The promotion potential and ambitions of staff.

(ii) Employee trainability, morale and motivation, which may influence productivity and flexibility

(iii) Organisational, technological, cultural, managerial and other changes which may positively or negatively affect employee productivity, loyalty and so on.

2.4 Closing the gap between demand and supply

Shortfalls or surpluses of labour/skills/productivity which emerge may be dealt with in various ways, in accordance with the organisation's specific HR and business objectives and policies (for example, equal opportunities), cultural values (for example about encouraging commitment, quality focus or developing people within the organisation) and available structures and technologies. Detailed action programmes may be drawn up for the following strategies.

***Shortfalls* may be met by:**	***Surplus* may be met by:**
Internal transfers and promotions, training and development (including individual career management and succession/promotion planning) External recruitment or improvement of recruitment methods (eg diversity programmes to encourage more applicants) The extension of temporary contracts, or the contracts of those about to retire Reducing labour turnover, by reviewing possible causes (including pay and conditions), improving induction/ socialisation measures	Running down manning levels by natural wastage or 'accelerated wastage' (encouraging labour turnover by withholding incentives to loyalty: eg pay freezes or barriers to promotion) Restricting or 'freezing' recruitment Redundancies (voluntary and/or compulsory) Early retirement incentives Short contract and flexible hours (eg annual hours contracts) to cover fluctuating demand Eliminating overtime and 'peripheral' workforce groups (freelance and temporary workers)

Shortfalls may be met by:	*Surplus* may be met by:
The use of freelance/temporary/agency staff to cover fluctuating demand Outsourcing appropriate activities to external contractors The development of flexible (or otherwise more productive) working methods and structures: multi-skilling, project structures, delayering Productivity bargaining encouraging overtime working or offering bonuses and incentives to increase productivity Review and adjustment of corporate culture, management style and organisation to increase productivity New technology (increasing productivity, and/or reducing the need for labour) Adjustment of corporate objectives: contracting in recognition of the constraints	Retraining and/or redeployment of staff to other areas of skill/productivity shortage. This may involve diversification by the organisation, to utilise existing skills/knowledge; retraining of employees in newly-needed skill areas; and/or multi-skilling, so that the workforce can be flexibly deployed in areas of labour shortage as and when they emerge

Bear in mind that there are also **external constraints** on HR planners in considering any or all of the above: UK legislation and EU directives, regulations and court rulings, the organisation's employer brand (reputation in the labour market) and other factors must be taken into account when planning to hire, 'fire', or alter working terms and conditions. These topics are covered in later chapters.

3 Labour turnover and retention

3.1 Measuring labour turnover

Labour turnover is the number of employees leaving an organisation and being replaced. The rate of turnover is often expressed as the number of people leaving as a percentage of the average number of people employed, in a given period. The term 'natural wastage' is used to describe a 'normal' flow of people out of an organisation through retirement, career or job change, relocation, illness and so on.

There are different ways of measuring labour turnover. Most simply, actual gross numbers of people leaving may provide a basis for recruitment/replacement – but this statistic does not say anything about whether or not these people need replacing! To measure labour turnover in a more systematic and useful way, an index such as the following may be used.

(a) **Crude labour turnover rate** (*the BIM Index, British Institute of Management*, 1949)

Here we express turnover as a percentage of the number of people employed.

$$\frac{\text{Number of leavers in a period}}{\text{Average number of people employed in the period}} \times 100 = \%\ \textit{turnover}$$

This is normally quoted as an annual rate and may be used to measure turnover per organisation, department or group of employees. The *advantage* of this index is that it can alert HR planners to unusually high percentages of the workforce leaving – compared with the HR plan, or with the industry average, say – which would suggest that something is wrong, or that more effort is needed to retain employees. The *disadvantage* of this index is that it does not indicate *who* is leaving the department or organisation: even a high turnover rate may not reflect any real instability if the core of experienced staff consistently remains. (In fact, most wastage occurs among young people and those in the early stages of their employment in an organisation: stability tends to increase with length of service.)

(b) **Labour stability**

Here we try to eliminate short-term employees from our analysis, thus obtaining a better picture of the significant movements in the workforce.

$$\frac{\text{Number of employees with one or more years' service}}{\text{Number of employees employed at the beginning of the year}} \times 100 = \%\ \textit{stability}$$

Particularly in times of rapid expansion, organisations should keep an eye on stability, as a meaningful measure.

(c) The labour stability index ignores new starts during the year and does not consider actual length of service, which may be added to the measurement via **length of service analysis**, or **survival rate analysis**. Here, the organisation calculates the proportion of employees who are engaged within a certain period who are still with the firm after various periods of time. There may be a survival rate of 70% after two years, for example, but only 50% in year three: the distribution of losses might be plotted on a survival curve to indicate trends.

ACTIVITY 3 — 20 mins

Suppose a company has 20 employees at the beginning of 2008, and 100 at the end of the year. Disliking the culture created by the expansion, 18 of the original experienced labour force resign.

Calculate:

(a) The crude labour turnover rate
(b) The stability rate

Comment on the significance of your results.

3.2 Causes of labour turnover

Some reasons for leaving will be largely unavoidable, or unforeseeable. '**Natural wastage**' occurs through:

(a) Illness or accident (although transfer to lighter duties, excusing the employee from shiftwork or other accommodations might be possible)

(b) A move from the locality for domestic, social or logistical reasons

(c) Changes to the family situation: for example, when an individual changes job or gives up work to accommodate parental responsibilities

(d) Retirement

(e) Career change.

Other causes of labour turnover, however, may be to do with the organisation, management, terms and conditions and so on: in other words, **job dissatisfaction**.

The technique used to discover an employee's reason for leaving is the exit interview. This is an interview held with an employee after they have resigned to discover their reasons for wanting to leave. However whilst exit interviews often provide valuable data for the Human Resources department, Taylor (2010) points out a number of risks:

1. Employees do not give completely honest answers, as they are often mindful of the need for a reference or even a job one day
2. Employees tend to focus on the pull factors (what attracted them to the job), rather than the push factors (what made them consider looking for a new job in the first place)
3. It is easier to say that the reason for leaving is other than a poor relationship with their existing manager as this avoids examining personal characteristics

ACTIVITY 4 — 15 mins

Suggest a number of factors that might contribute to labour turnover, which might broadly be grouped under the heading of 'job dissatisfaction'.

Which of these factors would be sufficient to make you leave an organisation: (a) in a market where you were reasonably sure of finding other employment and (b) in a market where other employment was scarce?

Labour turnover is also influenced by the following factors.

(a) **The economic climate and the state of the job market.** When unemployment is high and jobs are hard to find, labour turnover will be much lower.

(b) **The age structure and length of service of the work force.** An ageing workforce will have many people approaching retirement. However, it has been found in most companies that labour turnover is highest among:

   (i) Young people, especially unmarried people with no family responsibilities
   (ii) People who have been in the employment of the company for only a short time.

   The employment life cycle usually shows a decision point shortly after joining, when things are still new and perhaps difficult. This is called the **'first induction crisis'**. There is then a period of mutual accommodation and adjustment between employer and employee (called the **'differential transit'** period): in the settling of areas of conflict, there may be further turnover. A second (less significant) induction crisis occurs as both parties come to terms with the new status quo. Finally, the period of **'settled connection'** begins, and the likelihood of leaving is much less.

The CIPD table below shows the median turnover rates by industry and also illustrates these over time, giving an indication of the effect of the recent economic climate.

UK median labour turnover rates, by industry sector (%)						
	All leavers			Voluntary leavers		
Sector	2011 survey	2010 survey	2009 survey	2011 survey	2010 survey	2009 survey
Manufacturing and production	9.3	12.4	15.3	3.7	2.7	7.7
Private sector services	13.8	14.6	16.8	8.7	7.4	10.4
Public services	8.5	8.6	12.6	3.4	5.8	7.6
Voluntary, community, not-for-profit	13.1	15.9	16.4	7.0	10.2	11.0

TOYOTA

Toyota, the car manufacturer, wished to understand the impact of its performance management, career development, training and internal transfers policies on employee retention. It combined a statistical evaluation of leavers and an employee survey to understand the situation. The outcome of the survey was that the supposed beneficiaries saw little career advantage in taking up their options. Yet the statistical analysis showed that those who received more training or who made lateral moves within the organisation advanced more rapidly that those who did not. Toyota realised that there was a gap between the employees' perception of the policies and the actual career outcome. The focus of action changed therefore from revising the policies to focusing on improving the communication and understanding amongst employees.

So far, you may have got the impression that 'labour turnover' equals 'instability' and that, since it is caused by job dissatisfaction, it must be a bad thing for the organisation. But remember: earlier in this chapter we noted that an organisation may from time to time have a surplus of labour or particular skills, which it would like to be able to 'lose' through natural wastage instead of costly redundancies. And some organisations may be constantly creating and disbanding projects: forming loose, temporary or 'virtual' networks of people – without tying themselves to expectations of 'jobs' or 'careers'. So should organisations fight to retain employees – or not?

3.3 Is turnover a 'bad thing'?

The following table puts labour turnover in perspective.

Potential advantages of labour turnover	Potential disadvantages of labour turnover
Opportunities to inject 'new blood' into the organisation: new people bringing new ideas and outlooks, new skills and experience in different situations	Broken continuity of knowledge, relationships, culture and succession, where continuity could offer stability and predictability
Balance in the age structure of the workforce. Absence of labour turnover would create an increasingly aged workforce, often accompanied by an increasing wage/salary cost	Lead time and lost performance while a replacement is found and brought 'on line' to the level of expertise of the previous job-holder
The creation of opportunities for promotion and succession which offers an important incentive to more junior employees	Morale problems. Turnover may be perceived by other employees as a symptom of job dissatisfaction, causing the problem to escalate
The ability to cope with labour surpluses, in some grades of job, without having to make redundancies	The costs of turnover, including: • **Replacement costs**: recruiting, selecting and training; loss of output or efficiency • **Preventive costs**: the cost of retaining staff, through pay, benefits and welfare provisions, maintaining working conditions

It is common to hear that turnover is bad when it is high – but this cannot be assessed in isolation. What is an acceptable rate of turnover and what is excessive? There is no fixed percentage rate of turnover which is the borderline between acceptable and unacceptable. Labour turnover rates may be a signal that something is wrong when:

(a) They are higher than the turnover rates in another similar department of the organisation; for example, if the labour turnover rate is higher at branch A than at branches B, C and D in the same area, something might be wrong at branch A.

(b) They are higher than they were in previous years or months; in other words, the situation might be deteriorating.

(c) The costs of labour turnover are considered too high – although they will be relative to the costs of preventing high turnover by offering employees incentives to stay.

Otherwise, the organisation may live with high rates because they are the norm for a particular industry or job (think about call centres, for example); because the organisation culture accepts constant turnover (as in a project-based or 'virtual' network organisation); or because the cost of keeping employees is greater than the cost of replacing them!

Think of an organisation that you are familiar with; what are the major causes of turnover there? Do you know if reasons for leaving are formally recorded by the organisation? Do you see anything being done with the information?.

3.4 Costing employee turnover

The cost of employee turnover is a perpetual debate, and various studies have been conducted to calculate the costs. There is often a large variance in the costs to organisations, and this is primarily attributed to what is or is not included within the calculation. For example, advertising costs are direct costs which are invoiced and so easy to identify; the indirect cost of time spent arranging interviews (opportunity cost) is less easy to measure, and so sometimes is not included. Some of the more complex calculation methods estimate variances in employee productivity when first starting and during the wind-down after resignation. For the purposes of this study two elementary methods will be discussed.

The CIPD identified the following as the major cost categories:

- Administration of the resignation
- Recruitment and selection costs, including administration
- Covering the post during the period in which there is a vacancy
- Induction training for the new employee

Criteria included in cost per hire calculations (%)	
Advertising costs	81
Agency/search costs	75
Employee referrals	35
Travel expenses	30
Fixed costs of resourcing team	24
Opportunity costs of hiring managers' time	24
Relocation expenses	17
Don't know	4
Other	3

CIPD 2011

As shown above, over 80% of all companies include the cost of advertising when working out how much staff turnaround costs, whereas only 24% include the cost of the manager's time. This indicates that most organisations include only their most obvious costs when completing their calculations.

Method 1

This method simply looks at the *time* spent on replacing those who have left during the year. An example calculation is shown.

Assumptions, all annual employment costs:

HR manager	£35,000
HR administrative assistant (part time)	£10,000
Operations manager	£30,000
Average employee	£18,000

Percentage of time spent on resignation, recruitment, selection and induction activities		Cost £
HR manager	30%	10,500
HR administrative assistant	40%	4,000
Operations managers (x7)	5%	10,500
Employees (x150)	2%	54,000
Annual recruitment advertising		25,000
Total Annual Turnover Cost		**104,000**

Clearly this method is extremely simple and does not take account of the more subtle and harder to identify costs; it does however provide an organisation-specific amount that can be taken into consideration.

ACTIVITY 5

20 mins

Search the internet for employee turnover cost calculators, you will find free tools available. Use one of the tools and evaluate its functionality and ease of use

You could start with www.greatbiztools.com; be aware that it is American and so may use some terms that you are not familiar with, but these are explained.

Method 2

This approach focuses on greater detail than method 1 and places less reliance on assumed percentages, and looks at more directly identifiable costs.

Turnover cost for a retail assistant

Activity	Time	Cost £
Assistant time administering the resignation	2 hours	20
Management time conducting exit interview	1 hour	20
Other resignation-related management activities	2 hours	40
Management time writing and placing advertisement	1 hour	20
Advertisement in local paper		900
Management time shortlisting applicants	1 hour	20
Assistant time arranging the interviews	3 hours	30
Management time conducting interviews (x2 managers)	10 hours	200

Activity	Time	Cost £
Interview expenses		50
Assistant time administering new starter	2 hours	20
Management time on new starter administration	1 hour	20
Induction day for new starter	6 hours	60
Management time inducting new starter	4 hours	80
Staff time for on-the-job training	12 hours	120
Total cost per individual resignation		1,600
Total number of resignations per year		45
Total turnover cost for the year		**72,000**

This method produces a more accurate and reliable figure, however the effort to obtain all the costs may not be considered worthwhile.

Shown below is the result of CIPD research in 2011 for the estimated total costs for recruiting two categories of employees.

Estimated total costs (advertising costs, agency or search fees) per hire (£)				
	Median 2011 £	Minimum £	Maximum £	Median 2010 £
Senior managers/directors	7,000	251	55,000	8,333
Other employees	2,000	150	32,000	2,930

ACTIVITY 6 — 20 mins

How can there be such a great variance in the minimum and maximum cost of recruiting a senior manager/director?

4 Employee retention in action

In the late 1990s a US bank found that its most concerning HR problem was employee turnover. Annual employee attrition had reached 25%, and amongst key customer-facing employees it was reaching towards 40%. Given one of the bank's strategies was customer focus, this jeopardised its achievement. The turnover was higher than the industry norm and exacerbated by the bank operating in a number of tight labour markets.

Using employee surveys and exit interviews, the bank began to build a picture of what employees valued about their employment and why they were leaving. The results suggested that inadequate pay and heavy workloads were key reasons for leaving. Naturally the high level of employee attrition and the speed with which the vacancies were filled only compounded this issue. Whilst the bank tried to address these issues by more closely tracking local pay rates and trialling flexible working, this did not solve the problem. Indeed what concerned employers was that there was no clear cause for the turnover. Upon further analysis the bank concluded that employees were simply telling them their reason for leaving was salary as this was considered 'politically acceptable', and not the true cause. Therefore the bank concluded it had to delve deeper, and moved their focus of attention from what employees *said* to what they actually *did*.

The bank had a busy history of mergers and acquisitions which had often resulted in the consolidation of operations or closing of branches. Through an analysis of its activity the bank was able to see that the number of involuntary leavers that had left had undermined the confidence of those who stayed.

The bank consequently developed a multifaceted strategy to retention. Rather than immediately apply an increase in salaries, the bank utilised the information it had gleaned through its research.

Career development

Those employees who had been promoted or even taken lateral moves remained longest. The bank concluded that those employees who were able to broaden their experience while at the bank felt that they were enhancing their marketability. This protected them internally during periods of severances and externally should they choose to leave. In fact younger employees valued broad work experience over pay. The research also showed that the hiring policy and stability in management were two other crucial factors.

Promotion, job change and pay growth had the greatest impact on retention. Consequently the bank embarked on a deliberate strategy of enabling greater internal mobility through internal job fairs and internal vacancy postings. While it may have been anticipated that managers would resist the internal churn, they began to appreciate the confidence in knowing that the internal churn at least brought them employees who had good company knowledge and were proven performers. The bank also began a programme of career coaching to help employees manage transition within the organisation.

Pay and incentives

Pay was discovered to have the smallest impact on retention. The greatest impact on the individual was not their current level of pay, but how much their pay had grown in the past. The bank discovered that improving the bank's market position by 10% was far less important than increasing an individual's pay by 10%. This was because in some markets pay was already competitive and in others 10% wasn't enough. The bank abandoned market adjustments and implemented steady pay increases to those who performed well or exceptionally, and concentrated the messages around successful career progression and personal development.

The bank also began to offer its top performers inclusion in its incentive programmes. It discovered that the inclusion was more powerful than the financial reward. It concluded that inclusion suggested a commitment on the part of the bank to the employee, which in turn the employee reciprocated.

Management stability

The bank's research showed that there was a direct link between manager/supervisor attrition and employee retention. Any team that had a manager/supervisor leave was likely to double attrition in the following year. However it was unclear as to why. Was it because the team now felt disconnected to the organisation or because, if the supervisor believed better opportunities lay elsewhere, the team members should also consider their own positions. The bank had to investigate whether the outcome was the same for internal versus external moves and whether it related to the performance of the manager/supervisor. The research showed that there was only an impact if the manager was a recognised good performer by bosses and subordinates and the manager left the business.

The bank focused on how to retain good managers/supervisors. Career progression was again identified as key, and more important than base pay. However this level of employee did care about variable pay and how that pay was delivered. Performance-based cash bonuses were more highly valued than stock options. The bank therefore redesigned its reward programme to channel more cash bonuses to high performers.

Additionally, to reduce the impact on the teams of managers/supervisors leaving, the bank began to develop links with other managerial level staff. Consequently, if the manager did leave, the team had someone to turn to. This was also achieved through the development of coaching and mentoring programmes, again giving employees links to the bank outside their immediate team.

Hiring criteria

Through its research the bank identified attributes that were more likely to lead to higher retention. These were:

- Past stability. Employees who had remained with previous employers for long periods of time were more likely to remain with the bank for longer periods. The bank also identified higher levels of attrition in the first year and so enhanced the induction process and ensured that workloads were manageable. Heavy workloads had been a key reason for early leavers. Performance feedback was also given sooner for new recruits.
- Diversity. Woman and racial minorities were more likely to remain. The bank had already embarked on diversity programmes so these had the added benefit of compounding the retention effect.
- Referrals. Employees introduced through the referrals scheme were more likely to stay.

Conclusion

The bank found that the impact of its changes could be identified within the first eight months. It attributed its success to having firm data with which to present its arguments, and the data was compelling. It particularly valued hiring the 'right' type of employees and retaining valued managers/supervisors. The attrition rates reduced by up to 40%. For the key customer-facing employees the attrition rate reduced by 10% from 40% to 30%.

The bank was especially pleased that the changes had been low cost options; it had resisted simply throwing money at the problem and felt it had been proven correct. However as with all changes there were a number of unexpected outcomes, most noticeably that as attrition reduced, the internal job market shrank thus providing fewer opportunities for employees to move internally. At one time this had been a major leg of the strategy.

5 Organisational performance

5.1 Internal analysis

During any internal analysis an organisation will need to consider how well it is performing. As it develops its People Plan it will also want to identify how it hopes to perform in the future, and how this will be measured. To be able to evaluate any performance will require the use of measures.

The CIPD identifies three levels of data collection:

Basic	This includes examples such as staffing costs of HR, recruitment speed, cost of recruitment, employee attrition. The information is typically readily available and focuses on single points of measurement. The information is mostly analysed at a departmental level and provided to line managers. Trends and patterns are identified so that managers can identify problems and their causes and, following remedial action, improve their efficiency and effectiveness.
Intermediate	Information at this level is typically designed for purpose e.g. designing employee satisfaction surveys. The output from this data collection is the design of new policies or initiatives intended to increase employee satisfaction. Correlations are also investigated: for example, to find links between flexible working policies and employee retention. The information provided to line managers relates to which processes mostly influence the desired outcomes. Through this process HR is able to develop its plan and management behaviour is steered towards the most effective style.
Higher	At this level the information provides data for measuring performance against the Key Performance Indicators of the organisational strategy. The information collected is qualitative and quantitative. Managers are provided with a range of indicators on a range of measures which they can use to monitor the performance of their department.

Performance data can also be expressed as 'hard' or 'soft'. Hard data being number of new starters in a month; soft data being employee satisfaction for example below are some examples of such measures, which are often collected in an ad hoc manner and do not relate directly to the achievement of the People Plan.

Hard	Soft
• Cost to fill vacancies • Time to fill vacancies • Cost of HR as a % of total costs • Number of training days	• Employee satisfaction • Line manager satisfaction • Senior manager satisfaction • Customer satisfaction

Earlier in this chapter we looked at employee attrition; in a later chapter the measurement of diversity in the workforce is discussed, so they will not be considered now.

Organisations also have the option to benchmark themselves against other similar organisations. The purpose of the benchmarking will usually determine who is within the benchmarking group. For example if an organisation is evaluating employee satisfaction it can often draw upon a wider range of organisations; if it is trying to understand fee earner to support staff ratios it will wish to be industry and/or organisation-specific. Benchmarking can be extremely useful to an organisation to help it understand whether the People Plan is effective, for example when measured against the external environment rather than simply assessing internal measures. For example, the organisation's employee turnover may have reduced by 2% from 20% to 18%, yet the industry median is 12%. So whilst the organisation is improving it still has some way to go to even match the industry median.

5.2 The balanced scorecard

The final form of measurement recognised by the CIPD, the 'Higher' level, is the balanced-score-card, which is attributed to Kaplan and Norton. Kaplan and Norton identified the significance of **executed strategy** and the **implementation stage** of the strategic management process as key drivers in enhancing organisational performance. In so doing, they highlight the importance of having a realistic and achievable People Plan and only one that can be, and is implemented. Developing a plan that is unachievable and never implemented will not help an organisation achieve its strategic goals!

The balanced scorecard has four key measures:

1 Financial – 'to succeed financially, how should we appear to our shareholders?'

2 Customers – 'to achieve our vision, how should we appear to our customers?'

3 Internal business processes – 'to satisfy our shareholders and customers, what business processes must we excel at?'

4 Learning and growth – 'to achieve our vision, how will we sustain our ability to change and improve?'

Kaplan and Norton recognise the impact key HR activities can have on business performance in the fourth element. Employee skills, knowledge and satisfaction are identified as improved internal processes, and so in turn contribute to achieving customer satisfaction and added economic value.

Whilst the model is designed to apply to 'for profit' organisations, the principles are equally applicable to public service and 'not for profit' organisations. Such organisations also have to operate within financial parameters, such as available budget; they have people who receive the services and who are effectively customers; they also need to operate as efficiently and effectively as possible to extract best value out of the funds available; and they will also have the objective of continuing their operation and improving.

5.3 Benchmarking

Benchmarking is the 'establishment, through data gathering, of targets and comparators, that permit relative levels of performance (and particularly areas of underperformance) to be identified. Adoption of identified best practices should improve performance.'

Benchmarking is generally undertaken in order to improve organisational rather than individual performance. However, it may be seen as related to performance management since it involves much similar activity.

The benchmarking process

Benchmarking can be divided into stages.

step 1 The first stage is to ensure senior management commitment to the benchmarking process. This will only be genuinely available when the senior managers have a full appreciation of what is involved: senior people are quite capable of changing their minds when it becomes apparent that they did not anticipate the actual levels of cost or inconvenience, for example.

step 2 The areas to be benchmarked should be determined and objectives should be set. Note that here the objectives will not be in the form of aspirations for improvement to specific processes and practices, but more in the nature of stating the extent and depth of the enquiry.

step 3 Key performance measures must be established. This will require an understanding of the systems involved, which, in turn, will require discussion with key stakeholders and observation of the way work is carried out.

step 4 Select organisations to benchmark against. Internal benchmarking may be possible but, where internal departments have little in common, comparisons must be made against equivalent parts of other organisations.

step 5 Measure own and others' performance. Negotiation should take place to establish just who does the measurement: ideally, a joint team should do it, but there may be issues of confidentiality or convenience that mean each organisation does its own measuring.

step 6

Compare performance. Raw data must be carefully analysed if appropriate conclusions are to be drawn. It will be appropriate to discuss initial findings with the stakeholders concerned: they are likely both to have useful comment to offer and to be anxious about the possibility of adverse reflection upon them.

step 7

Design and implement improvement programmes. It may be possible to import complete systems; alternatively, it may be appropriate to move towards a synthesis that combines various elements of best practice. Sometimes, improvements require extensive reorganisation and restructuring. In any event, there is likely to be a requirement for training. Improvements in administrative systems often call for investment in new equipment, particularly in IT systems.

step 8

Monitor improvements. The continuing effectiveness of improvements must be monitored. At the same time, it must be understood that improvements are not 'once and for all' and that further adjustments may be beneficial.

Reasons for undertaking benchmarking

Benchmarking has the following advantages.

(a) Benchmarking can assess a firm's existing position, and provide a basis for establishing standards of performance.

(b) The comparisons are carried out by the managers who have to live with any changes implemented as a result of the exercise.

(c) Benchmarking focuses on improvement in key areas and sets targets which are challenging but evidently achievable.

(d) The sharing of information can be a spur to innovation.

(e) The result should be improved performance, particularly in cost control and delivering value.

Drawbacks of benchmarking

Many companies have gained significant benefits from benchmarking but it is worth pointing out a number of possible dangers.

(a) It can cloud perception of strategic purpose by attracting too much attention to the detail of what is measured, since it concentrates on doing things right rather than doing the right thing: the difference between efficiency and effectiveness. A process can be efficient but its output may not be useful.

(b) Benchmarking does not identify the reasons why performance is at a particular level, whether good or bad.

(c) It is a catching-up exercise rather than the development of anything distinctive. After the benchmarking exercise, the competitor might improve performance in a different way.

(d) It depends on accurate information about comparator companies.

(e) It is not cost-free and can divert management attention.

(f) It can become a hindrance and even a threat: sharing information with other companies can be a burden and a security risk.

Think of an organisation that you are familiar with; do they measure their organisational performance? If so, what measures do they use? Do they share these with the workforce? Does this improve the performance of the organisation?.

So far during this chapter we have considered many factors that contribute to the internal analysis by an organisation. Distilling this information into an easy-to-communicate and understand format is a useful tool to the People Planner; in the next section we will at method to achieve this.

6 Summarising and evaluating the current situation

6.1 Current situation

The current situation for an organisation can be analysed using the SWOT method (Strengths, Weaknesses, Opportunities and Threats). This is a classic business tool and can be applied in many situations. To obtain the maximum benefit it will be used in conjunction with the output from any other analytical tools that have been engaged to assess the internal and external situation.

The output from the SWOT can usefully be combined with a comparative analysis of performance.

(a) Anticipated and past performance can be compared.
(b) An organisation's performance can be assessed in relation to its competitors and sector norms.

6.2 Internal appraisal: strengths and weaknesses

The strengths and weaknesses analysis is internal to the organisation and intended to shape its approach to the external environment. The strengths and weaknesses part of the SWOT analysis involves looking at the findings of the internal audit. At the end of the internal audit an organisation should have some ideas as to its core competences. For instance, the identification of shortcomings in skills or resources could lead to a planned acquisition programme or staff recruitment and training.

Strengths

- Existing skill base
- Individual product, market, service expertise
- Lower employment costs
- Excellent retention

Weaknesses

- Insufficient skills
- Insufficient market knowledge
- Inflexible workforce
- High cost/benefits package

6.3 External appraisal: opportunities and threats

An external appraisal is required to identify profit-making or cost-effective service improvement opportunities that can be exploited by the organisation's strengths and also to anticipate environmental threats against which the organisation must protect itself. The external appraisal is the opportunities and threats part of SWOT analysis.

Opportunities

- New legislation that will require expert service providers
- Government subsidies to incentivise purchasing the product we make
- Global clients are seeking global service providers
- Weak currency is increasing demand for product

Threats

- New legislation is threatening long-term industry survival
- Overseas providers are able to produce same product at cheaper prices
- Competitor is able to attract key personnel
- Universities providing fewer degree places for vocational skills

6.4 Example of SWOT

Strengths	Weaknesses
• Strong corporate brand that supports recruitment • Above median pay and benefits • Graduate development scheme has excellent reputation within sector • Worldwide service provision insulating organisation from vagaries of any single market • Good cash flow and reserves	• Leadership team has most experience within single sector of the organisation – need greater knowledge of whole organisation • No successor identified for CEO • Core workers in product development are over 55 years old – need for succession plan • Too little knowledge of Asia Pacific market within the organisation
Opportunities	**Threats**
• New country to join European Union – could be good source of skilled workers • Local university has started to offer product-related course – summer student and future graduate pipeline • Recovery in major overseas market, have been approached about creating a Joint Venture	• New legislation will see demise of product in three years – need to redeploy 50 workers in next three years • New employer seeking similar skills is to open up new facility in the same city • Rival has won major worldwide recognised contract requiring additional resources

Chapter Roundup

- To be able to create any People Plan requires the careful identification and management of the key stakeholders, these will usually be internal but stakeholders can also be categorised as connected and external.
- Internal analysis can take two approaches, either bottom up or top down. Whatever the approach, they will need to consider: organisational objectives; staff characteristics; cost of labour.
- Employee turnover is both a cost to organisations and a key indicator of the employee perception of the organisation. Different measures can be used to evaluate the attrition and stability. Organisations need to understand the causes of employee turnover, especially those where employees voluntarily leave.
- The cost of employee turnover can be calculated through a variety of different methods. The annual cost will be often used as the base cost for justifying investment in Human Resources initiatives e.g. benefits improvement.
- Organisations need to understand their performance against either targets they have been set or against other competitors in the same sector. Performance data enables organisations to understand whether their performance is improving or deteriorating; and it can be used as a means of communicating and engaging with the workforce.
- SWOT analysis is a useful technique for informing an audience in an easily digestible format how an organisation stands when considering the internal and external factors that confront it.

Quick Quiz

1. What is a stakeholder?
2. What are the two approaches that can be taken to conducting internal analysis?
3. What is the calculation for Labour Stability?
4. Identify two risks associated with conducting exit interviews
5. Of the UK median turnover rates, which sector saw the smallest reduction in voluntary leavers between 2009 – 2011?
   - Manufacturing and production
   - Private sector services
   - Public services
   - Voluntary, community, not-for-profit
6. Identify two advantages of labour turnover
7. According to the CIPD, what is the most common criteria when calculating hiring costs?
8. What method of organisational performance measurement do you associate with Kaplan and Norton?

9 Which of the following are not benefits of benchmarking

(a) Benchmarking can assess a firm's existing position, and provide a basis for establishing standards of performance.

(b) Benchmarking information can be shared with competitors to enable them to achieve the same standard of performance

(c) Benchmarking focuses on improvement in key areas and sets targets which are challenging but evidently achievable.

(d) The sharing of information enables managers to compete internally with one another

(e) The result should be improved performance, particularly in cost control and delivering value.

10 What does SWOT stand for?

Answers to Quick Quiz

1 Any group or individual who can affect or [be] affected by the achievement of an organisation's objectives. (para 1.1)

2 'bottom up' or 'top down' (para 2.1)

3 $\frac{\text{Number of employees with one or more years' service}}{\text{Number of employees employed at the beginning of the year}} \times 100\% = \%\ \text{stability}$ (para 3.1)

4 You could have chosen from

1 Employees do not give completely honest answers, as they are often mindful of the need for a reference or even a job one day

2 Employees tend to focus on the pull factors (what attracted them to the job), rather than the push factors (what made them consider looking for a new job in the first place)

3 It is easier to say that the reason for leaving is other than a poor relationship with their existing manager as this avoids examining personal characteristics (para 3.2)

5 The private sector reducing from 10.4% to 8.7% (para 3.2)

6 You could have had: Opportunities to inject 'new blood' into the organisation; Balance in the age structure of the workforce; The creation of opportunities for promotion and succession; The ability to cope with labour surpluses, without having to make redundancies (para 3.3)

7 Advertising costs at 81% (para 3.4)

8 The Balanced Scorecard (para 5.2)

9 B) Benchmarking information can be shared with competitors to enable them to achieve the same standard of performance & D) The sharing of information enables managers to compete internally with one another (para 5.3)

10 Strengths, Weaknesses, Opportunities, Threats (para 6.1)

Answers to Activities

Activity 1

- Students, interested in receiving the qualification and the reputation of the college
- Lecturers, interested in job security, quality of students and reputation of the college
- Employers, either as they are paying the course fees, or want to be sure students are learning vocational skills they will be able to utilise
- Administrative staff, interested in job security and employer's reputation
- Parents, if they are helping to fund students
- Governing Board at the college, status of the college as a recognised learning institution, and financial security
- Competing colleges, number of students applying, income for their college
- The body that governs all higher education establishments to ensure that the correct standards are maintained

Activity 2

(a) The Internet is a rich source of statistical, environmental, benchmarking and other relevant information for HRP. Internal corporate databases (possibly integrated into Human Resource Information Systems) should provide data on current skills, workforce structure, productivity and so on. Expert and decision-support software is also available for manpower and 'Enterprise Resource Planning' (ERP). (You may like to do a web search on 'ERP' or 'Human Resource Planning' and check out some of the resources for yourself.)

(b) This may be useful as the beginnings of a research/information database. There are many potential sources of labour and environmental information. Just a few suggestions:

- CIPD and other HR journals (and their websites)
- News media
- Employment and industry journals (Employment Gazette, Employment Digest, specific industry journals, Industrial Relations Review, Labour Market Quarterly)
- Government statistical publications (census information, Social Trends)
- Publications, websites and contacts of relevant bodies: trade unions, trade associations, employers' associations, training bodies
- Competitors and other employers (websites, annual reports and accounts, personal contacts)

Activity 3

At the end of 2008, the company works out that it has:

BIM Index: $\dfrac{\text{18 leavers}}{\text{60 (average) employees}} \times 100 = 30\%$ turnover

This is not uncommon, and would cause no undue worries. However:

Stability index : $\dfrac{2-\text{year servers}}{20} \times 100 = 10\%$ stability

Only 10% of the labour force is stable (and therefore offering the benefits of experience and acclimatisation to the work and culture of the organisation). A crude turnover rate has disguised the significance of what has happened.

Activity 4

Everyone has their own personal reasons for wanting to leave an organisation, however the reasons typically fall into a number of categories:

- Lack of career development
- Change in personal circumstances
- Opportunity for promotion elsewhere, due to potential future positions not being available
- More money
- Working nearer to home
- Wishing to travel abroad

Activity 5

This is an activity for your own development. It should have given you insight as to what is available and the different methods that can be used.

Activity 6

Different methods used to calculate costs

- Agency fees are usually a percentage of salary package, not all senior managers/directors get paid the same, size of organisation and industry sector will be enormously important
- The typical statistical problems that are encountered when using minimum and maximums; better to use median
- Highly unusual outcomes, minimum could have be single advert in a local jobs board identified the correct candidate and no external agency was used; the other could have been a global search using a high profile headhunter

In such circumstances it would be important to know how many organisations participated and what size they are in terms of number of employees and turnover

Chapter 3

External analysis

To complement any internal analysis will require an understanding of the external environment. The external environment is important as, while this is the most likely source of any new labour, it is also impossible to control. Consequently it needs to be carefully monitored and understood as best as possible.

To help achieve a greater level of understanding, this chapter will firstly look at the external market at a macro level, which will provide an understanding of the long-term availability of labour and skills. The final section looks at the PESTEL tool as a method by which to analyse the external environment and understand how it may affect an organisation.

TOPIC LIST		LEARNING OUTCOMES
1	The labour market	3.1
2	Analysing the labour market	3.2
3	The changing workforce	3.2
4	The external environment	3.3
5	Applying PESTEL	3.4

1 The labour market

Implementing the People Plan will need to include an understanding of the current status of the labour market. The status of the market will form the basis for many of the decisions made around implementing the plan.

1.1 Changes in the labour market

The **labour market** is the sphere in which labour is 'bought' and 'sold', and in which market concepts such as supply, demand and price operate with regard to human resources.

The labour market has changed dramatically in the last few decades. Previously, writers suggested that a **'seller's market'** had been established, as technology increased the skills and therefore scarcity value of employees in certain jobs, and as the scale of state benefits blunted the fear of unemployment: the initiative seemed to be with the employee, or with organised groups of employees.

The decline of manufacturing, the increase of women in employment, the globalisation of business (allowing offshoring of production and service provision to low-cost labour countries) and the more general application of technology, among other factors, have changed that situation. A **'buyer's market'** for labour now gives employers considerable power, with a large pool of available labour created by unemployment and non-career (temporary, freelance) labour.

On the other hand, even in conditions of high overall employment, particular skill shortages still exist and may indeed be *more* acute because of economic pressures on education and training. The term 'war for talent' was coined to describe this phenomena, and while the recent economic downturn has seen the phrase used less vigorously, many employees still compete for people. Engineers and software designers, among other specialist and highly trained groups, are the target of fierce competition, forcing a re-evaluation of recruitment and retention policies amongst employers.

A number of observations can be made about the workforce in the Western economies, that have a macro impact on the labour market:

- **The baby boom generation** (a period of greatly higher birth rates during the period 1946 - 1964) **continues to age.**
- **Declining birth rates** for the post baby boom generation leading to a reducing young age population. This is partly being addressed through increasing immigration and births by immigrant mothers.
- Improved health and medical care leading to **increasing longevity.**
- **Increasing retirement ages**. The result of adults living longer and being able to continue to work has seen two major changes. The older workforce wishes to work longer in order to keep active and enjoy continuing income. The cost of supporting an aging population has required governments to increase the compulsory retirement age. This requirement has been necessary because governments cannot afford to provide pensions for the longer period and also the indigenous working population is declining, and hence the government is receiving less tax income.

ACTIVITY 1 — 10 mins

What are the implications for the Western economy employer of these four changes to workforce?

1.2 Differences in particular labour markets

Employers may compete for labour and skills in a number of different markets: local, national and international.

- Particular factors in the local labour market (people living in the 'travel to work area' or within reasonable commuting distance) may create pressure for flexibility. For example: geographical dispersion or lack of public transportation may require flexible starting hours, or work-from-home options.
- National/regional skill shortages and wage costs may encourage the outsourcing or 'offshoring' of operations to low-cost labour countries, or the co-opting of overseas team members through 'virtual' collaboration using ICT links.
- Different occupational structures and orientations (at local and national level) may also require different approaches to the employment relationship, career management and so on. Professionally and technically qualified staff, for example, may be treated differently (as 'core' employees) from lower-skilled and high mobility workers (who may be more flexibly contracted).

1.3 Demographic trends

Demography is an analysis of statistics on birth and death rates, the age structure of populations, ethnic groups within communities, population movements and so on.

(a) The **number of people who are economically active** in the UK is still increasing, principally due to immigration and the expanding number of women returning to, and remaining in, paid work (supported by diversity and family-friendly HR policies). Over the long term, however, the proportion of the population that is available for work is expected to shrink: birth rates continue to fall, and life expectancy to lengthen, creating an increasing retired population in proportion to those of working age.

(b) As a result, the **age profile of the workforce** is also changing: the population as a whole is getting older, with fewer young people entering the workforce (especially as a greater proportion of them remain longer in full-time education). This has been reinforced by the introduction of age diversity legislation in the UK in 2010, encouraging the selection and retention of mature workers, and the removal of the compulsory retirement age.

UK national statistics

The population of the UK is growing in size and becoming increasingly older. Ageing refers both to the ageing of the population and the increasing number of people reaching older age.

Over the period 1984-2009 the number of people aged 65 and over in the UK increased by 20 per cent to 10.1 million; in 2009, 16 per cent of the population were aged 65 and over. The number of people aged 85 and over more than doubled over the same period to 1.4 million and the percentage aged under 16 fell from 21 per cent to 19 per cent.

In 2009 the median age for women (40 years) was higher than for men (38 years). This is because, on average, women live longer than men. However, the gender gap has narrowed; in 1984 the median ages for women and men were 36 and 33 years respectively, a difference of 3 years.

Population ageing will continue for the next few decades. By 2034 the number of people aged 85 and over is projected to be 2.5 times larger than in 2009, reaching 3.5 million and accounting for 5 per cent of the total population. The population aged 65 and over will account for 23 per cent of the total population in 2034, while the proportion of the population aged between 16 and 64 is due to fall from 65 per cent to 59 per cent.

1.4 Diversity

The workforce is becoming increasingly diverse in its make up, in several respects.

(a) **Sex**. Increased female participation in the workforce has been a significant social trend since the Second World War. The employment rate for women of working age is currently just under 70%. Although a majority of managerial posts are still occupied by men, and there is a continued gap in overall pay levels, there has been an increase in the representation of women at all levels. There is still significant segregation in terms of the types of work performed, with particular areas of work dominated by either men or women. Women currently account for over 80% of part-time workers in the UK, which is in itself a growth sector.

(b) **Ethnic diversity**. Multi-racial representation has greatly increased in the UK workforce. The latest Workplace Employee Relations Survey (WERS) (2004) suggests that over 50% of workplaces are multi-racial compared to only 30% in 1980.

Total numbers of people coming into the UK and leaving, reported in 2010

Since the year 2000 518,000 people came into the UK in the year to end-June 2009 - down by 3% on the previous year. 317,000 people left the UK in the same year. Of the number coming in, 68,000 were from Eastern Europe (the A8 Accession countries), 58,000 left - the difference between the two (the migration balance) being 10,000.

Worker registrations by Eastern Europeans

Workers from the Accession countries have to register in the UK and the figures here show a decrease in recent years. In 2009, there were 106,390 applications accepted - down from 158,545 the year before. In total, there have been 703,620 applications accepted since 2006.

Workers from Romania and Bulgaria have a separate process - 20,180 workers applied for seasonal agricultural employment in 2009, up from 16,460 the year before.

UK immigration population by country of birth

Poland is now the second highest (behind India) with 503,000 people. In 2004 it wasn't in the top 60.

UK employment by country of birth and nationality

This shows that although numbers of Eastern Europeans have grown in the UK, they still form a comparatively small part of the workforce: 472,000 workers (or 1.63% of the workforce) by the end of 2009, compared to 13,000 (0.05% of workforce) at the end of 1997.

Major implications for employee resourcing include:

(a) The need to take account of anti-discrimination legislation and best practice in recruitment. As well as legal protection for groups which have traditionally been under-represented in the workplace, heightened sensitivity to such matters means that positive equal opportunity and diversity policies play an important part in building an employer brand which will enable organisations to attract quality labour.

(b) The need to take account of the needs of increasingly diverse family shapes and circumstances, in order to attract and retain people. Legislation has begun to address the needs of dual income families (e.g. parental leave and time off for emergencies) but proactive HR initiatives – such as career breaks and childcare support – contribute importantly to a 'family-friendly' employer brand (see Chapter 10).

1.5 Skills and qualifications

There has been a steady **decline** in the demand for skills in the **manufacturing** and **agricultural** sectors, and a corresponding growth in **managerial** and **professional** occupations and in **service** industries. A new premium has been placed on **interpersonal skills** (such as team-working, customer service and communication) and on **personal skills** (such as flexibility, time-management and self-motivation).

Since the early 1990s, there has been an increase in the number of graduates entering the labour market. However:

(a) The number of 'graduate jobs' has not kept pace with the increase in supply, making it difficult for new graduates to find employment.

(b) There remain specific skill shortages, creating difficulties for recruiters in filling vacancies. 'There are still too few graduates with high-level IT and scientific qualifications entering the labour market and far too many people lacking basic numeracy and literacy skills' (Torrington *et al*, 2002), despite ongoing policy initiatives to improve the skill base.

The implications for recruiters may be as follows:

1 The need to compete more aggressively for skilled candidates.

2 The need to re-define jobs to maximise the use of scarcer (or more expensive) skills.

3 The need to recruit (or relocate work) overseas.

4 The need to 'lower' recruitment requirements for specific skills and qualifications and invest in employee training and development in the required skills.

In May 2011 the Financial Times reported that the number of foreign-born workers filling low-skill jobs has more than doubled in nine years.

The Office for National Statistics (ONS) said 20.6 per cent of low-skill jobs were held by foreign-born workers in the first quarter of this year – up from 9 per cent in 2002. Workers from eastern or central Europe were the biggest factor.

The figure carried on rising through and beyond the recession, despite high unemployment and the fact that the total number of people in low-skill jobs remained steady at 3.2m. Separate figures from the ONS showed overall net migration had risen to a five-year high.

An extra 367,000 people born outside the UK are now working in low-skill jobs, taking the total to 666,000, up from 298,000 in 2002. The number of UK-born workers in these occupations fell 480,000 to 2.56m.

Workers from the eight eastern European countries that joined the European Union in 2004, who are subject to few immigration controls, were responsible for two-thirds of the rise. Their numbers in low-skill categories increased by 4,000 to 239,000.

Across all categories, UK-born workers have fallen by 223,000 over the past decade, while foreign-born workers have risen by 1.7m. Migrants from eastern Europe are concentrated in low-skill posts, whereas the extra 1.01m from non-EU countries are mainly in middle and upper categories.

ACTIVITY 2 — 10 mins

Identify two reasons why immigration can be an advantage for an employer and two reasons why it can be a disadvantage

1.6 Internal or external recruitment?

There is, however, a view that the labour market is not a simple economic market of demand and supply, where wages decrease where there is an oversupply of labour and increase when there is low unemployment. Such a model assumes perfect knowledge of the jobs available and wages being paid.

The situation is far more complex and in reality two markets operate, the external and the internal labour market.

Since 2008 employers have taken steps to reduce labour costs that have not been seen since the reduced working weeks of the 1970s. Employees have seen their wages reduced or frozen, and/or they have seen benefits reduced in order to contain costs. However, whilst these steps have been taken, and many workforces reduced through redundancy programmes, those in employment have not had the substantial reductions the economic model would indicate. There are a number of reasons for this:

- The need to motivate and engage the remaining workforce
- The need to remain competitive
- The contractual and employee morale difficulties of reducing employee wages

Additionally those who work in organisations with set grade and salary ranges have less scope for wage variation. The route most often taken is salary freeze which, when considering inflation, is a salary reduction in real terms.

There is limited data as to whether salaries are increasing or decreasing. Those who are unemployed and re-entering the market would appear to be accepting reduced salaries. Those who are prepared to move employer, in what can be an uncertain market, would not typically do so for a reduced income. Consequently the data is inconclusive and appears mostly anecdotal.

In the current, market internal opportunities have an appeal to both the employer and employee.

Employer	Employee
Advantages of internal recruitment • The candidate is a known quantity • They have operational knowledge of the organisation • They have the basic skills required • They understand the culture and what is expected • Cheaper, as no recruitment fees • Establishes succession programme, filling more senior positions with proven, experienced and loyal employees • Less risky than new hire who may have new and expensive ideas	Advantages of internal recruitment • The organisation is a known quantity • Less risky than external move as culture, management style, expectations are known • Service and existing service-related benefits are maintained • Greater opportunity for cross-functional move

Employer	Employee
Disadvantages of internal recruitment • Potentially the vacancy cascades down the organisation and so multiple internal appointments are made rather than a single one at the point of need • Creates internal churn when stability maybe sought • No new blood introducing new ideas or cross-industry experience • Existing employee's weaknesses are already known • No new injection of talent into the pipeline	Disadvantages of internal recruitment • New skills and experience are limited to the organisation • Salary limited by existing remuneration structures

Think about an organisation that you know; do they have a clear policy about promoting internally? Do you see this has any clear positive or negative impact on existing employees, contractors or agency workers?.

In a later section on PESTEL we will consider how these factors can be applied to consider the external environment in which an organisation operates.

2 Analysing the labour market

2.1 Planning decisions

When analysing the labour market and considering the requirements of their organisation the People Planner faces some difficult decision such as:

Location	• Does the organisation wish or need to be near the customers • Can the organisation manufacture or provide services away from customers • Can the organisation be split and part of the operations be located in lower cost areas, and retain the minimum presence in the high cost areas
Skills	• What skills are required • What level of skills are required • Can these skills be found concentrated in any particular geographical area • Can competitive advantage be gained by sourcing the skills away from the concentration and so pay lower wages • Can competitive advantage be found through investing in the development of skills away from the usual concentrations • Would offshoring the operations to a location of lower cost and/or greater supply of skilled workforce be a better option

If the People Planner needs to specifically consider where to locate an organisation they also need to include:

- Are there are any government or local incentives available when choosing an area
- What is the density of population
- What is the transport infrastructure to enable people to commute to work
- What is the transport infrastructure for travelling around the rest of the country
- Do all the workers have to be office-based could they be located at home
- Will work locations be sufficiently attractive for people to wish to work there
- Does the organisation rely on many specialist suppliers and so need to locate near to them
- Office/premises rental rates
- Does the population have any particular profile e.g. age, high density of graduates

2.2 Contingency planning

As organisations consider all the options and conduct feasibility studies, it is unlikely that all the objectives will be met. It is important, therefore, that contingency actions are planned for which overcome the issues or barriers encountered.

Desired outcome	Contingency action
A high number of low skilled workers available	Not enough suitably qualified resources are available: • Redesign the job, splitting them into part time roles and so appealing to a wider resource pool • Automate the processes as much as possible to reduce reliance on human resources • Design processes in order that decision making is minimised by the worker • Offshore to locations with high numbers of low skilled workers and accompanying low wages • Aim recruitment programme at immigrant workers who are more likely to be geographically mobile
A high number of intermediate skilled workers available	Not enough suitably qualified resources are available: • Create apprenticeship scheme to develop suitably skilled workers from within the organisation • Partner with local education institutions to provide suitable vocational courses • Provide in-house courses to improve skill levels • Outsource/offshore to organisations/locations with available workers with appropriate education levels
A high number of highly skilled workers available	Not enough suitably qualified resources are available: • Redesign the jobs so that the skilled resources are only required at key interactions • Outsource parts of the process or technical requirements to specialist organisations • Partner with local universities to provide work placement opportunities and graduate opportunities • Recruit workers from overseas with the necessary skills

NISSAN CARS

Why Nissan cars chose to locate in Sunderland, North East England.

As an incentive, grants for up to £100 million were available, although this was less than 10% of the investment. One of the attractions of the area was its manufacturing background. The region had recently undergone a period of industrial decline, with the closure of most of the shipyards on the Tyne and Wear, and the closure of many coal mines. The high unemployment this caused meant Nissan had a large, eager, manufacturing-skilled workforce to draw upon. The region had developed a strong reputation for engineering and, over the years, had built up a first class infrastructure of engineering universities and colleges. Additionally, there was no strong tradition of carmaking in the locality. Nissan specifically didn't want to recruit workers who had already been conditioned by their experiences of motor manufacturing within British or American owned companies.

The site, once the Sunderland Airfield, is close to large ports on the Tyne and Tees, within easy driving distance of the international Newcastle Airport. As well as the site having good transport links to the rest of the country, with the major roads, the A19 and A1 nearby, it also was in close proximity to two deepwater ports.

ACTIVITY 3 30 mins

You are opening a call centre to sell and manage the ongoing activities e.g. policy claims, related to car insurance.

What are going to be your top five criteria for selecting where to locate the centre? Using the people related data provided in the CBI report, select a part of the UK to base your centre.

It is not only due to demographics and the economy that the shape and nature of employment is changing. In the next section we will consider how the aspirations of how individuals want to live their lives can also have an effect.

3 The changing workforce

3.1 Why is the workforce changing?

Increased global competition, international recession, uncertainty about future markets and the effects of new technology undermined historical expectations of stable economic growth and the pace and complexity of such changes has continued to increase into the 21st century.

(a) **Increased global competition** has placed emphasis on quality, innovation and reducing the unit costs of production: job design and the organisation of work must both mobilise employees' energies for quality/innovation and reliable productivity.

(b) **Increased market uncertainty** means that organisations need to be more adaptable to changes in demand: able to vary the size and deployment of their workforces to meet demand as effectively and efficiently as possible.

(c) **Technological change**, particularly in the automation and computerisation of work processes and information flows, has eroded traditional demarcation boundaries between jobs: job design and the organisation of work must fit the new technology in order to secure its benefits for efficiency.

(d) **Demographic** (and related labour market) changes have highlighted the need for flexible job and career designs, in order to meet the needs of dual-income families, women and older workers for 'work life balance'.

The need for flexibility therefore underpinned new working practices:

(a) Increasing managerial ability to adapt the size and deployment of the workforce in line with changing demand and supply

(b) Increasing scope for flexible working for individual employees

(c) Raising the quality and/or quantity of workforce output.

3.2 The use of non-standard contracts

Research conducted in 2004 on workplace practices shows that the use of non-standard forms of employment has now become 'commonplace' in UK workplaces. 83% of workplaces employed **part-time** employees (less than 30 hours per week), up from 79% in 1998. Almost one third of workplaces had employees on **temporary** contracts. It is worth noting that those working on part time contracts is now 5% higher than before the economic downturn. Whilst this may be less attributable to a general change in working styles and more to do with the needs to control employment costs, it has meant that many people have remained in employment and continued to develop their skills.

The **increase** in the **service sector** has seen an **increase** in **non-traditional full-time jobs**. Compared to traditional manufacturing type employment there is not the requirement for the workforce to be in one place at one time. Service sector jobs often require a longer working day that cannot be undertaken by someone in single shift e.g. retail, call centres. Also by splitting such jobs the employer is able to avail themselves to a wider market of those seeking non-full-time hours.

There has also been an **increase** in **temporary contracts**. Research by Ford and Slater (2006) discovered that the use of temporary workers was less of a strategic people planning decision by employers but more driven by meeting short-term needs and managing costs. They also concluded that these type of contracts were mostly focused on low-paying entry level clerical and operative type work.

Research has also highlighted that many of those on temporary contracts were on such contracts as they could not find permanent employment. Additionally the use of such contracts is highly influenced by the current UK legislation. With increased protection afforded to employees there has been a greater motivation to circumvent this through the use of such temporary contracts. However, this practice is reducing as the UK Inland Revenue has been far stricter on interpreting the taxable status of employees and self-employed workers. Also, the introduction of the Agency Worker Directive is likely to have a knock-on effect.

Another developing practice is the **increase** in the **contracting out** or **outsourcing** of services such as cleaning, transport, security – and HR and training.

It has been observed that the employer and employee almost have diametrically opposed interests on this subject. The employer, faced with a rapidly evolving environment wants a deregulated market with loyalty and commitment from their flexible workforce. Yet the employee strives for job security and stability in employment during such periods of organisation and job restructuring.

AGENCY WORKERS

BBC 2009.

Angry agency staff have confronted union officials at BMW's MINI Cowley plant in Oxford, after the carmaker confirmed 850 job cuts at the site. The site will now close for a week, and weekend working has been scrapped.

A BMW spokesperson said weekend workers had effectively been given a week's notice as they would be paid for next weekend as well.

"MINI plant Oxford will be bringing in a new shift pattern in response to continuing volatile market conditions," a BMW statement said. "As of Monday 2 March, the plant will go from a three-shift to a two-shift pattern, operating five days per week instead of the current seven. The company regrets that this change will result in the release of around 850 agency workers from the business."

BMW had said that all staff at the factory, including remaining agency workers, would be paid their basic wages during the closure.

However, many agency workers said they were unclear what the future held after being told the weekend shift had been axed.

3.3 Regulation of working hours

The *Working Time Regulations 1998* and subsequent amendments set (currently negotiable) limits on working hours per week and entitlement to rest breaks and days. In order to cover equivalent workloads, employers may have to implement job-sharing and other flexible work patterns. The **EU Working Time Directive** regulates minimum holidays, paid breaks, rest periods and night work and creates a right to work not more than 48 hours per week on average. Workers can opt out of the 48 hour maximum.

Social Trends

People may work either full time or part time: in Q2 2009 1.9 million men and 5.7 million women reported that they worked part time, though this was defined according to their own perceptions rather than a specified number of hours. However, to analyse someone's working hours simply by whether they work full time or part time can mask a variety of work patterns, and the number of hours a week somebody in employment usually works can be more informative. The 1998 Working Time Regulations implemented the EU Working Time Directive on working time in the UK and these apply to full-time, part-time and temporary workers. Employers should limit working time to 48 hours a week (averaged over a 17-week period) unless they offer individuals the right to opt out of this maximum working week. In Q2 2009, 17 per cent of full-time employees in the UK usually worked more than 48 hours a week (including regular paid and unpaid overtime).

3.4 Work-life balance

Work-life balance is a concept which recognises the need for employers to support workers in achieving a balance between the demands of either their work and the demands of home and family or work and their aspirations outside the working environment.

WORK-LIFE BALANCE

Research for British Telecom Business conducted in 2006 indicated that more than a third of British workers (37 per cent of men and 34 per cent of women) would be prepared to forgo a pay increase for more flexible working options. The survey also found that 43 per cent of 18 to 29-year-olds are interested, compared to 31 per cent of the over-50s.

The research, conducted by YouGov, indicated that flexible working policies are valued across the age range, but with an above-average response from young people, more than three-quarters of whom agreed that it is an important benefit. Almost two-thirds of those aged 18 to 29 identified a better work-life balance as the main advantage, followed by less stress and fewer travel problems.

The opinions expressed in the 2006 research for BT may have changed given the shortages of jobs for young people, however a fundamental change in attitude is evident. There is other evidence to support that graduates select employers on the basis of their attitude towards work-life balance. Work-life balance strategies are often associated with the implementation of flexible working policies.

Conduct a mini-poll of your friends or fellow students; are flexible working practices most important to them either in employment or prospective employment?

If yes, why?

If no, why not? Why might they have a different opinion from those interviewed by YouGov for British Telecom?

Flexible working policies, designed to give employees options in regard to their hours and/or locations of work, have been supported in recent years by equal opportunity and family-friendly rights law. These have provided a package of entitlements including: annual leave; maximum working hours; parental leave and time off for dependent care; maternity/paternity leave and adoption leave; equal rights for part-time workers and so on.

'For years, best-practice organisations have taken an informal approach to fielding flexible working requests, with local line managers making decisions that best fit an individual or department, by involving other team members in the matter. In many cases, this method will continue to be the most effective in driving a flexible work culture while avoiding red tape' (Cartwright, 2003).

Availability of flexible working arrangements

Flexible working arrangements	Per cent of workplaces offering the arrangements to some employees
Reduced hours	70
Increased hours	57
Change working pattern	45
Flexi-time	35
Job sharing	31
Homeworking	26
Term-time only	20
Compressed hours	16

Kersley et al 2006

In the previous section we looked at how a number of factors can have an impact on the People Planner. In the section we mostly considered the composition and changes of the workforce, national demographics and worker aspirations. However the factors affecting an organisation can be far broader than those relating to people. In the next section we will look at a macro method of analysing the external environment to achieve a greater understanding of the influencing factors.

4 The external environment

4.1 PESTEL factors

All organisations exist in, interact with and are influenced by factors in their environment. It is important for organisations to identify and monitor these factors as they often have a direct effect on their current and future performance.

The macro-environment is generally out of the organisation's control. It includes all factors that can influence the organisation:

Political **E**conomic **S**ocial/Cultural **T**echnological **E**cological **L**egal (PESTEL)

Like many models, PESTEL is one of convenience. Environmental influences on an organisation do not appear in neatly packaged groups: they interact and take effect in complex ways. A good example is the way in which government policy affects economic factors. Economic policy is by definition a political matter, but it is inevitable that economic conditions and developments will be heavily influenced by policy developments.

4.2 The political environment

The political environment affects the organisation in a number of ways.

- A basic legal framework generally exists.
- The government can take a particular stance on an issue of direct relevance to a business or industry.
- The government's overall conduct of its economic policy is relevant to business.

Capacity expansion	Government policy can encourage organisations to increase or cut their capacity. (a) Tax systems encourage investment in equipment (b) A variety of incentives, funded by the EU and national governments, exist for locating capacity in a particular area (c) Incentives are used to encourage investment by overseas firms. Different countries in the EU have 'competed' for investment from Japan, for example
Demand	(a) The government is a major customer (b) Government can also influence demand by legislation, tax reliefs or subsidies
Divestment and rationalisation	In some European countries, the state takes many decisions regarding the selling off or closure of businesses e.g. telecommunications, defence supply

Emerging industries	Can be promoted by the government or damaged by it e.g. Wind farm technology
Entry barriers	Government policy can discourage firms from entering an industry, by restricting investment or competition or by making it harder, by use of quotas and tariffs, for overseas firms to compete in the domestic market.
Competition	(a) The government's purchasing decisions will have a strong influence on the strength of one firm relative to another in the market (e.g. armaments). (b) Regulations and controls in an industry will affect the growth and profits of the industry – e.g. minimum product quality standards. (c) As a supplier of infrastructure (e.g. roads), the government is also in a position to influence competition in an industry. (d) Governments and supra-national institutions such as the EU might impose policies which keep an industry fragmented, and prevent the concentration of too much market share in the hands of one or two producers.

In some industries, governments regulate the adoption of new products. This is well illustrated by the pharmaceuticals industry, where new drugs or medicines must in many countries undergo stringent testing and obtain government approval before they can be marketed.

QUOTAS

A good example of government quotas in action were those on Japanese car imports into the United States.

In March 1985 the limit on Japan's U.S. auto sales was 1.85 million cars a year; the limit was removed later that year. This was a self-imposed limit by the Japanese to maintain good relations with the US.

The Japanese companies did not suffer too badly. Since they could export only a limited number of autos, they began shipping more expensive premium models rather than small economy ones. In addition, Japanese firms could raise prices on their small cars because they were often in short supply. If there were no restraints, one U.S. study said, the average Japanese car would have cost $1,300 less in 1984.

But the International Trade Commission calculated cost of auto restraints, however, was high. The ITC reported that the four years of quotas cost the American consumer $15.7 billion while saving 44,000 auto workers' jobs. Whilst the restraints raised the cost of each Japanese by $1,300 they also allowed American auto makers to charge $600 more for their products.

There was, however, good news for the American car manufacturers who earned profits of $9.8 billion in 1984, vs. a loss of $4.2 billion in 1980. In 1984 sales rebounded to 7.9 million cars, vs. 5.7 million in 1982.

Allowing the Japanese controls to come off seemed to make no sense to most Detroit auto executives. Said Chrysler Chairman Lee Iacocca: "This is a sad day for America:-for American workers and American jobs."

The Japanese car manufacturers eventually set up manufacturing plants in the US to circumvent the issue.

Think about the government in your country; what examples of policies or legislation to promote certain industries can you think of? Likewise, what examples of policies or legislation can you think of that may harm or limit the growth of certain industries?.

4.3 The economic environment

The economic environment is an important influence at local and national level. Here are some factors that organisations must attend to.

Factor	Impact
Overall growth or fall in Gross Domestic Product	Increased/decreased demand for goods (e.g. dishwashers) and services (holidays).
Local economic trends	Type of industry in the area. Office/factory rents. Labour rates. House prices.
National economic trends:	
Inflation	Low in most countries; distorts business decisions; wage inflation compensates for price inflation.
Interest rates	How much it costs to borrow money affects cash flow. Some businesses carry a high level of debt. How much customers can afford to spend is also affected as rises in interest rates affect people's mortgage payments.
National economic trends:	
Tax levels	Corporation tax affects how much firms can invest or return to shareholders. Income tax and sales tax affect how much consumers have to spend, hence demand.
Government spending	Suppliers to the government (e.g. construction firms) are affected by spending.
The business cycle	Economic activity is always punctuated by periods of growth followed by decline, simply because of the nature of trade. Government policy can cause, exacerbate or mitigate such trends, but cannot abolish the business cycle. (Industries which prosper when others are declining are called counter-cyclical industries.)
Productivity	An economy cannot grow faster than the underlying growth in productivity, without risking inflation.

The **forecast state of the economy** will influence the planning process for organisations which operate within it. In times of boom and increased demand and consumption, the overall planning problem will be to **identify** the demand. Conversely, in times of recession, the emphasis will be on cost-effectiveness, continuing profitability, survival and competition.

Impact of international factors on a country's economy

Factor	Impact
Exchange rates	Cost of imports, selling prices and value of exports; cost of hedging against fluctuations
Characteristics of overseas markets. Different rates of economic growth and prosperity, tax etc	Desirable overseas markets (demand) or sources of supply
Capital flows and trade	Investment opportunities, free trade, cost of exporting
Globalisation	Increased competition, increasing prosperity

Government economic policy

Governments generally accept that they have a role to play in the management of the macro economy.

Their objectives are generally to achieve satisfactory and stable **growth**, while controlling **inflation** and avoiding significant changes in the value of their **currencies**. Growth is required since it enhances general economic **well-being** and provides for high levels of **employment**.

A government can use various policy tools as follows.

Fiscal policy	• Taxation and other sources of income • Government spending • Borrowing whenever spending exceeds income • Repaying debt when income exceeds expenditure
Monetary policy	• Interest rates • Exchange rates or exchange controls • Control of the money supply • Controls over bank lending and credit (rarely used nowadays)

Businesses are affected by a government's tax policy (eg corporation tax rates), and monetary policy (high interest rates increase the cost of investment, or depress consumer demand).

4.4 The social and cultural environment

Introduction

Social change involves changes in the nature, attitudes and habits of society. Social changes are continually happening, and trends can be identified, which may or may not be relevant to a business. Culture is often spoken of as 'the way we do things round here,' certainly in organisations. In society however culture is broader than this and encompasses customs, attitudes, characteristic ways of viewing the world and behaviour. Most countries contain several subcultures.

SOCIAL CHANGE

In January 2006, *Canterbury Foods*, a manufacturer of food products such as pastries, sausages and hamburgers, collapsed into insolvency with debts of £15m. The Chief Executive, Paul Ainsworth, had said in September 2005 that the TV campaign by celebrity chef Jamie Oliver to drive up the quality of school meals had helped to undermine the company's position. *Compass*, the international contract caterer, said that sales of several food companies had been hit by the school meals campaign: 'there has been a move away from Turkey Twizzlers'.

Demography

Demography is important for these reasons.

- Labour is a factor of production
- People create demand for goods, services and resources
- It has a long-term impact on government policies
- There is a relationship between population growth and living standards

Here are some statistics, which might help to explain the importance many businesses are placing on overseas markets. The figures are taken from *Social Trends*.

	1994 Population Millions	*2025* Population (estimated) Millions	*Increase* 1994–2025 %
World population	5,665.5	8,472.4	49
Europe (including Baltic states)	512.0	541.9	5
Former USSR (excluding Baltic states)	284.5	344.5	21
Canada and USA	282.7	360.5	27
Africa	681.7	1,582.5	132
Asia	3,233.0	4,900.3	52
Latin America	457.7	701.6	53
Oceania (including Australia)	27.5	41.3	50

ACTIVITY 4 — 20 mins

You are a manufacturer of a tablet-type electronic device, similar to an Apple iPad. Africa clearly has the greatest potential population growth in the next decade. List two reasons why you may wish to promote your product in Africa and two reasons why you may not.

The following demographic factors are important to organisational planners.

Factor	Comment
Growth	The rate of growth or decline in a national population and in regional populations.
Age	Changes in the age distribution of the population.
Geography	The concentration of population into certain geographical areas.
Ethnicity	A population might contain groups with different ethnic origins from the majority. In the UK, about 5% come from ethnic minorities, although most of these live in London and the South East.
Household and family structure	A household is the basic social unit and its size might be determined by the number of children, whether elderly parents live at home etc. In the UK, there has been an increase in single-person households and lone-parent families.
Social structure	The population of a society can be broken down into a number of subgroups, with different attitudes and access to economic resources. Social class, however, is hard to measure (as people's subjective perceptions vary).
Employment	In part, this is related to changes in the workplace.
Wealth	Rising standards of living lead to increased demand for certain types of consumer good. This is why developing countries are attractive as markets.

Implications of demographic change

(a) **Changes in patterns of demand**: an ageing population suggests increased demand for health care services: a 'young' growing population has a growing demand for schools, housing and work. The UK disposable nappy market turnover fell by 18% to £344m between 1999 and 2003, according to *Mintel*, a market research company. This fall echoes a 15% fall in live births between 1998 and 2004.

(b) **Location of demand**: people are moving to the suburbs and small towns.

(c) **Recruitment policies**: there are relatively fewer young people, so firms will have to recruit from less familiar sources of labour.

(d) Wealth and tax.

Culture

Culture is 'the sum total of the beliefs, knowledge, attitudes of mind and customs to which people are exposed in their social conditioning.'

Through contact with a particular culture, individuals learn a language, acquire values and learn habits of behaviour and thought. Culture has the following characteristics.

(a) Beliefs and values. Beliefs are what we feel to be the case on the basis of objective and subjective information (eg people can believe the world is round or flat). Values are beliefs which are relatively enduring, relatively general and fairly widely accepted as a guide to culturally appropriate behaviour.

(b) Customs: modes of behaviour which represent culturally accepted ways of behaving in response to given situations.

(c) Artefacts: all the physical tools designed by human beings for their physical and psychological well-being: works of art, technology, products.

(d) Rituals. A ritual is a type of activity which takes on symbolic meaning, consisting of a fixed sequence of behaviour repeated over time.

The learning and sharing of culture is made possible by language (both written and spoken, verbal and non-verbal).

Individualism: emphasis is on the individual and individual contribution, the 'I' identity and independence.

Collectivism: emphasis is on the group/team contribution, the 'we' identity (firm, family) and interdependence.

TURKISH CULTURE AND RECRUITING

The cultural environment in Turkey and the impact on recruitment.

A study was conducted to find the recruitment practices in Turkey as it prepared for entry into the European Union.

Turkish society and organisational culture is a blend of "Western" and "Eastern" values. Some organisations that attempt to adopt the new human resource management trends experience difficulties due to some characteristics of these cultures. Generally, Middle Eastern countries are characterised by a collectivistic value dimension. In many Middle Eastern cultures, where a very close knit community exists, some managers feel that they cannot apply formal staffing methods because there is so much social pressure to help out friends in need.

The research observed that in collectivistic cultures organisations can expect more cases of in-group recruitment. In Eastern cultures the collectivistic managers seek trustworthiness, loyalty and compatibility with present employees as key characteristics of job applicant; whereas in the West individualist managers seek competence as a key applicant characteristic. Many small firms in Turkey employ a large portion of the owner's family because the owner feels an obligation to take care of the less fortunate members of the family, even though they may be less capable than someone that could be hired from outside the family.

How would you describe the culture at your place of study eg College. Are there any particular routines that you observe eg everyone arrives early to classes? Are there any stories that symbolise what happens there eg many former students have gone on to lead major local businesses? Do you observe any symbols eg parking spaces all have names on them?

How does this compare to other places of study you have been at? How are they different, and what do they tell you about the different cultures?.

4.5 The technological environment

Introduction

In the most general sense, technology contributes to overall economic growth, by enabling:

- Gains in productivity (more output per units of input)
- Reduced costs (e.g. transportation technology, preservatives)
- New types of product

Technological change is rapid, and organisations must adapt themselves to it. Technological change can affect the activities of organisations as follows.

(a) The type of products or services that are made and sold. For example, consumer markets have seen the emergence of personal computers, DVDs, digital cameras and digital TV; industrial markets have seen the emergence of custom-built microchips, robots and local area networks for office information systems.

The development of the transistor made valve radios obsolete. Japanese firms were thus able easily to enter the consumer electronics market, where they are now key competitors. Japanese firms had no previous investment in valve radio production.

(b) The way in which products are made:

(i) Modern production equipment reduces the need for labour.
(ii) Technology can also develop new raw materials

(c) The way in which services are provided, for example travel agencies over the internet.

(d) The way in which markets are identified. Database systems make it much easier to analyse the market place.

(e) The way in which firms are managed. IT has helped in the 'delayering' of organisational hierarchies (in other words, the reduction of management layers between the senior managers and the workforce), but requires greater workforce skills. Using technology often requires changes in working methods. Information technology, in particular, requires skills at manipulating and interpreting abstract data.

(f) The means and extent of communications with external clients.

Impact of technological change

The impact of technological change also has potentially important social consequences.

(a) Whereas people were once collected together to work in factories, home working will become more important.

(b) Certain sorts of skill, related to interpretation of data and information processes, are likely to become more valued than manual or physical skills.

(c) Technology increases manufacturing productivity, so that more people will be involved in service jobs.

Bookselling with the arrival of Amazon

A neat example of technological change in action concerns the book-publishing and book-retailing sector. Bookselling has already been vigorously attacked, in effect, by the arrival of Amazon, leading, directly or otherwise, to the closure of many independent book retailers and even some larger firms like Borders and Sussex Stationers. The future of Waterstones, the UK's last major book retailer, is by no means clear. Then a further onslaught has taken the form of electronic book readers, led once more by Amazon with its Kindle range of products. Already Amazon is selling more electronic books than paper books. These are unstoppable changes.

4.6 The ecological environment

Introduction

For many decades there has been an awareness of the impact of man on the environment, the air pollution acts (Clean Air Act 1956 UK), fishing quotas in the North Sea to limit stock depletion, and concern about deforestation and the knock-on effects on indigenous people, endangered animals and the climate.

In more recent times there is a growing awareness and slower formal recognition that climate change is an issue. The issue means that organisations are more conscious of their actions and what needs to be done. Organisations need to consider whether the rising sea levels could affect their operations.

Additional to the impact of man on the climate there are also the natural disasters that also occur. Hurricanes, floods, tidal waves all occur and, in areas where these are more likely, organisations need to plan around the risk of such occurrences.

Planning

Mankind has always planned around exploiting areas of maximum potential, for example river deltas, river crossings and other natural crossroads. The challenge is little different today with organisations needing to be conscious of where they locate their operations and the risk they face from flooding, earthquakes etc.

- The city of London has the Thames Barrier to prevent a tidal rush caused by exceptionally high tides and storm surges coming in from the North Sea
- Japanese buildings are specifically designed to withstand earth tremors
- Insurance companies are in the business of evaluating such risks and attributing a risk factor to them

Reacting to disaster

Organisations conduct operations where they are aware that a risk is present. For some this is drilling in the ocean, or transporting hazardous materials. For other organisation they may be unaware of the risk until it is 'exposed', such as the case of exploiting cheap labour in under-developed countries.

For many organisations the damage incurred or lack of it is determined by their response to the disaster. Where a risk is known, they can plan for this and so the quality of their response is determined by their planning and their ability to implement a rapid and appropriate response. Or they simply have to react on the ground and their response is determined by the quality of their management.

There are however also commercial opportunities associated with responding to disaster. Organisations are able to provide rapid response units to meet the immediate needs of the disaster victims. Also the reconstruction after the event can provide long-term development opportunities and sources of income and job creation.

Political activities

Already in this section we have identified how governments can influence the activities of organisations and this topic is no different.

Proactive action

Governments can take a position to influence the activities of organisations through the use of tax incentives or restrictions. For example the UK government is making the generation of environmentally friendly electricity attractive though tax benefits on electricity generated through wind power or solar panels. They are also encouraging the use of electrical cars by making them exempt from road tax.

Reactive action

Governments however will react to events either as a form of political appeasement or learning from the lessons of others.

THE CONSEQUENCES OF THE JAPANESE TSUNAMI

Reuters May 2011.

Germany plans to shut all nuclear reactors by 2022, Chancellor Angela Merkel's ruling coalition announced on Monday, in a policy reversal drawn up in a rush after the Fukushima disaster in Japan.

The coalition, sensitive to accusations it may increase dependence on highly polluting brown coal, said it planned to cut power use by 10 percent by 2020 and further expand the use of renewables such as wind and solar power.

Customer outcomes

The effect on customers is three-fold

1. Their power as consumers. It is increasingly recognised that consumers have the power to influence organisations through their purchasing choices. Consumers are now more conscious of what crops are grown, or the welfare of animals during their rearing. Through their choice of spending there are able to influence the providers
2. Their power as voters. Political parties increasing have an environmental agenda as they seek to be both conscious of the impact their decisions can have on the environment but also as a way to win the votes of the environmentally conscious voter. This has developed to the point where there are 'green' parties.
3. The impact on them as consumers. The outcomes of disasters and measures to protect the environment can impact the consumer in a number of ways, but mainly by limiting the supply and therefore increasing the price. Additionally being re-educated to accept alternatives that are more sustainable

IKEA

IKEA is a Swedish international home products company that designs and sells ready-to-assemble furniture. The company is the world's largest furniture retailer.

IKEA works towards sustainability goals by:

- Providing tips and ideas for a sustainable home life on its website

- Aiming for zero landfill waste, reduced wastewater treatment and less water use
- Cutting carbon footprint through less transport and packaging
- Showing social responsibility, for example, through its works to support charities.

4.7 The legal environment

The legislation can have a number of effects on the way organisations operate:

- The **ways of doing business** e.g. weights and measures, opening hours, ages of who can be served
- **Specific laws** exist for particular areas of **economic activity** e.g. legislation associated with financial advice and transactions
- Legislation and judicial decisions increase the **customer's rights**
- Particular classes of customer may be protected in some cases (e.g. funeral services).

Laws come from common law, parliamentary legislation and government regulations derived from it, and obligations under treaties such as those establishing the European Union.

Some legal factors affect **all companies**, for example tax law (corporation tax, sales tax, income tax); employment law; health and safety law. Other legal and regulatory factors affect **particular industries,** where the public interest is served by doing so. For example, electricity, gas, telecommunications, water and rail transport are subject to regulators in the UK (Ofgem, Ofcom, Ofwat, Office of Rail Regulation) who have influence over market access, competition and pricing policy (can restrict price increase)

This is because either:

- The industries are, effectively, monopolies
- Large sums of public money are involved (e.g. in subsidies to rail companies)

National and EU institutions also affect the operating activities of some organisations, for example:

- Anti-discrimination legislation
- Health and safety legislation
- Product safety and standardisation (especially EU standards)
- Workers' rights (eg unfair dismissal, maternity leave)
- Training and education policies can determine the 'standard' of recruits

5 Applying PESTEL

British American Tobacco (BAT) is the second largest tobacco company in the world, with more than 200 brands and operating in over 180 markets. BAT have 45 cigarette factories in 39 countries with over 60,000 employees worldwide. The brand portfolio includes Dunhill, Kent, Lucky Strike and Pall Mall.

This review will reference many statistics from the UK, but the outcomes apply equally to many western European countries

Political	• The UK government tobacco policies include banning smoking in all workplaces; a commitment to maintain, and maximise use of, the stop smoking clinics; greater enforcement of the law to stop sales of tobacco to children; plans for pictorial health warnings and further efforts to combat tobacco smuggling. • In the UK the government and the National Health Service are highly connected. The NHS recognises smoking to be a major contributor to prevalence of cancer and hence sets out targets for improving prevention. • The government in China appears to be encouraging smoking by allowing tobacco companies to actively market in their country.
Economic	• Tax, both excise duty and VAT on tobacco products, continue to be a major source of revenue for the government. BAT estimate they pay £30 billion per year in excise duties to governments around the world. • The value of pound sterling (£). BAT purchase 90% of their raw materials from overseas, the value of sterling will impact their costs and profits. • Purchasing power of consumers, whilst reduced during economic downturn, would not appear to have directly impacted sales.
Social	• As individuals become more health conscious and aware of the health risks, the numbers of those smoking in the UK reduced between 1999 and 2009, male smokers reduced by 7.5% and female smokers reduced by 5.5%. • In 2010 in the UK 22% of adult men smoke and 21% of adult women. In 1974 51% of adult men smoked and 41% of adult women. • Increasing awareness of 'passive smoking' allows for more acceptance of changes around public smoking etc. • Population growth in many countries that have less negative perceptions of smoking are the markets of the future. • Illegal trade in cigarettes sales increasing, threatening profits for BAT.
Technical	• New pesticides on tobacco to reduce amount of pesticides currently used and so create 'healthier cigarettes'. • E-cigarettes, claim to enable a less toxic way of smoking cigarettes. • 'Snus' is tobacco-based product that is held in the mouth, increasingly popular as cheaper than cigarettes. • Nicotine patches that can be used to help people stop smoking.
Environment	• New uses for tobacco as a pesticide. • Climate change is making it more difficult to achieve predictable crop growth and harvests.
Legal	Numerous pieces of legislation have been introduced: • Banning cigarette advertising (2002) • Banning smoking in public places (2007) • Cigarette packets to have public health warnings • Cigarettes to be have plain packaging • Cigarettes to not be displayed in large shops (2012)

In conclusion from a people recruiting plan there maybe a number of conclusions drawn:

- Due to social perceptions, the business is likely to struggle to attract all the candidates it wishes. This may require higher levels of pay and intense social programmes to counter the negative perception.
- Future markets are likely to be in the Far East so experience of working in those markets will be valuable.
- For management, skills in dealing with public perception and negative perception will be important.
- The business may even wish to actively recruit smokers as they know they are aligned to the product

ACTIVITY 5 60 mins

Conduct a PESTEL analysis for the airline industry e.g. Virgin Atlantic, Ryanair

Chapter Roundup

- The labour market needs to be analysed and understood before any resourcing plan can be designed.
- Labour markets vary by geography, skill type and demographic mix. The influence of immigration and education are also important factors.
- The demographic mix is a combination of the working population, the age profile, the mix of sexes, the ethnic diversity.
- The skills and qualification of those in the market and those entering the market in the future is a point of key concern; will sufficient numbers be available to meet the organisation's needs?
- The workforce is changing both in terms of the type of employee eg sex, race etc but also their aspirations for the workplace eg looking after children, worklife balance. This change and the changing requirements of employers has seen a change in how people are employed – typically far more flexibly.
- A method for analysing the external environment is **P**olitical **E**conomic **S**ocial/Cultural **T**echnological **E**cological **L**egal (PESTEL). The impact of any of these factors can influence the strategic decisions an organisation makes, as well as the People related decisions. Often strategic decisions automatically impact any People related planning.

Quick Quiz

1 During which years are the 'baby boomers' associated with?

2 What percentage of part-time workers are women?

3 In 2011 from which area did most foreign-born low-skilled workers in the UK come?

- North Africa
- India
- Eastern or central Europe
- Western Europe

4 Identify two reasons why the workforce is changing.

5 What is the most popular method offered as flexible working?

6 Identify three ways that a government can influence the external environment

7 What international factors influence a country's economy?

8 Which continent is going to see the greatest population growth between 1995 – 2025?

- Asia
- Latin America
- Africa
- Oceania

9 What is the social impact of technology change?

10 What does PESTEL stand for?

Answers to Quick Quiz

1	1946 – 1964	(para 1.1)
2	80%	(para 1.4)
3	Eastern or central Europe	(para 1.5)
4	You could have chosen from: increased global competition; market uncertainty requiring greater flexibility; changes in technology; demographic changes in the workforce	(para 3.1)
5	Reduced hours (70%)	(para 3.4)
6	You could have chosen from: Capacity expansion; Demand; Entry barriers; Competition (regulation and promotion)	(para 4.2)
7	Exchange rates; characteristics of overseas markets; capital flows and trade; globalisation	(para 4.3)
8	Africa 132%	(para 4.4)
9	People will no longer have to work in one place; mental skills will become more valuable than manual or physical skills; more people will be involved in service jobs	(para 4.5)
10	Political, Economic, Social, Technical, Environment, Legal	(section 5)

Answers to Activities

Activity 1

- Baby boomers continue to age; high level of knowledge resides in a cohort of employees who will all progress through the organisation at the same time – need to ensure that knowledge is disseminated. Their benefits costs of medical, pensions etc will increase together.
- Risk of greater competition for limited supply of candidates – increasing wages and therefore costs of the organisation. Need to be able to employ those from outside the usual recruitment pools. Need to be able to extend the working lives of those in employment now.
- Increased longevity will require policies to allow and encourage and enable longer careers. Increased pressure on medical programmes and retirement plans.

Activity 2

Advantages:

- New sources of labour for areas with people or skills shortages
- Potentially cheaper sources of labour
- New customers for goods and services within which they are working
- Greater diversity in the workforce reflects greater diversity in the population, a positive attribute for customer-facing organisations
- Source of tax and social security payments for the government

Disadvantages

- Administrative burden to manage visas and comply with other statutory requirements
- Political issue of employing non-nationals during periods of high unemployment
- Political issues of immigrants not aligning into main society and appearing alien in society
- Communications and cultural issues

Activity 3

- Low cost of employment
- Low cost of office accommodation
- Area attracting subsidies
- Good local infrastructure to enable employees to get to work
- Highly diverse population to relate to the broad customer base of the business

Activity 4

Reasons why

- Product especially appeals to a younger population, the continent will have a high proportion of young users relative to the rest of the world
- Populations of likely purchasers concentrated in urban areas, easing sales and distribution

Reasons why not

- Limited infrastructure to support the product sales and distribution in a number of countries
- Whether sufficient disposable income is distributed across the population

Activity 5

Political **E**conomic **S**ocial/Cultural **T**echnological **E**cological **L**egal

P

- UK government decision not to build third runway at Heathrow limits capacity in major airport.
- Governments will intervene in airline mergers if they believe they are against the interests of passengers or even national interest.
- EU-US Open Skies Agreement allows US to offer services in the EU market.

E

- The recession has seen a reduction in flights, however low-cost carriers have seen an increase in traffic.
- Fuel surcharges are passed onto passengers due to unpredictable increases in aviation fuel due to increasing cost of oil.
- Income comes from all around the world, currency fluctuations can have an enormous impact. Oil for example is priced in US Dollars and so the Dollar exchange rate is important.
- Governments taxing flights and so increasing the overall cost of travel.

S

- Since 9/11 passengers are increasingly aware of the terrorist risk in flying. The security measures that have been subsequently implemented now making flying more arduous and less attractive.
- A number of social changes have occurred in past decades, the 'package tour' was abroad and included a flight; the rise of cheap airlines has meant people have brought properties abroad that can be accessed via cheap flights.
- Many people fly to go on holiday seeing peaks of demands at certain times in the year.
- Trade union activity is increasing, and strikes by certain categories of workers can bring a whole country to a standstill e.g. air traffic controllers.

T

- New generations of engines are more fuel efficient.
- Growth in the internet since mid 1990s provides opportunities for both marketing and tickets sales.
- Video conferencing technology provides alternative to flying to meetings.
- New planes can carry more passengers more fuel efficiently and more quietly (Airbus A380).
- New technology in planes eg video or ability to use phones is a way that airlines try to compete with one another.

E

- UK government say aviation emissions must not rise above 2005 levels.
- Businesses are increasingly conscious of their environmental credentials, reducing air miles helps demonstrate them taking action.
- Passengers are increasingly aware of emissions caused by plans.
- Natural incidents like the Icelandic volcano and a harsh snow fall can paralyse airspace or airports, these are unpredictable and need contingency planning.

L

- EU compensation law for delayed flights.

Chapter 4

People resourcing

In this chapter we will look at the options available to organisations to achieve their strategic objectives. Firstly the organisation needs to determine how best to resource to meet these. The options available do not always include recruitment and growth, they can be to remain as is, or to reduce headcount. Sometimes reduction is necessary for survival, the reduction in people leads to a reduction in costs. However organisations can also reduce their headcount, and often costs, if they decide to outsource their service requirements to a third party.

In the previous chapter of this study text we looked at the changing nature of the workforce; we have noted the increasing number of women in the workplace, the number of migrants and the greater longevity of the population as a whole. In this chapter we consider the value of diversity and some of the issues associated with international recruitment. In the next chapter we will look at the legislation that protects people from discrimination.

Where organisations are expanding internationally or cannot find the skills they require in their own country they look abroad, this chapter will also look at the benefits and challenges of international resourcing.

TOPIC LIST		LEARNING OUTCOMES
1	People resourcing and achieving strategic objectives	4.1, 4.2, 6.5, 7.3
2	Talent management	4.2
3	Managing diversity	4.3
4	International resourcing	5.3
5	International recruitment	5.3

1 People resourcing and achieving strategic objectives

1.1 Rightsizing

Rightsizing Finding the optimal size and composition of the workforce to meet the strategic requirements of the business is known as rightsizing.

Prior to 2008, many economies had seen a long period of sustained growth; for many organisations during this period their People Planning focused on the need to find resources and retain them. During this period the phrase **'war for talent'** was pertinent to many industries at all levels, and in both the private and public sectors. After 2008 the requirements rapidly changed and many HR professionals found themselves managing large-scale redundancies for the first time.

However, simply because many organisations have experienced a downturn this is not the case for all. Some organisations have found that their products or services are in greater demand due to their lower costs or meeting a new need. Consequently during the same economic period different organisations can find themselves planning for different outcomes, growth, stability and decline.

1.2 Growth

If an organisation is planning a period of expansion the issues it will face are going to be: are there enough potential employees in the market with the appropriate skills, are the potential employees located where we require them, are we able to attract sufficient applicants to meet our current demands?

The answers to these questions will start to determine the responses. If the market has an oversupply of suitable applicants and these are readily to hand and actively seeking employment, the organisation is unlikely to be too concerned. Especially if the number of applicants for any current vacancies far exceeds the number of jobs on offer.

However, if the skills required are scarce, or located in other areas the challenges are going to be greater. The HR professional is going to have to plan how to source more candidates. The questions to consider are:

Are there sufficient skilled resources in the local market?	If yes, how many, what is the typical rate of pay, how quickly would they be available If no, need to look elsewhere or grow our own skilled workforce
Are sufficiently skilled resources elsewhere in the country?	If yes, in which parts and in what numbers, are they likely to be mobile ie move to us, or do we need to relocate to them. What is the typical rate of pay ie do we need to increase our anticipated costs, or will our proposed rates of pay be sufficient to encourage employees to relocate If no, need to look overseas, or grow our own, or actively engage with universities and colleges to develop programmes that produce suitably skilled resources

Are sufficiently skilled resources available overseas?	If yes, where in the world, educated to what standard, are their skills immediately transferable, what is their typical rate of pay, are they mobile and willing to relocate, what is the standard of their language skills. If we are to plan to meet our requirements with overseas employees, what actions are needed to be able to obtain visas to allow foreign workers to work in the country, will there be limits on the numbers we can bring in. If no, can the job be redesigned in order to match the requirements with skills available. Is there a third party outsourcer who is able to meet our requirements through their own existing workforce.

1.3 Stability

The organisation that is expecting stability in the workforce will still have a number of strategic decisions it wishes to make. Is the current rate of attrition acceptable or does it wish to reduce this, or possibly increase it? Whichever objective is agreed, plans can be put in place to either improve the retention of employees, or to increase the turnover in order to get an injection of 'new blood'. This type of increased turnover would usually be achieved through a more rigorous application of the performance management process.

Additionally trends towards flexibility and multi-skilling have encouraged a different approach as to who to recruit, which is oriented more towards **'fitting the job to the person'** than **'fitting the person to the job'**. In a highly innovative market, technological environment or transformational change (see the next section), for example, rigid job descriptions would not be suitable. In order to creatively exploit the opportunities or such environments, organisations should be able to look at the skills and attributes of the people they employ, and those of gifted outsiders, and ask: 'What needs doing, that this person would do best?'

In a relatively informal environment, where all-round knowledge/skills and experience are highly valued and suitable external labour resources are scarce (say, in management consultancy), this approach would give much-needed flexibility. The organisation would try to recruit excellent, flexible, motivated and multi-skilled personnel, without reference to any specific job, as defined by a job description. They would form an available resource for any task or requirement that arose on a project or 'virtual project team' basis.

However, the **'selection' approach** ('fitting the person to the job') is still by far the most common, and is suitable for most organisations with fairly defined goals and structures.

Have you seen examples of an organisation 'fitting the job to the person'; what was the situation and why do you think they did it?.

Transformational change. Any organisation will have the number of people leaving annually to recruit for, but as part of an organisational strategy of change it may wish to upgrade the quality and skill levels of new employees joining the organisation. Alternatively it may wish to increase the general skill levels of all existing employees and embark on a skills development initiative. This process can be challenging for the organisation and the new individuals joining it. The organisation will find itself for a period of time with two types of employees, the existing workforce who understand the 'old' organisation but are not the type of employee now sought; and the new employees who have joined believing the organisation is embarked on a change journey only to find the organisation appears very staid.

HR TRANSFORMATION AT THE ROYAL MAIL

The Royal Mail is national postal services provider in the UK.

When Royal Mail Group's losses reached £1.5m a day, it launched a renewal plan intended to return it to profitability – and its HR department was one of many to face major upheaval.

To return to profitability and prepare for full postal competition – which came into effect on 1 January 2006 – the business embarked on a major change programme to improve efficiency and service.

The Human Resources (HR) Transformation programme was just one part of the response. This involved a corporate shake-up from the top down, combined with an inevitable reduction in staff numbers – always a sensitive operation in a unionised public company.

At the time, each operational unit within Royal Mail had its own personnel team. This may have been logical when the structure was first introduced a number of years earlier – in a bid to make each unit a pseudo profit-and-loss entity – but it had led instead to a bloating of staff numbers in many duplicate activities, as well as rising costs.

Indeed, the HR community had reached 3,200 in total – covering a total workforce of about 220,000 – but despite their numbers, performance was not highly rated, coming in the bottom quartile of most objective benchmark data, including:

- Employee/HR ratio
- Cost of HR
- Cycle time of key HR processes
- Effectiveness of HR interventions.

In addition, this structure also encouraged HR teams to become inward-looking and to concentrate on their own activities rather than community effectiveness. Process performance in terms of demand levels was used as a justification for resourcing levels, rather than cycle time or capability.

Project objective

The HR contribution to Royal Mail's transformation programme was to be:

- A 40 per cent reduction in the costs of the HR service – equating to a reduction of 1,400 staff
- An improved employee/HR ratio of 1:140
- Improved satisfaction with HR services.

Easier said than done. From a knowledge perspective, the incumbent HR community was poorly equipped to manage the transformation. While it had a wealth of process-related information it had little experience of viewing HR performance through other lenses, such as customers and people.

The first step in the transformation was to appoint a new management team for the services arm of the HR operation. They would be responsible for delivering the programme's objectives. This management team was selected because its members had the experience of delivering an equivalent transactional-services transformation to similar timescales.

The application of external best practice was integral to the project, so an external programme director was contracted to lead the initiative, bringing with them experience of establishing HR shared services and process rigour through the Six Sigma quality-management methodology. The introduction of Six Sigma was an important element in improving the information quality, giving the initiative a focus on process-performance data as opposed to process volumes – that is to say, doing it right, first time.

During transformation

A key principle throughout the transformation was that commitments would be met and the pace of change maintained – there could be no let-up or relaxation until the programme was satisfactorily completed. A critical element of this was a rapid restructuring of business processes at the same time as the 40 per cent reduction in staff numbers over a two-year period.

Barker and Shepherd (2007)

1.4 Reduction

The amount an organisation needs to reduce is difficult to predict, especially when the calculations are based on the state on the economy. Many organisations have found themselves having to implement consecutive waves of reduction programmes as the low level of economy activity has been unable to sustain the organisation. Organisation that are closing locations, or ceasing certain types of production or service are able to make more informed decisions about numbers and so are able to plan better how to make the reductions. The People Planner faces a number of options as to how to reduce the headcount painlessly to those affected, with minimum disruption to the business and at the lowest cost.

Natural attrition	This has a high level of appeal, as the cost to the organisation is minimal both in terms of cost and disruption. However if large-scale reductions are required the rate of attrition is often not high enough. Additionally, if the whole market is slowing down the future employers that most current employees would expect to depart to will reduce their recruitment activity; consequently the market 'locks up'. Finally, if employees believe that severance payments are to be made, they may be inclined to continue in employment hoping to receive a payment.
Retirement and early retirement	Retirement also appeals as the retiree appears to own the decision rather than it being forced upon them. However, as has been highlighted in previous chapters, employees are less enthusiastic to retire than previously. Expecting to live longer means that older employees are conscious of how much they require in funds; pension schemes have not performed well and so those who are not on 'final salary' schemes are facing a funding shortfall. Finally, changes in legislation mean that employees are no longer facing compulsory retirements as they once would have expected. For employers to enhance the 'pot' to make it more attractive for employees to retire early can mean a substantial increase in costs.
Voluntary redundancy	Many employers will attempt to reduce their headcount through a voluntary redundancy programme. Enabling the employee to choose is less confrontational. To make the proposal more attractive, employers will often enhance the redundancy package; this increases the costs, but these are hopefully recovered through less management time than would be involved in a compulsory programme. The downsides to a voluntary programme are there is less control as to who volunteers and often the most capable employees volunteer as they are confident of finding employment elsewhere, or those with long service and organisational knowledge volunteer as they will receive the biggest payment.

Compulsory redundancy	Compulsory redundancy is the most confrontational and disruptive reduction method an organisation faces. The organisation is typically required to consult with employee representatives and the employees themselves. Particular attention has to be given to timing, the selection criteria chosen and ensuring fairness. Even after following all these procedures there is no guarantee that an employee will not make a claim for unfair dismissal or discrimination. Such programmes require careful planning, and draw upon the change management skills of the HR professional.

Whilst early retirement and voluntary redundancy may have an immediate it needs to be remembered that both have advantages and disadvantages

	Advantages	Disadvantages
Early retirement	• Avoids the potential stigma of being made redundant • Maybe appealing to the employee who was considering retiring soon anyway • Is a useful method of allowing new and often younger employees in the workforce to move up through the organisation	• Can be expensive if the retirement package is enhanced to encourage volunteers • The loss of the knowledge and experience within the organisation can be severely detrimental, this can often not be retrained into someone else • Customers lose confidence in an organisation as experience and expertise leaves
Voluntary redundancy	• Reduces antagonism and confrontation between management and workforce representatives • Allows employees the dignity of choosing to leave rather than being forced • The workforce consider that management are acting reasonably to achieve the savings, and so minimises disruption	• Can be expensive as severance package is usually enhanced to encourage volunteers • Employees who the organisation would rather retain volunteer, management lose control • Leavers often depart quickly requiring their former colleagues to adapt and pick up workload • Survivor syndrome (see section 1.5)

Minimising compulsory redundancies

Unemployment can represent not only an economic threat to livelihood and lifestyle, but a source of stress, insecurity and loss of self-esteem. On grounds of social responsibility, therefore, as well as reduced cost and preserved morale, the organisation should attempt to minimise compulsory redundancy as far as possible. There are various ways by which this can be done.

(a) **Advance HR planning**, so that foreseen seasonal or other contractions in demand for labour can be taken into account, and natural wastage can be allowed to downsize the organisation.

(b) **Adjusting HR plans** to ban non-essential recruitment; reduce overtime working; develop job-sharing (people alternating or splitting days of work in the same job); encourage short-contract working; restrict the use of subcontracted temporary and casual staff; and, if necessary, implement temporary layoffs.

(c) Encouraging **voluntary redundancy**.

(d) **Retraining and redeployment programmes**. This may be a solution where alternative jobs are available, employees have some of the skills (or at least aptitudes) required and retraining facilities are available. The organisation may use outplacement agencies, or liaison with other employers in the same industry, supply chain or area, with a view to securing redeployment within a network of organisations.

(e) Encouraging **early retirement**.

Most claims for unfair dismissal in respect of redundancy are for unfair selection and lack of consultation: we will look at these two areas next.

Selection for compulsory redundancy

Traditionally there have been two basic approaches to selection for redundancy, which have proved acceptable to tribunals and trade unions.

(a) **Point score systems.** These allow **retention by merit** – retaining good performers and dismissing less effective ones – while supporting the objectivity of the process.

   (i) Clear criteria should be chosen, and ideally agreed in advance with trade unions or the employee representatives. They may be based on aspects such as attendance records, disciplinary records, competence assessments, range of work experience and other objectively measurable factors.

   (ii) Each employee is scored on each criteria to build up a points score.

   (iii) Managers implementing the system should have clear definitions of criteria; points available for different degrees of fulfilment of each criterion; and weighting of criteria to reflect their relative importance and value to the organisation.

   (iv) Once all scores have been calculated, employees with the lowest scores are selected for redundancy.

   From the organisation's point of view, selection criteria should ensure that the skills needed for organisational survival and regrowth are not lost through redundancy, and if possible that the best people are retained in the most value-adding jobs.

   Employees who are employed on special projects or who have special skills required by the organisation may need to be removed from the pool prior to selection, or this should be provided for in the selection criteria.

(b) **'Last in, first out' (LIFO)**: newcomers are dismissed before long-serving employees. In countries with age discrimination legislation this is a high-risk strategy.

ACTIVITY 1 15 mins

When choosing selection criteria, emphasis is placed on choosing fair and measurable criteria; why are problems encountered when using appraisal ratings or 'manager's opinion' as criteria?

Employee rights and redundancy procedures

The UK has enshrined in law the process that must be followed before an employee can be made redundant, the law also stipulates the minimal payments that must be made in such circumstances. The requirements vary around the world, some countries having more requirements on the employer whilst in others the concept of redundancy does not exist, and employees are dismissed without compensation.

Armstrong (2009) notes that redundancy procedures have three key aims.

(a) To treat employees as fairly as possible.
(b) To reduce hardship as much as possible.
(c) To protect management's ability to run the business effectively.

In addition any procedure must take into account the employee's legal rights in redundancy situations. Many large organisations provide services and benefits well in excess of the statutory minimum with regard to consultation periods, terms, notice periods, counselling and aid with job search and so on.

Prior to consultation, employees or their representatives must have been provided with information about: the reason for redundancies; numbers to be dismissed; proposed methods of selection for redundancy; timescale and methods of the redundancy programme; and method to be used in calculating redundancy pay. The consultation period is not deemed to have started until sufficient information is provided on all these matters.

Consultation must be 'genuine', with the intention of reaching agreement with the employee representatives. It has to explore whether there are other options open to the business.

(a) Are there ways of avoiding dismissals altogether?
(b) Can the numbers to be dismissed be reduced?
(c) How can the impact of redundancy on those who must be dismissed be minimised?

Compassionate exit management

A number of measures may be taken to alleviate the consequences of redundancy for employees.

(a) **Informing employees** who are to be dismissed of their selection should be managed with as much sensitivity as possible. Managers should be given training and/or guidance in how to handle the difficult situation sensitively. They should also be given information about any special circumstances that might make the employee react particularly badly.

(b) **Counselling** may be offered to employees, to aid their readjustment and job search. The employee will be guided in reinforcing his or her sense of employability, redefining career objectives, devising strategies for job search, and working through personal issues (including anger and grief) around job loss.

(c) **Outplacement services** may be offered, often through external consultancies, to help redundant employees to find alternative work. The HR department or consultancy may offer services such as:

    (i) Seeking specific job opportunities in the local area

    (ii) Training employees in CV preparation, selection interview techniques and application filling

    (iii) Helping employees to draw up skill or competence inventories, personal success/attainment inventories and other aids to applications

    (iv) Carrying out psychometric assessments and helping employees to set career and job objectives

    (v) Matching of employee details to advertised vacancies or network opportunities

    (vi) Helping the employee to plan a focused job-search campaign

(d) **Information** on job, self-employment and retraining opportunities and funding should be made available. Individuals should be made aware of the role and accessibility of the Department of Works and Pensions facilities, and private sector services for careers counselling, recruitment, CV preparation and so on.

1.5 Survivor syndrome

The term **survivor syndrome** has been coined for a psychological state which involves long-term anxiety about job loss, increased loyalty to co-workers and reduced loyalty to the employer.

The impact of any redundancy programme is also felt by those who were *not* selected. 'Survivors' may suffer guilt and anxiety, insecurity about their own jobs and a loss of loyalty to the organisation: they may tend to identify more closely with fellow workers and less with the organisation. Efforts will have to be made to reinforce survivors' loyalty and morale by acknowledging their worth to the employer – particularly since, despite the concept underlying 'redundancy', remaining workers may in fact have to shoulder an increased workload!

Have you seen 'survivor syndrome' at your place of work or heard others talking about it? What examples can you give? And what has management done to try and build loyalty and morale back up?

TALENT SHORTAGE AND COMPETITION

Employers are struggling to recruit because they are being swamped by unsuitable candidates, while the talented individuals they are looking for are staying put, fearing that the economy is too volatile to risk changing jobs.

These are the main findings from the annual Chartered Institute of Personnel and Development (CIPD) resourcing and talent planning survey, produced in partnership with Hays.

Three-quarters (73%) of organisations have highlighted an increase in the number of unsuitable candidates, fuelled by the sheer weight of applications. More than half (52%) of employers believe that competition for talent is even greater than previously, compared with 41% and 20% in 2010 and 2009 respectively.

Claire McCartney, resourcing and talent planning adviser at the CIPD, said: "High levels of unemployment have boosted quantity, but employers are still struggling with quality. Headlines focus on high levels of unemployment, but those stark statistics mask an ongoing struggle for employers to find the skills and experience they need to drive their businesses forward. Shortages of specialist and technical skills run the risk of slamming an unwelcome brake on the long-term competitiveness of the UK economy."

This year, exactly three-quarters of organisations experienced recruitment difficulties. As in previous years, the main reason for these recruitment difficulties is a lack of necessary specialist or technical skills (72% in 2011 compared with 67% in 2010), with managers/professionals and technical positions being the most difficult to fill.

The researchers said that a clear contributing factor to the talent shortage issue is that those who are in work are reluctant to leave in a volatile market.

Personnel Today 2011

Even within the three classic situations of growth, stable and reduction, the People Planner now also finds themselves considering other options as how best to resource the organisation.

1.6 Outsourcing

Outsourcing the contracting out, to a third party, a function or activity that was, typically, previously performed within the organisation

Outsourcing is an alternative approach that organisations utilise to meet their requirements. In Europe, to enter into an outsourcing arrangement will mean that the employees will transfer to the new employer, and hence come off the original organisation's headcount. Organisations will look to outsource services for a variety of reasons but these primarily fall within:

Cost reduction	Many organisations follow a competitive tender route to finding an outsourcing provider. The competitive tender enables them to understand what services are being provided at what price and agree the arrangements for service monitoring and compliance. However the primary advantage is the opportunity to drive down cost whilst retaining an acceptable level of quality.
Greater flexibility	Some organisations recognise that due to the fluctuating levels of demand for certain services they either understaff or overstaff depending on the cycle. This is often cost-inefficient and quality of service fluctuates. Through outsourcing the organisation shifts the burden on meeting the fluctuating demand onto an outsourced provider. The outsourcing provider, through managing multiple such contracts, has a larger core workforce that it can allocate to clients in accordance with demand. It is also incentivised to focus on maximising process efficiencies as this is its core business.
Access to expertise or systems	Some organisations recognise that in order to transform their service provision they need to invest in new technology and redesign their processes. This poses a risk in terms of cost of the new IT system, cost of manpower commitment and of not getting it right. By appointing an outsourcing provider, organisations find they can bypass these issues. The period of an outsourcing contract is often longer than the payment period for a new IT system, and so defers the cost impact on the organisation. The outsource provider will already use the IT system and so is experienced in its application, it has already bought the major licenses and so a new outsourcing contract is an incremental cost. Given the outsource provider has a track record of moving existing processes onto the system, the project risks are reduced and improvements are likely to be realised quicker.
Improved quality	It is expected that the service being outsourced is a core capability for the service provider. They are expected to have expertise in process design and service provision. Through outsourcing, these benefits can be realised and at a reduced cost to the outsourcing organisation.
Strategically to focus on core capabilities	Some organisations reach the conclusion that they need to focus on their core capabilities and non-core activities are a distraction and absorb too much management time. Whilst they will seek maximum value for money and service efficiency this is not their primary motivation.

From a planning perspective the decision to outsource is a project within itself. In Europe the **legislation** associated with the **transfer of employment** has as many requirements as those for redundancy. In many ways the requirements are more onerous. Whilst the employees may be terminating their direct employment with the organisation, they could well still be providing services or products back it, and so the link is not entirely severed. Additionally, as the terms and conditions of employment have to transfer across to the new employer, the HR department have to be diligent to ensure that the correct information is given about each employee and that all obligations are met.

The outsourcing process needs with dedicated resources, a project plan and a governance body. Indeed to manage the outsourcing contract may need a new set of skills in the organisation, and sourcing contract management skills will be an HR objective.

The disadvantages of outsourcing may be summarised as follows.

- External advisers/providers must be carefully chosen, contracted and managed, in order to maintain standards and organisational values
- External advisers/providers may lack understanding or flexibility to be able to tailor their offering to reflect the organisation's objectives, culture or brand
- Outsourcing may be carried out for short-term cost saving without defining which activities are (or may become) 'core' to the business or role of HRM in the organisation
- The horizontal integration and consistency of application across the range of HR policy and practice may be lost
- Recognising that a contract is in place, it needs to be managed accordingly; this requires a different skill set from managing an in-house function and includes the ability to ensure good third party relationship management. If differences occur this can ultimately lead to dissolution of the contract

It is highly likely that your organisation or one you are familiar with has outsourced some HR function whether it be payroll, training, recruitment. Describe to other members of your group:

1 The outsourced service

2 The quality of the service e.g. responsiveness, accuracy, knowledge of your organisation, level of expertise, suitable advice, value for money

3 Should the service remain outsourced or brought back in-house and why?

ACTIVITY 2 — 60 mins

Research the major requirements for outsourcing a service provision. In Europe, the legislation is called the Acquired Rights Directive

1.7 Flexible employment

In the previous chapter, we identified the increasing use of non-permanent workers as part of the changes that are occurring in the modern workforce, and the issues that arise from this. However in this chapter we focus on the operational options they provide in resourcing decisions.

Atkinson (1984) is recognised as developing the model for the 'flexible firm'. The model provides a perspective on how human resources can be employed and engaged by an organisation. It also considers the value they provide to the organisation and therefore how they are to be treated.

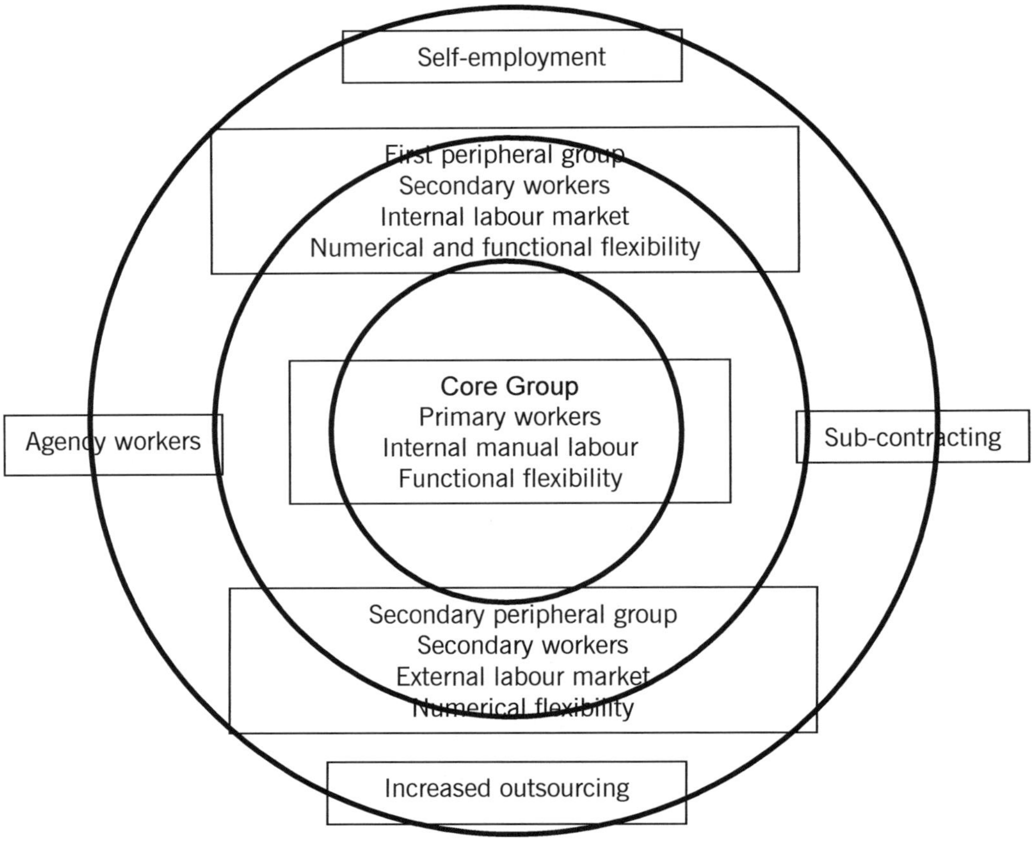

Figure 4.1: Atkinson's 'flexible firm' model

Numerical flexibility. This allows the organisation to respond quickly to a changing environment in terms of the numbers of people employed. To achieve this, full-time permanent employees are replaced by short-term contract staff, staff with rolling contracts etc. This design enables the organisation to quickly expand or contract with little additional cost.

The flexible firm has a number of options as to how best to resource itself.

The **core workers** form the primary labour market, they are on permanent contracts. They are highly valued by the employer, well rewarded and are involved in those activities that are unique to the employing organisation. As this group is of core importance to the employer they can expect longer-term career prospects. In return they are expected to be functionally flexible (see below) and apply their skills across a wide range of tasks.

The **peripheral workers** fall into two groups. First are those who have skills that are needed but are not specific to the employing organisation. This group is sourced from the external market, they are employed to conduct specific tasks, and so the focus is on the job and not career. They have some degree of permanence within the organisation, but their skills are not core to the organisation and can be replaced from the external market. Due to their non-core skills, they are vulnerable to be being released quickly, especially as they can be replaced with relative ease.

The second group contains those workers on short-term or part-time contracts. This group has a low likelihood of securing employment security. Those that do move into the internal labour market have to be good at their job and a cultural fit.

Beyond the second group, workers are either employed by another employer or are self-employed. An alternative method to achieve the numerical flexibility for this group is to use agency workers or outsource the function. This type of worker has seen growth in the last decade, partly owing to more people choosing to work this way, but also in response to employers resourcing their organisation through peripheral workers.

Temporal flexibility. This is focused on flexibility achieved through varying patterns of hours worked, both to respond to employers' demands and employee needs. This flexibility is demonstrated in annual hours contracts, part-time working and flexible working hours.

Functional flexibility.This is where an employee has the capability to undertake a variety of tasks rather than specialising in one. **Horizontal** flexibility involves each employee becoming multiskilled so that they can be deployed as and where required across a range of tasks. **Vertical** flexibility means the employee gains the capability to undertake work that would be performed by colleagues above or below them in the organisational structure. At one time the multiskilled employee was seen as effective solution to employee utilisation and increased productivity. However the use of multiskilled workers would appear to be declining in part due to a reluctance on the part of employers to invest in the skills development programmes and in part to the increasing technical specialisation of roles requiring deep technical knowledge.

Atkinson's model has been criticised by some as:

- Classifying part-time workers as peripheral, and therefore not core to the organisation. Is it true that no core workers in an organisation work part time?
- Is this type of model more productive, how easy is it to manage such a complex organisation?
- The model (1984) is outdated, it only sees a direct relationship between employer and worker, yet the outsourced relationship can be far more complex.

What do you think?

The UK government department for Business and Enterprise and Regulatory Reform published a study of agency workers in October 2008:

- The best estimate for the number of agency workers shows there are between 1.1 and 1.5 million agency workers. The high turnover, the seasonality and the flexibility of agency work make it difficult to come to a definitive figure.
- Agency workers are more likely to work in the manufacturing, transport, and financial services sectors and less likely to work in distribution, hotels, restaurants and the public sector compared with all employees.
- Agency working is concentrated in larger organisations of 50+ employees.
- The estimated duration of an assignment is less than three months for around 55 per cent of agency workers who knew the length of time they had been on their current assignment.
- The overall hourly earnings of agency workers were 94 per cent of the level for all employees with less than two years in their company.
- Agency workers are more likely to be younger, from an ethnic minority group but with broadly similar qualifications compared with all employees.
- Workers are most likely to be found in professional, administrative, secretarial, personal services (e.g. social carers, class room assistants and workers in hospitality) and process/plant/machine operations.

CBI - Mapping the route to growth: rebalancing employment June 2011

The considerable resilience shown by the UK labour market in the early stages of the recent recession is in part explained by the flexibility provided by temporary workers. As the economy slowed there was a sharp reduction in the number of temps engaged by firms, but as the recession eased firms took on temps to meet growing staffing needs while mindful of the continued economic uncertainty. The number of temps, and their share of the labour force, are both now higher than pre-recession levels

1.8 Consultants

The flexible firm mostly focuses upon the concept of workers within the organisation helping achieve the primary objectives, organisations can also decide to use consultants who are expected to apply **particular expertise** to address particular issues.

Organisations often have the necessary resources in-house, however there are a number of reasons for choosing consultants over existing employees:

- Existing in-house resources are already fully utilised, and the effort to redeploy them is greater than appointing consultants.
- Consultants can be seen as politically neutral and impartial, and so avoid the issue being embroiled in organisational political infighting.
- Consultants with particular expertise and greater breadth of experience in addressing the issue will have greater creativity and the necessary resources to achieve the desired outcome.
- Consultants can act as a catalyst within an organisation to achieve change; through their processes they are able to build consensus and navigate through the organisation.
- The outcome is likely to be unpopular and packaging the outcome as a third party expert solution is easier to implement.

There are many types of consultants ranging from large international organisations to single operators. They are typically expensive and so the organisation has to be very conscious as to what outcomes are sought and timescales or/and budget available.

1.9 Interim managers

Interim managers are different from consultants in that they come into an organisation to fill a **vacancy** or **role** on a **temporary basis**. Many interim managers have high levels of expertise and can often be employed for the purpose of affecting change, however they are doing this whilst occupying a line role.

The advantages of interims are:

- Provide a resource at shorter timescale than would be required if selecting a permanent role
- Provide in-depth knowledge and able to operate at the required level within the organisation and so provide a 'safe pair of hands' during a period of need
- They are often able to provide an objective and impartial view of the organisation and so identify opportunities for developmental change in the organisation
- Expect to leave the organisation at the end of the assignment and so departure can be easily effected with minimal impact on the organisation.

So far this chapter has focused on the resourcing needs of the organisation as a whole entity. However reflecting the difficulties faced in the 'war for talent' organisations can adopt a people-centric strategy, one in which they focus on obtaining the best people for the organisation and provide an environment in which they can flourish.

2 Talent management

2.1 Introduction

Talent management is a term that is subject to a wide range of interpretations; these range from:

> The strategic and integrated approach to developing a skilled and competent workforce, involving targeted recruitment, development and retention.

To the more focused:

> The process to identify the individuals within the organisation with the potential to fill the most senior jobs.

Whatever definition an organisation may give to talent management the results of a CIPD survey, conducted in 2010, identified that more than half the respondents said they had a programme in place.

An organisation's values and strategy will determine whether an organisation adopts an **inclusive approach**, where all employees are believed to have an inherent potential that can be developed to enable them to achieve their potential; or whether the programme is highly focused on identifying and developing the **future leadership cadre**.

	Advantages	Disadvantages
Inclusive approach	• Demonstrates the cultural value that people are our most important asset • Organisations need different types of talent at different levels throughout the organisation • Employees can see that the employer is interested and investing in their development • People all have inherit potential which may mature at different rates, inclusive approach allows for different development levels	• Expensive especially if additional programmes are included concerning talent development • Being able to internally resource the requirements e.g. providing mentors • Administrative effort required to manage and co-ordinate the programme • Raising unrealistic expectations amongst employees as to what they can expect from the programme
Future leadership cadre	• Focuses on the critical business need of identifying and developing future leaders • Is targeted on a reduced number of individuals and so is more economic and cost effective • Allows the organisation to focus effort and resources on where it will see the greatest return	• Risks missing talent through over prescriptive criteria • Becomes a 'self-fulfilling prophecy' as the interesting jobs go to those on the scheme • Risks alienating those who believe they should be on the programme but have not been included • Organisation may have serious shock as it realises has little or no high potential talent within the organisation

An organisation will have a number of internal and external factors influencing its decision to launch a talent programme:

- The intention to expand internationally
- Increasingly competitive global markets
- Current and/or predicted skills shortages
- Demographic trends
- Lack of senior management successors.

The focus for the organisation needs to be aligned to strategic goals, what **skills** and **capabilities** are needed for the **long-term plans**, not to meet the more immediate needs. However it can pose a serious challenge for an organisation to identify the skills and behaviours required in the future. Some may be easier than others: if an organisation wishes to expand internationally, overseas experience would be beneficial, if they wish to sell 'solutions' rather than products or services they need people who can articulate this to customers and can design integrated solutions. The question will be revisited as to what is 'talent' and what is the organisation trying to achieve through the programme?

The starting point is defining what is the requirement for the organisation. What do they wish a talent programme to provide? While some organisations may follow the route of treating all employees within the workforce as talented, most define the scope to those jobs or roles that will help an organisation achieve its strategic goals.

2.2 Identifying talent

Assuming an organisation is able to identify the job or roles, and how these will look in the future, the next challenge is what do the individuals who will fill these roles look like? The two most common measures are potential and performance. The following indicators were identified by the CIPD:

High-potential indicators
• Has the respect and trust of peers, supervisors and subordinates • Maintains a high level of competence in their role/job • Has a bias for action and is a proactive catalyst for change • Thinks and solves problems creatively and from a position of inquiry (versus advocacy) • Is open to constructive criticism and feedback • Uses critical judgement • Has a broad understanding of the organisation's business and their role in achieving its goals • Has high capacity to learn
High-performance indicators
• Consistently produces measurable results above expectations • Self-manages in a manner that fosters learning and high performance • Ensures that team goals are achieved within ethical and cultural guidelines • Manages and leads teams that demonstrate a sense of loyalty and community • Strives to deliver and exceed customers' needs • Arranges and leverages resources within an organisation • Has high resilience

To 'measure' these, any organisation has a number of choices: it can run assessment centres designed to identify and measure the indicators. Alternatively an organisation may use the current performance ratings from its performance appraisal scheme and ask managers to assess who they believe demonstrates the greatest potential, using a set of predesigned descriptions. Applying the two measures to all employees in the organisation, the results are then mapped to a matrix. The matrix is crude and generates plenty of debate around B+ players and on whether potential should be weighted more greatly than performance, however it is a starting point.

Such exercises usually demonstrate that there are **very few** fully rounded individuals, some may have outstanding strengths and equally demonstrable weaknesses. Those managing the process will need to determine whether certain weaknesses are critical flaws and so excluded from any programme. Also whether individuals can be developed and so overcome their weaknesses or alternatively can jobs designed that exploit their strengths and yet avoid their weaknesses? Such situations maybe where an individual is brilliant at designing systems, yet struggles to engage with others let alone supervise or motivate them. They may be given a standalone design role, that sits within a team, but the team is supervised by a manager who manages to act as a bridge between the individual and the rest of the team.

Potential				
Low	Medium	High		
C players	B players	A players	High	Performance
C players	B players	B players	Medium	
C players	C players	C players	Low	

An organisation may conclude that it has insufficient numbers of suitable individuals currently within the organisation. This will require the recruitment of talent. In later chapters we consider the different methods to recruit and select individuals, but the same challenges apply when recruiting talent.

2.3 Developing talent

Once a cohort of individuals has been identified, the next question is what to do with them. Some organisations simply make a note of who are the individuals identified as 'talented' and keep a watching brief, others automatically enroll them onto a programme; others invite applicants from the workforce to apply to be enrolled.

Those enrolled on programmes can expect:

- Mentors
- Greater levels of training
- A greater variety of assignments
- External secondments
- Accelerated promotion

A risk for such programmes is that they become a self-fulfilling prophesy. The individuals on the programme enjoy interesting and challenging work - this is clearly developing them. They are feeling highly valued by their employer and receiving special attention. It can be argued it would be hard for any employee not to feel motivated and engaged with their employer. A risk for the organisation is that those who are not enrolled feel exactly the opposite. While many may not want the additional responsibility or recognise that they do not have the required capabilities, there will be a number who feel disengaged by not being selected for the programme.

Does an organisation you know have a Talent Programme? Is it successful in what it tries to achieve or has it created disharmony?

Talent programmes are not the only way organisations can enrich the pool of human resources in an organisation, this can also be achieved through employing a broader and more diverse workforce. The concepts are not mutually exclusive and can complement one other. Before considering diversity management it is best first to understand equal opportunities.

3 Managing diversity

3.1 Equal opportunities

Equal opportunities is a situation in which people have the same opportunities in life as other people, without being treated in an unfair way because of their race, sex, sexuality, religion, age etc.

Equal opportunities seeks to achieve the correct **moral outcome** through creating the **right behaviour**, it seeks to achieve this through **legislation**. The emphasis is on the **equality of opportunity** rather than the **equality of outcome**. The approach is based on the understanding that some individuals are discriminated against due to **irrelevant criteria**, this is especially important during any resourcing exercise of course. The irrelevant criteria arise from assumptions based on stereotypical characteristics, for example women will be less flexible due to home commitments, or that black males are poorly educated. The equal opportunities approach seeks to **formalise procedures** so that any selection process only includes **job-based relevant criteria**. The assumption is that following a criteria-based selection process will be inherently fair and the best person will be selected for the job.

Some of the characteristics associated with equal opportunities are the application of strict criteria, an emphasis on monitoring and positive action. Positive action is where organisations seek to improve the representation within their workforce by deliberately seeking applications from minorities. They seek to achieve this by advertising in minority press publications for example. The action however is limited to encouraging applications; the selection process adheres to criteria that have been identified, as to do otherwise would be discrimination in favour of the minority applicants.

Equal Opportunities faces a number of problems.

- **Assumes fair practice**. The establishment of selection criteria and robust process should ensure equality. However, the inherent prejudices of people are more difficult to overcome than through criteria and process selection. For example the belief that certain of the sexes are inherently better at certain tasks than others e.g. nursing for women, armed combat for men. Also research has shown that managers and even HR will work to circumvent the requirements to get the 'right' outcome. Training and careful selection of recruiters is required.
- **Assumes organisational enlightenment**. Once the minority individual is within the workplace it is assumed that their qualities and skills will become self-evident and that their co-workers will become more enlightened and more open to diversity.
- **Responsibility borne by HR**. Since equal opportunities is regarded as a legislative-driven process that is not connected to achieving organisational objectives, there is the assumption that responsibility falls within the remit of HR.
- **Risks alienating minorities**. In the US (where the legislation is different to Europe), the drive to improve the representation of minorities has had a negative impact. Research showed that in certain situations minority individuals were resented simply because their co-workers believed they had been afforded an unfair advantage in the selection process, and the most qualified people for the job had not been selected.
- **Increases employers costs**. The 'increased costs' argument comes in two forms.
  - Firstly, legislation to create fairness in the workplace requires greater bureaucracy and management time. For example in the UK, a request for flexible working has a statutory procedure that needs to be followed.
  - The other argument is that within the current economic climate many organisations are facing cost pressures, the requirements to demonstrate a good process e.g. advertising in a wide range of press journals is incurring additional expense.

Another feature that is typically associated with Equal Opportunities is **monitoring**. This is the systematic collect and analysis of data on the composition of the workforce, particularly concerning recruitment and promotion. The rationale for monitoring is - how can an organisation make decisions as to how to improve a situation without data? The counter-argument is that managers will correctly engage with the practices and do not need to be required to do so.

MONITORING AT WALMART

Walmart's US operations provides a good example of why monitoring is necessary.

Walmart is a company with a culture that likes to think of all employees as a family and vows to treat everyone with respect. However Walmart found itself facing a discrimination suit due to its operating practices. Part of the culture is to minimise bureaucracy and empower and trust their store managers; managers were allowed to recruit and promote who they wished, as it was assumed they would do the right thing. Part of minimising bureaucracy was not to monitor the composition of the workforce. It was alleged, however, that this working culture partly resulted in only 14.5% of managers being women, compared to 66% of the workforce, and earning 19% less than their male counterparts.

As can be imagined, organisations, especially those outside the public sector, engage at different levels with equal opportunities. Beardwell (2010) identifies the following four types:

The Negative Organisation	Has no equal opportunities policy Makes no claims of being an equal opportunities employer Might not be complying with the law
The Minimalist Organisation	Claims to be an equal opportunities employer Has no written equal opportunities policy Has no procedure or initiatives, but will react to claims of discrimination as they arise
The Compliant Organisation	Has a written equal opportunities policy Has procedure or initiatives in place to comply with some aspects of good practice recommendations
The Proactive Organisation	Has a written equal opportunities policy backed up with procedures and initiatives Monitors the outcomes of initiatives to assess their impact Promotes equality using full set of good practices guidelines, and might even go beyond these

3.2 Diversity management

Managing diversity accepts that the workforce consists of a diverse population consisting of visible and non-visible differences. It is founded on the premise that harnessing such differences will create a productive environment in which everyone feels valued, where all talents are fully utilised and in which organisational goals are met.

The approach to diversity management is to **focus** on the **individual** rather than groups and includes the improvement of opportunities for all individuals not just those in minority groups. The outcomes are therefore beneficial for everyone, without any single groups being identified. Also in contrast to equal opportunities where differences are minimised in diversity management they are seen as positive assets.

A 'managing diversity' orientation implies the need to be proactive in managing the needs of a diverse workforce in areas (beyond equal opportunity and discrimination) such as:

(a) Tolerance of individual differences
(b) Communicating effectively with (and motivating) culturally diverse workforces
(c) Managing workers with diverse family structures and responsibility
(d) Managing the adjustments to be made by the ageing workforce
(e) Managing diverse career aspirations and paths
(f) Confronting literacy, numeracy and qualifications issues in an international workforce
(g) Managing co-operative working in ethnically diverse teams.

The other major difference is that having a diverse workforce is seen as being beneficial to an organisation in terms of its economic or service provision. Essentially there are considered to be six key benefits:

Cost	Organisations have observed that, through employing a more diverse workforce, the productivity levels are high, attrition and absence rates are lower. Certainly in the UK B&Q found attrition and absence were improved when employing an older workforce.
Resource acquisition	Organisations that develop a reputation for excelling in diversity management, will attract the best qualified employees from the minority groups. In turn a diverse and highly capable organisation will become more successful, which will in turn attract even more applicants.
Marketing	A diverse organisation will be able to understand the needs of different market segments better than a less diverse organisation. Thus if computer games companies want to sell more games to women they would be sensible to employ female game designers.
Creativity	The argument suggests that a diverse organisation will be more creative and innovative. The more homogeneous the group, the more the norms and accepted thinking will limit the ability of the group to think creatively. Additionally the group will not be coming into contact with new ideas and stimuli from a broader environment as they will typically sit within the same one.
Problem solving	The greater and more diverse the pool of those trying to solve the problem, the more information and different perspectives available. Less diverse organisations will have fewer reference points and so will risk being stifled in their scope of thought.
Flexibility	A by-product of an organisation seeking to become more diverse, it must also become more flexible in order to accommodate the broad range of employees. The flexibility in turn becomes a strength as the flexible organisation is more effectively able to respond to its external environment.

This argument for diverse workforce is especially powerful for customer-facing organisations, where a customer would expect to see the diversity of their environment reflected in the workforce.

The success of diversity management can often be linked to the culture of the organisation. Ideally the culture of the organisation is one that sees all individuals as a valuable resource and as someone who can be helped to achieve their potential. What needs to be recognised is that to help everyone achieve their potential is unlikely to be enrolling everyone through the same programmes or necessarily creating the same work environment.

The ways in which people are meaningfully different in the workplace include personality, preferred working style and individual needs and drives. These things do not necessarily correlate with racial or gender differences in any way. For example, it would be a gross oversimplification to say that all women in an organisation require assertiveness training: it may be less appropriate for many women than for some men. Thus, the organisation will educating the managers to seek to understand the job-relevant ways in which employees differ and should seek to manage their performance in ways which recognise those differences as far as possible. Managers need to understand the unique contribution each person – not each 'category or person' – can make to the organisation.

It is recognised that during the initial phases of moving to a diverse environment that conflicts will occur. As with any group forming there will be a storming phase and this is the same for organisations. However it has been found that after the conflict phase as the organisation becomes more accustomed to the diversity the value it can bring begins to emerge, and the organisation itself becomes multicultural.

During the recruitment the manner in which an organisation is operating with diversity at the heart of its operations will become apparent and applicants can be expected to pick up this.

DIVERSITY AT PITNEY BOWES

Kramer, McGraw and Schuler (1997) describe the award-winning diversity strategy of USA multi-national, Pitney Bowes.

The vision statement on diversity reads

Pitney Bowes will provide an open, flexible and supportive work environment that values the uniqueness of each of its employees. Through leadership, communication and training programs, Pitney Bowes will aggressively promote an understanding of individual difference, including (but not limited to) age, gender, race, religion, ethnicity, disability, sexual orientation and family circumstances.

The five goals of the Pitney Bowes strategic plan on diversity, and examples of the actions the company has taken to achieve these, are set out below.

- **Goal 1: Communications**: 'Our vision of diversity and its implications for the organisation will be clearly communicated to all of us'. Actions:
  - Formed diversity councils throughout the company
  - Engaged in widespread promotional activity to promote diversity
  - Development of diversity marketing guidelines for Pitney Bowes products and services.
- **Goal 2: Education and training**: 'We will become sensitive to and demonstrate an understanding of the value of differences through education and training'. Actions:
  - Provided multiple training opportunities for the stimulation of diversity awareness
  - Identified high profile minority customers to address employees on diversity issues.
- **Goal 3: Career development**: 'We will create a culture that enables and encourages the development and upward mobility of all of us'. Actions:
  - Introduced new succession planning process based on 'assessing competencies for tomorrow'
  - Published career networking directory
  - Increased opportunities for rotational assignments and cross-training
  - Increased participation in employee mentoring programme.
- **Goal 4: Recruitment and hiring**: 'We will further increase the diversity of our employees so that our organisation reflects the demographic changes in our labour force'. Actions:
  - Developed new minority recruitment campaigns including new promotional material and specific recruitment from schools with diverse populations
  - Supported minority scholarships and intern programs

- Increased funding support for external organisations promoting the diversity agenda
- Tied management bonuses to diversity recruitment goals.

- **Goal 5: Work/life balance**: 'We will provide a flexible and supportive work environment for employees in achieving a balance of work/life issues'. Actions:
  - Developed training to enhance flexible work environment for all employees
  - Expanded child care, elderly care and school referral programs
  - Supported emergency sick child care
  - Conducted employee surveys on work/life balance
  - Piloted telecommuting program.

In order to achieve the five goals of diversity, the business units at Pitney Bowes have tied the concept of diversity to management performance ratings. Part of the incentive compensation plan for the corporate management committee, for instance, includes a diversity component directly linked to the business unit's diversity action plan, and all managers are held accountable for diversity through the performance appraisal system.

ACTIVITY 3 — 10 mins

Complete the following table comparing and contrasting the two approaches of equal opportunities and managing diversity by allocating the following words and phrases to a category:

Reduce discrimination; Utilise employee potential to maximum advantage

Strategic; Operational

Business objectives, improve profitability; Moral and ethical

All managers; HR/personnel function

Individuals; Groups

Dealing with different needs of different groups; Integrated

Improved opportunities for all employees; Improved opportunities for disadvantaged employees primarily through setting targets

Managing; Recruitment

Changing systems and practices; Changing corporate culture

Business outcomes; Changed processes

	Equal opportunities	Managing diversity
Purpose		
Approach		
Case argued		
Responsibility		
Focuses on		
Perspective		
Benefits for employees		
Focus of management activity		
Remedies		
Monitoring		

Much has been written about this subject and the tendency has been for diversity management to be presented as the superior outcome, however as has been shown with the necessity for legislation and the inherent risks of assuming that managers will do 'the right thing' there is a need for a blended approach.

However organisations that ignore this topic can do so at severe risk to themselves, the next example looks at the poor publicity that Nike, the sportswear manufacturer, has received through the 'exploitation' of their workers. The company now monitors, audits and publishes its working conditions.

NIKE

BBC 2007

Nike has pledged to crack down on the amount of overtime done at factories it used worldwide as part of efforts to improve working conditions.

The sportswear firm will seek to abolish "excessive" overtime at its 700 contract factories by 2011, a move which would affect 800,000 workers.

Nike gave details of all such factories for the first time in 2005 after claims of poor conditions at some plants.

Compliance standards

Publishing its annual corporate responsibility report, Nike said the issue of excessive overtime was one of the "most serious" facing the company and the industry as a whole.

Nike uses more than 130 factories in China, where its other major contractors, which manufacture Nike-branded products ranging from trainers to footballs, include India, Vietnam, Malaysia, Brazil and Indonesia.

Nike said improving conditions at these factories was a priority, citing its decision to publish details of its procedure for auditing their compliance with its standards on pay, working conditions and employee benefits.

Earlier this month Nike said it was resuming production of hand-stitched leather footballs in Pakistan, previously suspended due to concerns about the use of child labour.

"We see corporate responsibility as a catalyst for growth and innovation," said Nike's chief executive Mark Parker.

To broaden the talent net as widely as possible and to enjoy the full benefits of a diverse workforce, organisations will often look overseas. These are not the only reasons of course; skills, cost and availability of labour are equally important.

4 International resourcing

4.1 The global employment context

People are increasingly likely to work in an organisation that has multinational or multi-ethnic elements, whether based in their own country or abroad. In some respects, a global labour market has developed in recent decades, because of such factors as:

- **Domestic skill/education shortages**, encouraging international recruitment – which in turn has been facilitated by social policy harmonisation (eg freedom of labour movement within the European Economic Area).

- The emergence, with political change, of **new markets** in areas such as Eastern Europe, South-East Asia and China.
- The development of **integrated trading blocs** such as NAFTA (North American Free Trade Agreement) and the European Union.
- The 'shrinking' of the world through **Information and Communication Technology** (ICT) developments and travel. There are now 'virtual organisations' scattered around the globe, in which people work together via e-mail, the Internet, web-conferencing and so on.
- **The pressures of globalised competition**. Under the ethos of globalisation, local markets are considered too small to justify the costs of developing and marketing new products. This has encouraged the growth of multinational corporations operating outside national boundaries, and an increase in international mergers, acquisitions, joint ventures and strategic alliances.

ACTIVITY 4 — 15 mins

What barriers to a common, global employment environment can you foresee? What, for example, might prevent a UK organisation from recruiting in China?

4.2 People Planning and internationalisation strategy

People Planning issues will have a key influence on the strategic management of multi-national organisations. The choice of a base of foreign operations, or the decision of whether to set up a foreign subsidiary or enter into a joint venture or strategic alliance with foreign partners, for example, might be influenced by a number of people-related factors, including:

(a) Labour costs

(b) Skills available in the local or national labour market: government policy on education and training, available recruitment avenues and media and so on

(c) Employment legislation, controlling the employment relationships (eg health and safety regulation, minimum wage)

(d) Industrial relations culture, trade union power

(e) Language, cultural and social differences that would make transfer of HR practices (and/or the use of expatriate staff) difficult to implement.

4.3 Human Resources strategy

Multi-nationals have to develop specific human resourcing strategies about whether to use 'local' labour, or labour from the 'parent' (head office) country, especially in regard to:

(a) Managerial staff, in order to transfer consistent HR (and business) culture and practices to the international operation

(b) Technical and professional staff, since equivalent skills or qualifications may not be available in all nations in which the firm wishes to operate.

The range of strategies may be broadly summarised as follows.

Strategy	Advantages	Disadvantages
Key positions are filled with nationals of the 'parent' country. e.g: a US multinational transfers US employees to key positions in foreign subsidiaries.	Facilitates the transfer of the distinctive culture and practices of the parent company to the overseas subsidiary (or project), especially where straight-forward overseas expansion is involved.	• Expatriates find it difficult to adjust to the environment and culture of work/management in the foreign country. • May alienate local employees, because of reward disparity or lack of promotion opportunities.
Key positions are filled by local nationals, although overall control is retained by senior management in the 'parent' country. e.g: a US multinational recruits within Italy to find managers for its Italian subsidiary.	Avoids difficulties of expatriate employment.	• May be cultural/ linguistic/priority barriers to co-operation between local and 'parent' country management. • Little genuine cross-cultural experience on either side.
Key positions are filled by the best available people, regardless of nationality. e.g: a US multinational recruits a German to manage a UK subsidiary.	Develops genuine cross-cultural experience.	• Difficult to implement, given 'protectionist' employment policies. • Requires strong corporate culture, communication and co-ordination.

'**Offshoring**' is a major trend of globalisation, whereby organisations in developed countries outsource functions to another group company or third-party provider overseas, in order to take advantage of large, low-cost and increasingly well-educated labour forces in countries such as India and China. This has been traditional in areas such as manufacturing and printing, but has more recently spread to financial services and other service industries: call centres, research and 'back-office' operations are extensively offshored, using ICT developments such as the Internet to co-ordinate and control operations.

OFFSHORING AT IBM

As part of workforce restructuring, IBM recently 'offshored' a large number of highly-skilled IT jobs from developed economies – mainly the United States – to Bangalore in India, Shanghai and the north-eastern city of Dalian in China and to Sumare in Brazil.

'Where the IBM initiative differs from what has gone before is that it highlights the fact that developed countries are losing skilled service-sector jobs that have hitherto been seen as offering secure and well-paid employment opportunities. Such services have traditionally been seen as non-tradeable but increasingly more and more jobs in the sector have, thanks largely to the globalising power of the Internet, become internationally mobile. All knowledge-based activities – financial services, communications, health, education, architecture, the law, media – are discovering that the natural protection they have enjoyed in the past is fast diminishing...'

(Walsh, 2004)

ACTIVITY 5 — 10 mins

What are the HRM implications raised by the example given above?

5 International recruitment

5.1 Why recruit internationally

Organisations need to recruit internationally for a variety of reasons:

1. Expansion abroad requires local managers who understand the market
2. Expansion abroad requires personnel to staff the organisation
3. Succession planning requires local personnel to succeed expatriate managers
4. Skills required cannot be resourced locally and so need to imported

The exact resources required and the particular set of circumstances will vary for each organisation. An organisation that is seeking to source individuals with particular technical skills will be most concerned with the technical ability and the transferability of that skill set to the requirements of the recruiter. An organisation that is looking to create an overseas operation and needing to source a number of local managers to help launch the enterprise will be looking for a different set of competencies. In this instance the requirements may be:

- Ability to speak English
- Experience of having worked/been employed by overseas employers
- Experience of having worked in a start-up environment with little direct management
- Knowledge of the product or service
- Is the employee able to travel and spend time in the recruiting country to learn about the organisation, and products or services

A major barrier for any organisation planning to locate in a new market and simply recruit from that market is limited knowledge and capability. A European organisation is likely to feel more comfortable expanding into another European country, than say China or Korea. First time expansion into such countries will see concern arising as to:

- Language
- Local legislation
- Knowledge of the local market conditions
- Local country culture

We will look at Hofstede's influential model of national cultural differences.

5.2 Recruitment and cultural differences

Hofstede (1984, 1991) carried out cross-cultural research at 66 national offices of IBM and formulated one of the most influential models of work-related cultural differences.

The Hofstede model describes four primary dimensions of differences (predominant traits) between national cultures, which impact on all aspects of organisational behaviour: motivation, team working, leadership style, conflict management, HR practices and so on.

Power distance (PD): the extent to which unequal distribution of power is accepted.	
High PD cultures accept greater centralisation, a top-down chain of command and closer supervision. Subordinates have little expectation of influencing decisions. White collar jobs are valued more than blue collar jobs.	*Low* PD cultures expect less centralisation and flatter organisational structures. Subordinates expect involvement and participation in decision-making. Clerical and manual jobs are equally valued.
Uncertainty avoidance (UA): the extent to which security, order and control are preferred to ambiguity, uncertainty and change.	
High UA cultures respect control, certainty and ritual. They value task structure, written rules and regulations, specialists and experts, and standardisation. There is a strong need for consensus: deviance and dissent are not tolerated. The work ethic is strong. People are risk-averse and experience more stress.	*Low* UA cultures respect flexibility and creativity. They have less task structure and written rules; more generalists and greater variability. There is more tolerance of risk, dissent, conflict and deviance from norms. People take each day as it comes: there is less stress.
Individualism: the extent to which people prefer to live and work in individualist (focusing on the 'I' identity) or collectivist (focusing on the 'we' identity) ways.	
High Individualism cultures emphasise autonomy and individual choice and responsibility. They prize individual initiative. The organisation is impersonal and tends to defend business interests: task achievement is more important than relationships. Management is seen in an individual context.	*Low* Individualism (or Collectivist) cultures interdependence, reciprocal obligation and social acceptability. The organisation is seen as a 'family' and tends to defend employees' interests: relationships are more important than task achievement. Management is seen in a team context.
Masculinity: the extent to which social gender roles are distinct. (Note that this is different from the usual sense in which the terms 'masculine' and 'feminine' are used.)	
High Masculinity cultures clearly differentiate gender roles. Masculine values of assertiveness, competition, decisiveness and material success are dominant. Feminine values of modesty, tenderness, consensus, focus on relationships and quality of working life are secondary (and confined to women).	*Low* Masculinity (or Femininity) cultures minimise gender roles. Feminine values are dominant and both men and women are allowed to behave accordingly.

ACTIVITY 6

10 mins

According to the Hofstede model, what issues might arise in the following cases?

(a) A Swedish company sets up a subsidiary in Brazil under a Swedish general manager, who wishes to import Scandinavian decision-making styles.

(b) The newly appointed Spanish HR manager of a UK firm asks to see the Rules and Procedures Manual for the HR department.

(c) A US-trained HR manager attempts to implement a system of Management By Objectives in Thailand.

(d) A Dutch HR manager of a US subsidiary in the Netherlands is instructed to implement downsizing measures

5.3 Selecting overseas candidates

Most organisations select individuals according to:

1 Technical ability
2 Cross-cultural suitability
3 Language skills
4 Personal circumstances

These requirements can all be assessed through the usual methods that are described in later chapters in this study text, however it is important to understand the process that local candidates may expect to go through. Such information can be learnt through recruitment agencies with international presence or organisational bodies or networks.

It is also important to have clearly established the selection process: if the position is senior, will the candidates be expected to fly to the employing organisation's head offices? Will this require a flight and overnight accommodation, who will they meet and what will the process be? As referenced in other chapters of this study text, how many meetings are arranged and the preparation that goes into them will be informing the candidate as much about the recruiting organisation, as the organisation will be learning about them.

5.4 Issues when considering overseas candidates

Purpose. A primary issue for the recruiter is what is the purpose of the recruitment? The case study below shows the primary reasons identified through research, yet as part of People Planning the organisation maybe seeking a long-term talent investment. Are the objectives of the individual and the organisation matched? Does the candidate have an interest in a long-term career, or are they seeking international experience to enhance their market value?

Personal circumstances. The personal circumstances of the individual also need to be considered. The recruiting organisation may have no international mobility policy and simply expect the candidate to attend work on their first day. However many overseas assignments fail because the employee's partner is unhappy in their new location.

Qualifications. It can be difficult to establish the equivalent status of qualifications around the world. In recent years there has been a growth in the global reach of various Institutes, and many universities have overseas partners or branches. It is important to understand what level of qualification is required for the recruitment.

Visas. European organisations recruiting within Europe have little difficulty in employee mobility. However in the cases where non-EU applicants are being sought, a good understanding is required as to whether they would receive a visa to work in the employing country and how long that would last. The requirements of the UK are discussed further in Chapter 5.

INTERNATIONAL RECRUITMENT

Why employers recruit internationally?

- Because they are an international company : 52%
- To source specific skills : 41%
- To fill international roles : 40%
- Local skills shortages : 24%
- Local labour shortage : 20%
- Cheaper staff : 5%

Occupational areas that are particularly difficult to fill

- Research, Development & Science
- Engineering & Technical Professions
- Banking & Financial Services
- Transport & Logistics
- IT & Telecommunications

Research, Development & Science

Positions require very specialised, highly skilled workers. Engineering & Technical and IT & Telecommunication positions are also hard to fill, because in many countries the demand for workers with the right qualifications for these positions greatly exceeds the supply.

Checklist for International Recruitment Campaign

1 **Target audience**

Know the target audience: who are they and where can they be found? Define the target audience as specifically as possible.

2 **Language**

Think carefully about the language to be used in the campaign. English is the most common language used to attract international workers, but when it is required that a candidate is also fluent in another language (e.g. the local language) it might be useful to run the campaign in that specific language as well. This ensures that the candidates responding meet the language requirements.

3 **Company branding**

Company branding is a very important factor in the campaign. No matter if the organisation is trying to recruit people from abroad or if the organisation is relocating their activities, be aware that most people will not have a clear image of the recruiting organisation. (This is discussed in Chapter 10)

4 **Job-related elements**

Job title - Job description - Qualification description - Application process - Offer - Contact for more info

"A study on how to recruit efficiently and effectively in the European Labour Market" By: LY Stamet , G.J. M Waasdorp

Chapter Roundup

- Organisations need to ensure that their resourcing strategy reflects their organisation's strategy whether that be growth, stability or reduction.
- Workforces reduce by either natural attrition, retirement, voluntary or compulsory redundancy.
- Successful redundancy programmes ensure that employees are treated fairly, that the process is transparent and that all parties are appropriately consulted with – those who lose their jobs need support and advice.
- Organisations can achieve some strategic objectives through outsourcing i.e. contracting out activities to a third party.
- Flexible employment is another option that enables achievement of strategic objectives, this can provide numerical, available working hours and skills flexibility.
- Talent management is subject to a variety of interpretations, each organisation needs to determine what their talent management strategy is, if they choose to have one.
- Diversity management is different from equal opportunities. Diversity management looks to create an environment where difference is embraced and valued as means of achieving a productive environment , whilst equal opportunities is based on achieving equality through legislation and monitoring.
- International resourcing is increasingly common as commercial globalisation occurs, organisations become multinational and the labour market has more freedom of movement.
- To achieve their strategic objectives many organisations also recruit internationally to source skills unavailable locally or to support international expansion.

Quick Quiz

1 What is meant by the phrase 'fitting the job to the person'?

2 What is meant by 'survivor syndrome'?

3 Identify two reasons an organisation would look to outsource.

4 Agency workers are concentrated in what size of organisations?

5 When identifying talent what are the two primary factors that are assessed?

6 Identify two of the problems facing equal opportunities

7 Identify three benefits of diversity management

8 Why do organisations 'offshore'?

9 Name the four primary dimensions in the Hofstede Model.

10 Place the following in order of importance to an organisation recruiting overseas candidates

(1) Cross-cultural suitability
(2) Personal circumstances
(3) Language skills
(4) Technical ability

Answers to Quick Quiz

1 This is the recognition that as situations change and evolve it can be more important for an organisation to recruit someone with the right characteristics who can adapt to the changing environment rather than simply with the necessary skills for the job (para 1.3)

2 Survivor syndrome describes the psychological state for those workers remaining in an organisation after redundancies which involves long-term anxiety about job loss, increased loyalty to co-workers and reduced loyalty to the employer (para 1.5)

3 Cost reduction; Access to expertise or systems; Improved quality (para 1.6)

4 Larger organisations of 50+ employees (para 1.7)

5 Potential and Performance (para 2.2)

6 Assumes fair practice; assumes organisational enlightenment; risks alienating minorities (para 3.1)

7 Lower operating costs due to reduced attrition; improved resource acquisition; increased creativity; more flexible organisation (para 3.2)

8 To take advantage of large, low-cost and increasingly well-educated labour forces (para 5.3)

9 Power distance; Uncertainty avoidance; Individualism; Masculinity (para 5.2)

10 (1) Technical ability
(2) Cross cultural suitability
(3) Language skills
(4) Personal circumstances (para 5.3)

Answers to Activities

Activity 1

- The problem with using appraisal ratings are those that are associated with the appraisal process most of the time:
  - The goals and objectives were not clear and achievable (i.e. not SMART)
  - The employee was too new into the job
  - The manager who gave the rating was too new/didn't know the employee
  - No appraisal was actually conducted – so there is no record
  - The appraisal was conducted too long ago, the employee has developed since then
  - Appraisal process is inconsistent across the organisation and so there is no confidence the ratings equally measured
  - Appraisals are meant to be used for development, if the people knew they were to be used for this purpose a different approach should have been taken
  - Appraisals are at best subjective and so using an appraisal rating is not using a truly measurable value
- Manager's opinion is likely to be subjective, managers have favourite employees, they may be using different criteria to evaluate a 'good' employee, they have selective memories and they suffer from prejudice.

Activity 2

(1) To preserve the continuity of employment and terms and conditions of those employees who are transferred to a new employer when a relevant transfer takes place. This means that employees employed by the previous employer ('the transferor') when the transfer takes effect automatically become employees of the new employer (the 'transferee') on the same terms and conditions (except for certain occupational pension rights). It is as if their contracts of employment had originally been made with the transferee employer. However, the Regulations provide some limited opportunity for the transferee or transferor to vary, with the agreement of the employees concerned.

(2) The Regulations contain specific provisions to protect employees from dismissal before or after the relevant transfer.

(3) Representatives of affected employees have a right to be informed about a prospective transfer. They must also be consulted about any measures which the transferor or transferee employer envisages taking, concerning the affected employees.

- Trade union representatives or elected representatives of the affected employees must be consulted. If there are no representatives in place it is expected that representatives will be elected for this purpose. Where the number of employees is small it is possible, with their agreement, to consult directly with them.
- The information must be provided sufficiently in advance of the transfer to give adequate time for consultation and must include:

  (a) Notification that the transfer will take place, approximate timing and the reasons

  (b) The legal, economic and social implications of the transfer for the affected employees

  (c) Whether the employer intends to take any action which will affect the employees and, if so what action will be taken

  (d) Where the previous employer is required to give the information, he or she must disclose whether the prospective new employer envisages carrying out any action which will affect the employees, and if so, what.

  The term 'measures' is used in the legislation; these can mean actions or changes, for example, a relocation of the employees to the new employer's office, or a change the way that work is processed or a new organisation structure.

  Where the previous employer is required to give the information, they must disclose whether the prospective new employer envisages carrying out any action which will affect the employees, and if so, what. The new employer must give the previous employer the necessary information to meet the requirement.

  The consultation with the representatives of employees must be **in good time** with **a view to reaching agreement**. It is important to understand that there is no stipulated time requirement, and that the consultation periods for redundancy are not to be treated as a guidance. The length of time will be determined by the complexity of the transfer, whether any measures are required, the frequency with which the representatives can be consulted and how well the consultations progress. (Note: the parties do not have to reach agreement.)

(4) The Regulations also place a duty on the transferor employer to provide information about the transferring workforce to the new employer before the transfer occurs. This information includes:

(a) The identity of the employee who will transfer

(b) The age of those employees

(c) Information relating to any collective agreements which apply to those employees

(d) Information contained in the statements of employment particulars for those employees

(e) Instances of any disciplinary action within the preceding two years taken by the Transferor in respect of those employees in circumstances where the statutory dispute resolution procedure apply

(f) Instances of any grievances raised by those employees within the preceding two years in circumstances where the statutory dispute resolution procedures apply

(g) Instances of any legal actions taken by those employees against the Transferor in the previous two years, and instances of potential legal actions which may be brought by those employees where the Transferor has reasonable grounds to believe such actions might occur.

The information must be given in writing or in other forms accessible to the Transferee at least two weeks before the transfer unless special circumstances exist.

Activity 3

	Equal opportunities	Managing diversity
Purpose	Reduce discrimination	Utilise employee potential to maximum advantage
Approach	Operational	Strategic
Case argued	Moral and ethical	Business objectives: improve profitability
Responsibility	HR/personnel function	All managers
Focuses on	Groups	Individuals
Perspective	Dealing with different needs of different groups	Integrated
Benefits for employees	Improved opportunities for disadvantaged employees primarily through setting targets	Improved opportunities for all employees
Focus of management activity	Recruitment	Managing
Remedies	Changing systems and practices	Changing corporate culture
Monitoring	Changed processes	Business outcomes

Activity 4

- Language, ability to communicate the requirements to the local population
- Lack of knowledge of how to advertise positions, and the usual process for employment
- Not understanding how local qualifications compare to the UK
- Inability to manage the process, how to interview, take up references
- Lack of knowledge of how a 'contract of employment' is formed
- Lack of knowledge as to local labour laws and how they are enforced
- Lack of knowledge as to market rates of pay and typical benefits

Activity 5

Some of the *positive* outcomes you may have identified for offshoring include:

(a) Access to a highly motivated workforce

(b) Access to specialised skills and infrastructure development (in cities or areas in which facilities such as IT and call-centre services are concentrated)

(c) Lower HR costs, due to lower costs of wages, benefits and welfare provision

(d) Potential for greater productivity, due to workforce motivation, work culture, specialisation etc

(e) Corporate Social Responsibility and sustainability: creating employment and income flow in developing economies; transfer of technology and management know-how to developing economies etc.

Some of the *negative* issues you might have identified include:

(a) The requirement to consult with employee representatives on redundancies, together with other redundancy procedures and compensation

(b) Likely trade union resistance to the loss of jobs

(c) Encouragement of trade union recruiting within the company, and potential loss of morale (because of the erosion of job security) in surviving employees

(d) Claims of unfair dismissal by redundant employees, if relocation cannot be shown to be a justifiable 'economic, technical or organisational' reason

(e) Impact on employer branding, given likely poor publicity, impacting on future recruitment

(f) Poor PR in general, since off-shoring is a highly political issue.

Activity 6

(a) A low-PD manager is likely to attempt consultative joint decision-making: high PD workers will be inexperienced and uncomfortable with such styles, preferring authoritative instruction.

(b) A high-UA manager, expecting to find detailed and generally adhered-to rules for everything, may be horrified by the adhocracy of a low-UA organisation: if (s)he attempts to impose a high-UA culture, there may be resistance from low-UA employees and management.

(c) A high-individuality manager may implement MBO on the basis of individual performance targets, results and rewards: this may fail to motivate low-individuality workers, for whom group processes and performance is more important.

(d) A low-masculinity manager may try to shelter the workforce from the effects of downsizing, taking time for consultation, retraining, voluntary measures and so on: this may seem unacceptably 'soft' to a high-masculinity parent firm.

Chapter 5

Recruitment and selection overview

As organisations establish their resourcing needs to meet their strategic objectives expectations begin to increase as to what type of candidates may apply and what capabilities the new employees may bring to the organisation.

It is important to ensure that when planning any recruitment and selection activities they have to be cost-effective and legally compliant. The reputation of any resourcing specialist will be based on sourcing and selecting good candidates at the most effective cost. In addition to this the process must be both lawful and fair.

In this chapter we will examine these aspects and consider practices to keep recruitment and selection effective and lawful.

	TOPIC LIST	LEARNING OUTCOMES
1	Cost-effective recruitment and selection	5.1, 6.4
		4.3, 5.2
2	Avoiding discrimination during the recruitment and selection process	5.2
3	Employing foreign workers	4.3
4	Outsourcing recruitment	6.5

1 Cost-effective recruitment and selection

1.1 Is recruitment necessary?

Before any recruitment process is begun, the first question that should arise is – is it necessary to fill the vacancy?

The 'vacant' position may have occurred for any number of reasons:

- Resignation
- Internal promotion
- Retirement
- Re-organisation
- New job design

The person proposing to fill the vacancy may believe that recruitment is the most obvious solution, yet it is important to understand their motivation and knowledge:

Motivation	They do not believe anyone in the department can take on any additional duties and so a new person is required They wish to maintain or increase the number in their department due to budget and prestige associated with managing a large department To deliver on the budget requirements they need to recruit now not later They believe workloads will increase in the future and they wish to start preparing now
Knowledge	Are they aware of surplus employees elsewhere in the organisation who could be redeployed? Are they aware of the organisation's financial performance and the impending need to reduce costs? Are they aware of the People Plan to upskill in many positions in the organization? Are they aware of the policy change to fill more positions through job shares?

Many organisations go through a cycle of centralising their recruitment (to save costs, ensure greater co-ordination, promote the organization more effectively to the market) and then decentralising (centralised recruitment provided poor service, local unit can achieve same outcome for lower costs).

Regardless of this cycle, an important **control** mechanism is for the organisation to be able to control its recruitment through an **authorisation** process. Essentially this will be a single point in the organisation which is able to co-ordinate the numbers in the organisation against the current plan and confirm whether a vacancy should be filled. In very large organisations this process tends to be monitored against the approved headcount for the financial year.

Once a process is in place to monitor and ensure that any recruitment complies with the organisation's plans, the attention can then turn as to what is cost effective. The two most typical costs incurred are time and expense.

1.2 The cost factors for recruitment and selection

When considering how to recruit for a position, many organisations will intuitively determine what type of approach to adopt. For example, if recruiting a receptionist for a local office, it may advertise in a local paper or local internet job board. There may be a maximum of two interviews, and possibly a typing skills test if word processing is a requirement. The focus of the selection criteria are likely to be:

reliable, ability to use the equipment, pleasant telephone manner, pleasant demeanor when greeting visitors, able to type. The process will be relatively short and not overly time-consuming.

If recruiting a chief executive officer, the organisation may appoint a headhunter, they may advertise in a top Sunday newspaper, the interview process will include the chairman, non-executive board members; the candidate may also be invited to meet other executive board members, the process is likely to be lengthy and possibly protracted. The candidate's track record will be considered in detail and informal references may be taken from reliable sources.

Organisations rationalise the level of effort, and therefore cost, on the basis of risk to the business. The receptionist presents no great risk to the business; if the wrong choice is made, a replacement will be relatively convenient and inexpensive to find. The CEO however is a different proposition. If the wrong choice is made, significant cost has been incurred in the advertising and time of all those involved in the selection; not only that, but the CEO's wrong decisions could cause immense damage and reputational damage. Selecting the wrong person could take years to recover from. The greater the risk, the more diligent and cautious an organisation is going to be.

The typical time and expense issues are:

	Issue	Possible solution
Time	Wrong candidates applying	• Wrongly designed job – redesign job with comparable duties and less broad range, may need to split role; role may need to have greater flexibility to attract broader range of applicants • Wrong advertising media – choice of media sends message as to importance of role to the organisation, select media more aligned to type of person expected to apply • Salary too high or too low for the role – obtain benchmarking salary data to confirm rate; determine whether to include rate in advert (adverts with salary range will have significant effect on who applies)
	Insufficient candidates applying	• Organisation fails to understand current market activity and level of demand for suitably qualified candidates – need to redesign jobs so that technical skills required by fewer roles; redesign job so greater element of self-management; increase salary on offer; look further afield; offer training • High local employment results in minimum applications – offer more flexible employment; introduce 'family friendly' policies; develop employer brand and reputation to raise recruitment profile
	Too many candidates applying	• Advertisement worded too vaguely – greater explanation of duties and person specification, explain selection criteria • Salary too high for role – reduce salary in line with duties, or greater explanation of job (It should be acknowledged that in the current economic climate there will inevitably be a high number of applicants for advertised job. The employer will need to have clear criteria and apply them strictly to the applications)

	Issue	Possible solution
	Candidates reject offer when made	• Too much time is taken in recruitment process, candidate loses interest or is offered elsewhere • Job attracts candidates wishing to work flexibly yet is only on offer as full-time working – ensure basis of job on offer is clearly expressed; consider whether job has to be done on full-time basis, working at single location or could be redesigned • Failure to sell role and organisation to candidate. Better educated and trained interviewing managers • Interviewers fail to reflect brand values during selection process – better informed interviewing managers, time spent considering how process can reflect values
	Candidates get offered elsewhere first	• Organisation fails to understand current market activity and level of demand for suitably qualified candidates, rival organisations interview and offer more quickly – educate line managers about market and need to respond quickly – process is redesigned so that good candidates can be seen quickly rather than waiting for designated interview date • Too many stakeholders in the interview process, key decision maker is too senior and not available enough for interview – redesign process so that designated managers are empowered to interview and offer without senior manager approval • Too many interviews – design panel interview approach, or book interview dates in advance and ensure managers are available
	Process too complex for level of job	• Process has too many stages or elements than the role warrants – streamline process to minimum stages necessary • Testing process too long and expensive for level of job – review process, identify key competencies and most effective method for identifying these versus cost of interviewing and/or testing • Poor relationship with recruitment agencies means they prefer to send candidates to quicker processing organisations – a good relationship will elicit honest feedback, agencies are attracted to organisations that have short recruitment process times as it means they can place more candidates for equal effort
	Recruitment department ineffective	• The recruitment department is failing to attract and recruit suitable candidates – department under-resourced for recruitment volumes; department failing to maintain good relationship with stakeholders resulting in poor communications; department not aware of changing requirements in the organisation; department poorly led resulting in poor reputation

	Issue	Possible solution
Expense	Advertising costs too high	• Too much reliance on using expensive and even outmoded recruitment media – need to renegotiate rates; identify different choices of media to reach target audiences e.g. internet job sites; need to develop own corporate web-site
	Too much reliance on recruitment agencies	• The organisation has become over-reliant on recruitment agencies, this has resulted in above market rates being paid, too many managers appointing their own preferred agency on poor contractual terms – a Preferred Supplier List process would identify a small number of selected agencies that are offering competitive rates and standard service terms and who can become highly familiar with the organisation's needs • Organisation recruits directly through internet job boards and leverage of employer brand
	Poor relationship with agencies	• Whilst organisation uses agencies it is failing to maximise the relationship with them and so suitable candidates are being steered towards other organisations – need to improve relationship either through greater communications or change in mindset from client-service provider to partnership
	Wrong approach for type of job	• The organisation is failing to use the correct type of recruitment campaign, campaign pitched too high or too low, wrong choice of media, wrong choice of agency type. Greater time needs to be spent considering campaign strategy maybe requiring expert advice
	Agency rates too high	• The organisation is paying premium agency rates – organisation either needs to negotiate with existing supplier or conduct a Preferred Supplier List process would identify a small number of selected agencies that are offering competitive rates, standards service terms and who can become highly familiar with the organisation's needs
	Process too complex	• Organisation has evolved to a position where too many stakeholders are involved in process, their time in attending the interviews and the time spent organising the appointments is more complex than is justified for the role – organisation agrees approved recruiting managers and delegating authority to these individuals

Think about an organisation with whom you are familiar. What changes have they made to improve their recruitment processes? How have they measured their results?

Recruiting organisations also have to be conscious of the cost of making the wrong choice. The time spent having to terminate the employment of the appointed person and the need to start the process all over again can be immense and tiresome. Consequently, the cost of getting it wrong cannot be ignored.

2 Avoiding discrimination during the recruitment and selection process

Ensuring that discrimination does not enter the process is critical in effectively managing the employment relationship - beginning with recruitment/selection, right through to termination of contract.

While allegations of discrimination can arise at any stage in the employment relationship, the early stages of recruitment and selection are particularly prone to pitfalls. These can often be as a result of the subjective methods of selection adopted by managers. To overcome the risk of accusations of subjectivity, an objective approach should be taken with setting the job criteria, consistent treatment of candidates, questions asked, short-listing criteria and any tests undertaken.

Applications should be processed in exactly the same way. Careful records of interviews should be kept, where practicable, showing why applicants were or were not appointed.

2.1 Arrangements for recruitment and selection

For many employers the recruitment process can take a number of approaches, from the highly informal to the highly formal. Discrimination can occur at any point, but the main areas of risk are:

- Informal methods of recruitment
- Job descriptions, person specifications and competency frameworks
- Job advertisements
- Selection criteria
- Application forms
- Interviews
- Testing

2.2 Informal methods of recruitment

This is potentially one of the most discriminatory employment practices. This method can include:

(i) Recruitment by 'word of mouth' from friends and families of existing employees
(ii) The supply by a trade union of job applicants by use of a 'list' or 'word of mouth'
(iii) Filling vacancies through unsolicited letters from applicants
(iv) Recruitment by internal appointments or transfers.

The primary risk with 'word of mouth' is that if the workforce consists predominantly of one sex or race this method of recruitment prevents members of the other sex or race from applying. These informal 'networks' are likely to exclude women, ethnic minorities and the disabled, and their use is likely to result in imbalances in the composition of the workforce.

It should be emphasised that not all of the above are unjustifiable by employers. For example, a small employer may rely on an unsolicited application when filling a single post. For employers of all sizes internal appointments may be perfectly justifiable when 'ring-fencing' vacancies in a redundancy exercise or when attempting to provide internal career paths to retain good calibre staff. But employers must be careful not to allow these methods to become standard for all vacancies, and they must be able to justify them on sound 'business' grounds.

EHRC guidance on recruitment

The Equality and Human Rights Commission regulates employer conduct in all areas of discrimination in the UK. It is unlawful for an employer to discriminate against a candidate for a job because of their age, disability, race, religion or belief, sexual orientation, trans background or gender in any part of the recruitment process – in job descriptions, person specifications, application forms, during interviews, in tests, or in shortlisting.

For example, application forms should not ask for details that are not relevant to the job, such as country of birth or sexual orientation (except where such questions are contained in monitoring forms that are separated from application forms before assessment). During interviews, questions about a woman's plans for starting a family, or asking an applicant whether they think that they will 'fit in' with the organisation, may also be evidence of discrimination.

However, an employer can ask if you have a disability so they can make special arrangements for you to attend an interview.

Evidence of discrimination

There is no obligation on an employer to show that they have selected the best candidate for the job. However, all employers are recommended to keep records that allow them, if challenged, to justify their decisions to select particular candidates and reject others. The former Commission for Racial Equality's code of practice on employment contains useful information on this and other areas, which may also be relevant to issues other than race.

Employers need to be able to show that each selection is based on objective evidence of a person's ability to do the job satisfactorily, and not on assumptions or prejudices about race, gender, disability, sexual orientation, religion or belief, or age. An employer is unlikely to tell you that they rejected you for these reasons. But if you believe there is evidence of discrimination, you may be able to make a complaint.

2.3 Job descriptions, person specifications and competency frameworks

Job descriptions and person specifications should be drafted using factual, objectively gathered information. Likewise, competency frameworks should be drafted in a similar fashion ensuring that cultural bias is not involved.

Qualifications and personal attributes sought in candidates should be appropriate to the job, otherwise direct discrimination could result. For example, a good standard of English for a manual or unskilled/semi-skilled job could discriminate against those with English as a second language. Generally speaking, the requirement for higher qualifications, such as a degree, is not discriminatory.

The sensible employer will not use 'sexually connotated' job titles. As the job description and person specification are often subsequently used to create advertisements and selection criteria, avoiding these at the start reduces future risk. Examples of these are storeman, which becomes storekeeper; cameraman becomes camera operator.

Some countries in Far East Asia are not restrained in how they treat their employees by equality legislation, they are 'free to trade'. With some economies in the Far East doing better than those in Europe, is equality legislation a step in the wrong direction?

2.4 Job advertisements

It is unlawful to advertise a job vacancy in a way which indicates the job is only available to members of one group based on gender, racial origin, age, disability, marital status, religion/belief, or sexual orientation

Just as with the job descriptions and person specifications, the emphasis should be on skills, competencies and relevant experience. Consequently advertisements should avoid age limits or ranges, and the use of words that imply age, for example 'young' or 'mature'. It can be argued that words such as 'bright' and 'lively' imply an intention to discriminate by recruiting younger people, just as 'mature' and 'dependable' imply a preference for older workers.

Placing a job advertisement in a certain publication could amount to indirect discrimination, for example advertising a job in a magazine aimed at young people may constitute discrimination on grounds of age. Additionally the inclusion of photographs of only one group could also lead people to conclude that only one type of applicant is being sought.

Where a role requires a particular ability, the advertisement should focus on the requirement, for example '*a very high standard of written and spoken English*', or, alternatively, '*fluent English*', rather than wording which invites applicants only who speak English *as their mother tongue*. This phraseology discriminates indirectly against people who speak English fluently, but not as their mother tongue.

If the employer is using a Recruitment Advertising Agency the agency should be able to provide advice on copy and visual work that will achieve the commercial objectives and avoid infringing the anti-discrimination legislation.

Employment and recruitment agencies

Employment agencies will not avoid liability under the anti-discrimination statutes because they simply relied on a statement by the employer that an advertisement was not unlawful. Such a reliance must be reasonable, so where it is clear and obvious that an advertisement' is discriminatory the agency should query it, and if necessary refuse to handle the advertisement unless it is amended. The same process should be applied where instructions are received from the employer, e.g. 'do not put any women forward for interview'.

2.5 Selection criteria

The criteria chosen should be clear, objective, fair and relevant. Proper job analysis and an objective assessment of higher performing employees should proceed the drawing-up of selection criteria. Subjective 'gut feelings' about whether people will 'fit in' or not should definitely be avoided.

Conditions or requirements which may have a disproportionate effect on one sex, or racial group, or those with disabilities should be avoided. It is possible that applying unnecessary height requirements (eg, no applicants under 5 foot 6 inches (1.7 metres), or no applicants over 5 feet 6 inches (1.7 metres) could indirectly discriminate, in the first example against women, and in the second example against men.

2.6 Application forms

Questions on the application form should not suggest that the employer will take into account any factors which could amount to discrimination. Only questions that are relevant to the job should be asked. If the information required is justifiable and relevant, it must be asked for all applicants regardless of sex, racial origin, age, disability, marital status, religion/belief and sexual orientation.

It is recommended that questions on marital status, responsibility for children and domestic obligations are not included. If it is necessary to obtain information relating to the applicant's family for example, for pension purposes, these questions should be asked **after** the successful applicant has been selected.

Where employers are monitoring information such as gender, racial origin, age, disability, marital status, religion/belief and sexual orientation etc then this should be included on a tear-off slip which is removed before those involved in the selection process review the application form.

Employers who require applicants for certain types of job to demonstrate irrelevant and unnecessary skills may indirectly discriminate.

2.7 Interviews

Research studies over a number of years have demonstrated that the interview as a predictive device is an extremely fallible method. Nevertheless, they have also shown that **trained interviewers** produce better results than untrained interviewers and are less susceptible to the **biases** and **stereotyped** perceptions. No interviewer is totally free from bias but they should realise this and attempt to minimise any tendency towards their personal preferences.

To achieve selecting the 'best' candidate the employer should:

1. Focus on the skills, abilities, competencies, potential and the enthusiasm of candidates when making shortlists and selection decisions.
2. Ensure interviewers are trained to avoid age-related bias in questioning and suppress any stereotypes of older (or younger) persons they hold; indeed, training on equal opportunities should include age diversity, and should help them to ask appropriate, probing questions.
3. Use, wherever possible, a mixed-age interviewing panel.
4. Finally, select on merit, based on the application of each candidate and their individual performance during the selection process.

It is worth noting that the candidate cannot take the prospective employer to an Employment Tribunal on the basis of asking questions that are prohibited. However, if the interviewer does ask such questions, and does not employ the candidate, should that person bring a claim the burden of proof will be on the employer to demonstrate that they had not acted in discriminatory manner.

2.8 Selection tests

Selection tests are normally used in recruitment to measure the attitudes, abilities and interests of job applicants and obtain a profile of their personality to obtain a 'best fit'. Tests of personality are more properly referred to as 'personality questionnaires'. The ability tests include measuring literacy, numerical reasoning, spatial awareness and trainability. If tests are carefully chosen, professionally designed and properly used by trained administrators they can minimise bias in the selection process and be a valuable tool for employers in making recruitment decisions. Their key strength is by bringing enhanced **validity, objectivity** and **reliability** to the selection process.

Irrelevant questions in tests should be avoided, particularly if they are about matters which may be unfamiliar to applicants from different ethnic backgrounds, for example, questions which assume a knowledge of English history. This important characteristic of tests is known as being **'culture fair'**.

Other examples of unfairness would be using national or regional colloquialisms which might confuse people who have not spent many years living in the UK.

Information should be collected on the way that men and women and members of different racial groups perform in comparison to each other. This is known as **'norm referencing'**. For example, if the test to be used is to select personnel managers, it is inappropriate to use a test norm referenced with engineers. This process should assist employers to assess whether the tests adversely affect certain groups.

When sourcing candidate from abroad, there are also legal rules that have to be complied with. This next section focuses on the issues relating to overseas employees coming to work in the UK.

3 Employing foreign workers

3.1 Foreign nationals who wish to work in the UK fall into three main categories:

(a) **Nationals of the European Economic Area (EEA)**

The European Economic Area

Austria, Belgium, Bulgaria, Cyprus, Czech Republic, Denmark, Estonia, Finland, France, Germany, Greece, Hungary, Iceland, Irish Republic, Italy, Latvia, Liechtenstein, Lithuania, Luxembourg, Malta, Netherlands, Norway, Poland, Portugal, Romania, Slovakia, Slovenia, Spain, Sweden, United Kingdom.

Iceland, Liechtenstein and Norway are not members of the European Union (EU) but citizens of these countries have the same rights to enter, live in and work in the United Kingdom as EU citizens.

All EEA and Swiss nationals can enter and live in the UK without needing to apply for permission.

Certain EEA nationals do not automatically have the right to work in the UK:

- Nationals of a country that joined the European Union (EU) in 2004 may need to register with the Borders Agency when starting work.
- Bulgarian and Romanian nationals may need to apply for permission before they can start work.
- All other EEA and Swiss nationals are free to take work in the UK without needing to apply for permission.

Some States such as Turkey have Association status with limited rights.

(b) **Non-EEA nationals for whom a work visa is not necessary**

Some categories of non-EEA persons do not require work permits, the **two main examples are:**

1 **Business visitor**

2 **A citizen of a Commonwealth country and one grandparent was born in the UK**

(c) **Non-EEA nationals requiring a work visa**

To update the immigration issues facing the UK the Labour government revised the previous systems and over time introduced a five-tier points-based system. However, reflecting the political sensitivity of immigration, the tiers are already subject to suspension and modification having only been fully implemented for a number of months.

Some organisations may mistakenly believe that they can unburden themselves of responsibility for all of the worries relating to legislative compliance by outsourcing the process. In fact there is little evidence that any organisations try to achieve that. However, outsourcing the recruitment and selection processes can offer potential benefits to many organisations, but they will still find themselves having to act in a legally compliant manner!

4 Outsourcing recruitment

In Chapter 4 we considered the benefits to an organisation of outsourcing to achieve its strategic objectives. Recruitment and, to a lesser extent, selection are both seen as ripe for outsourcing.

4.1 The benefits of outsourcing recruitment

What benefits would an organisation expect to gain from outsourcing its recruitment?

Flexibility	A dedicated recruitment function in an organisation can be a highly prized asset for the purposes of recruiting the right candidates and future talent pool. However it can also become a fixed cost, particularly an issue when recruitment volumes reduce. An outsourced provider is contracted to provide a service and so the scaling of resources to support any recruitment rests with them. They are expected to have sufficient resources to be able to respond to any sudden increase in demand. This is often achieved by managing many accounts and scheduling resources across the accounts in line with demand. Outsourced providers often provide both permanent and temporary resources, and so offer a 'one stop shop' solution.
Reduced cost	Often the decision to outsource will be with a single provider. Included within the contract negotiations will be an indication of anticipated volumes. Based on a single provider status and expected volumes the provider will offer recruitment costs considerably below 'one-off' exercises. Advertising rates will also be cheaper, either because the outsource provider is bulk purchasing; or because they have pre-bought space within which they will advertise any vacancies they have.
Global reach	Many of the larger agencies have international branches, so using their pre-existing network makes it easier for client organisations to understand what is available overseas and what the process would involve.
Greater pool of applicants	The agency may be a more recognised brand than the organisation they are recruiting on behalf of and so they may be able to attract candidates who may not have heard of, or considered, the employer before.
Expertise	Many larger agencies are organised by sector and so are familiar with the recruitment requirements of the sector and will often be familiar with candidates. They can also provide head hunter services for more senior or specialist roles. The larger agencies are also able to provide specialist advertising design skills and advice on employer brand etc
Use of IT infrastructure	Many large employers have invested in their own e-recruitment platform, however for many organisations this can be a major cost. The outsourced provider has already invested in this system and is highly familiar with its configuration. They will brand the 'front end' pages to appear as if they are the employing organisation, and these pages will be located on the employing organisation's corporate website. Applicants will perceive they are applying directly to the organisation when, in fact, the applications and data will all be managed by the outsourced provider.

4.2 The disadvantages of outsourcing recruitment

The disadvantages are:

- **Loss of control and direct ownership**, needing to convey messages about the organisation through a third party.
- **Loss of in-house expertise**, the transferred employees are now employees of the outsourcer and can be moved onto other accounts or terminated. Whilst clauses can be included within the contract to ensure discussion, the decisions ultimately rest with the service provider. If the original employer wishes to bring the service back in-house there is no guarantee the former employees will also return.
- **Total reliance on outsourcer** especially if using their IT platform. All the data and the technology with which it is managed is held by the outsourcer. If the organisation wishes to bring the service in-house, it needs to buy the licenses and build the data.

ACTIVITY 1 — 60 mins

You have been asked to create a list of criteria that will be used to select a short list of potential outsourced suppliers. Rank the following list in order of importance:

(a) Range of services and method of delivery
(b) Scalability, ability to increase capacity to reflect growth in the business
(c) Account management and service performance information
(d) Management Information
(e) Candidate attraction and resource planning strategy
(f) Technology
(g) Fee structure
(h) Applicant monitoring (legislation compliance)
(i) Sector experience
(j) Implementation of new contract and management of transition/change programme

Chapter Roundup

- Before organisations commence any recruitment process they need to ensure there is a need to recruit.
- The two cost factors in recruitment and selection are the time spent involved in the process and the expense incurred such as advertising, agency rates.
- It is important when recruiting to follow pre identified criteria and follow a process that is fair and equally applied to all candidates. Care should be taken to avoid discrimination, the focus is on objective evidence.
- When recruiting foreign workers it is important to ensure that any immigration requirements are understood before offering a position. Different rules apply to people from different countries; different rules also apply depending upon why the person is planning to enter the country and what they will do once in the country.
- Organisations can achieve a number of financial and operational advantages from outsourcing their recruitment and potential selection processes. There are also risks involved in outsourcing.

Quick Quiz

1. Identify two 'time' reasons why recruitment and selection takes longer than ideal
2. Identify two reasons why too many applicants may apply for a job
3. What is the primary risk of sourcing applicants through 'word of mouth'?
4. What does EHRC stand for?
5. It is unlawful to discriminate against someone on the basis of their weight and appearance – true or false?
6. Give an example of a 'sexually connotated' job title
7. Managers should be encouraged to recruit based on their gut instinct – true or false
8. When selecting a candidate what should an employer focus upon?
9. What key strength do tests bring to the selection process?
10. Identify two benefits of outsourcing recruitment

Answers to Quick Quiz

1 You could have chosen from: insufficient candidates applying; too many candidates applying; process too complex for level of job (para 1.2)

2 Advertisement worded too vaguely; salary too high for the job; a reflection of the current economic situation (para 1.2)

3 If the workforce consists predominantly of one gender or race this method of recruitment prevents members of the other gender or race from applying. (para 2.2)

4 The Equality and Human Rights Commission (EHRC) (para 2.2)

5 False – it is only unlawful to discriminate against someone on the basis of race, gender, disability, sexual orientation, religion or belief, or age (para 2.2)

6 Storeman, sales girl (para 2.3)

7 False – they need to recruit according to pre identified criteria (para 2.5)

8 Skills, abilities, competencies, potential and enthusiasm (para 2..8)

9 Validity, objectivity and reliability (para 2.8)

10 You could have chosen from: flexibility; reduced cost; use of IT infrastructure (para 4.1)

Answers to Activities

Activity 1

Each organisation will have their own agenda as to why they wish to outsource their recruitment services, however as an indicative answer:

1 Fee structure (Cost saving is a primary consideration and reason for looking at outsourcing)

2 Range of services and method of delivery (The business has a wide range of services, and outsourcing provider is to be only provider, therefore it needs a wide range of services)

3 Applicant monitoring (legislation compliance) (The organisation has been poor on diversity and monitoring, these need to improve and this is an opportunity)

4 Implementation of new contract and management of transition/change programme (The organisation neither has the resources nor a good track record of implementing such a change, heavy reliance will be put upon the outsource provuder)

5 Sector experience (The sector is relatively small and so providers with prior experience would be valued)

6 Candidate attraction and resource planning strategy (An ability to demonstrate capability would be valued)

7 Technology (Any technology would be valued, however all providers offer a technology solution)

8 Account management and service performance information (This is effectively an expected service delivery item)

9 Scalability, ability to increase capacity to reflect growth in the business (The business does not expect much growth in the next three years and so is not a priority, however things may change)

10 Management Information (No management information is available currently, so valued; however all providers supply this)

Chapter 6

Recruitment

Recruitment is the process whereby an organisation communicates opportunities and information to the labour market in order to attract the quantity and quality of potential employees it requires to fulfil its human resource plan. However before that it needs to determine what is included within the job and the attributes of the most suitable person for the job. This chapter outlines a systematic approach to this task.

The process of deciding which of the candidates short-listed by the recruitment process are suitable is called **selection**: this will be discussed in Chapter 7.

TOPIC LIST		LEARNING OUTCOMES
1	The recruitment process	6.1
2	Job analysis	6.1
3	Job description	6.1
4	Person Specification and Competencies	6.1
5	Recruitment methods and media	6.1, 6.2
6	Evaluating recruitment	5.4, 6.3

1 The recruitment process

Recruitment is the part of the human resourcing process concerned with finding the applicants: it is a positive action by management, going into the labour market, communicating opportunities and information, and encouraging applications from suitable candidates.

Aims of the recruitment process

The aims of the recruitment process may be divided into three main areas.

The creation of a pool of suitable candidates. Recruitment is about attracting applications from sufficient candidates with the appropriate qualifications, skills, experience and personal qualities. The aim is to create a pool of candidates for each vacancy that arises so that the most suitable can be appointed.

The management of the recruitment process itself. Those responsible for recruitment will also be charged with the development and refinement of the procedures and practices in use. These must be clear, effective and applied consistently. All applicants must be treated fairly and equitably.

The basis of selection. The recruitment process feeds into selection and must support the requirement that selection is made on merit and in accordance with the stated requirements of each job to be filled.

1.1 A systematic approach

The overall aim of the recruitment process in an organisation is to obtain the quantity and quality of candidates required to fulfil the objectives of the organisation.

A systematic approach to recruitment will involve the following stages.

(a) Detailed **human resource planning** defining what resources the organisation needs to meet its objectives.

(b) **Job analysis** (or variants), so that for any given job or role there is a definition of the skills, knowledge and attributes required to perform the job.

  (i) A **job description**: a statement of the component tasks, duties, objectives and standards of the job

  (ii) A **person specification**: a reworking of the job description in terms of the kind of person needed to perform the job

  (iii) Some other appropriate definition of the requirement, such as a **competence or role definition**

  If such documents already exist, they may need to be updated or confirmed.

(c) An identification of **vacancies**, from the requirements of the human resource plan or by an approved authorisation to recruit.

(d) Evaluation of the **sources of skills,** which again should be identified in the human resource plan. Internal and external sources, and media for reaching them (eg through **job advertisement** or e-recruitment, say) will be considered.

(e) Preparation and publication of recruitment **information**, which will:

  (i) Attract the attention and interest of potentially suitable candidates

  (ii) Give a favourable (but accurate) impression of the job and the organisation

  (iii) Equip interested candidates to make an application (how and to whom to apply, desired skills, qualifications and so on).

(f) **Processing applications** prior to the selection process. This may include:

   (i) Screening replies at the end of the specified period for application
   (ii) Short-listing candidates for initial consideration
   (iii) Advising applicants of the progress of their application
   (iv) Drawing up a programme for the selection process which follows.

1.2 Recruitment policy and best practice

Detailed procedures for recruitment should only be devised and implemented within the context of a coherent **policy**, or code of conduct. Policy decisions will have already been made as to whether all vacancies are advertised internally first and how much emphasis is going to be placed on diversity.

A typical recruitment policy might deal with:

(a) Internal advertisement of vacancies

(b) Efficient and courteous processing of applications

(c) Fair and accurate provision of information to potential recruits

(d) Selection of candidates on the basis of qualification, without discrimination on any grounds

(e) Recruitment of labour reflecting the composition of society as a whole, and perhaps local labour where possible (supporting diversity and social sustainability targets, eg in the public sector).

Detailed procedures should be devised in order to make recruitment activity systematic and consistent throughout the organisation (especially where it is devolved to line managers).

1.3 Influences on recruitment policy

Recruitment policy will be influenced by the following considerations.

(a) The **People Plan** and subsidiary plans

(b) **Fairness, courtesy and professionalism** in dealing with applicants, as defined by 'best practice' benchmark evidence.

(c) **Legislation and regulations** affecting:

   (i) **Terms and conditions** able to be offered to (or imposed on) potential employees (for example, minimal wage, working hours, holiday entitlements)

   (ii) **Equal opportunities** and **diversity**

   (iii) **Labour mobility** – for example, discrimination on the basis of nationality or national origin against candidates from the European Economic Area.

(d) The **cultural values** of the organisation, as well as the national culture in which it operates. These are often reflected in the attributes considered essential or desirable in candidates; the importance attached to educational, vocational or professional qualifications; and/or identification with the organisation's self-image (responsible, fun, fast-paced, flexible or whatever).

(e) The organisation's **image** in the community, market-place and labour market: its **'employer brand'** and identity as an employer. Recruitment advertising, in particular, is a public relations exercise: it must reflect the organisation's values and professionalism – and, where appropriate, its marketing message (quality, products/services and so on). (We look at employer branding in Chapter 10)

JAPANESE VS MALAYSIAN RECRUITMENT PRACTICES

In a study carried out by Hooi (2006) regarding how recruitment practices of Malaysian-based Japanese companies in comparison with the recruitment practices of Malaysian companies.

Japanese practice

As you may expect, Japanese companies have traditionally placed a high reliance on life-time employment. This has been achieved through recruiting graduates and then committing to a life time of training and development. Indeed many companies expect the male employees to remain until compulsory retirement age, and for female employees to leave either when they get married or have children.

For large Japanese companies (250+ employees) their primary source of new employees is to recruit new graduates from colleges and universities. The recruiters would be basing their numbers on long and medium range forecasts and anticipated retirements.

It is acknowledged that larger Japanese corporations are now recruiting mid-career candidates especially where those companies are competing for specialist technical skills or knowledge of foreign markets. However the primary focus has been to source top quality graduates from the best colleges and those who demonstrated interests such as membership of sports clubs.

The personal qualities sought included:

- Enthusiasm
- Good common knowledge
- Co-operative spirit
- Drive

While in the past emphasis for certain careers was placed on the academic tutors making personal recommendations, it is recognised that now job boards and internships play a major role in sourcing candidates.

As the study points out:

'Thus, although traditional practices continue to dominate, more and more companies are beginning to experiment with unconventional employment methods such as mid-career hiring, lateral hiring from other Japanese companies, outsourcing for special skills, as well as increased use of temporary employees...'

Malaysian practice

The study observed that in comparison to Japanese practice Malaysian recruitment was highly orientated to immediate need and without the consideration to life-time employment. This is partly attributed to them not having long-term people planning practices. Consequently the emphasis was placed on the candidate's prior experience and what they could immediately bring to the role. It was noted that as Malaysian companies do not particularly invest in employee training and development to support life-time employment, expertise had to be bought in. Malaysian recruiters, when interviewing, placed less emphasis on formal qualification than their Japanese counterparts, and were more focused on personal traits and attitudes.

It was also noted that even when Malaysian companies did recruit graduates direct from colleges again it was not with the expectation of life-time employment. The study pointed out that employees recognise their current skills create their personal market value, therefore they value the experience they gain from their current employer and remain with the employer to develop these. However as the employers do not have long-term development programmes, the employees recognise that to develop they have to move to new employers to gain broader experience. This behaviour, in turn, feeds the employer's belief that employee development is not a good investment as employees are committed to job-hopping to progress. As so a job-hopping culture is perpetuated.

Another outcome of the non-life-time employment expectation is that the Malaysian employer has a greater preparedness to terminate under-performing employees. This contrasts to the Japanese situation where the employee, with an expectation of life-long employment, focuses on developing their career within the company and acts more flexibly and is willing to participate in learning and development.

Again as Japanese companies are often recruiting for life-long employment there is not a particular practice of having probation periods. In contrast the Malaysian companies have probation periods as standard practice.

2 Job analysis

Job analysis is 'the determination of the essential characteristics of a job', the process of examining a job to identify its component parts and the circumstances in which it is performed (*British Standards Institute*).

2.1 Uses of job analysis

Job analysis, and the job specification resulting from it, may be used by managers:

(a) In **recruitment and selection** – for a detailed description of the vacant job to provide a source of information for the preparation of job descriptions and personnel specifications

(b) For **appraisal** – to assess how well an employee has fulfilled the requirements of the job

(c) In devising **training programmes** – to assess the knowledge and skills necessary in a job

(d) In establishing **rates of pay** – this will be discussed later in connection with job evaluation

(e) In eliminating **risks** – identifying hazards in the job

(f) In re-organisation of the **organisational structure** – by reappraising the purpose and necessity of jobs and their relationship to each other.

2.2 Content of job analysis

Information which should be elicited from a job appraisal is both task-oriented and worker-oriented, including:

(a) **Initial requirements of the employee:** aptitudes, qualifications, experience, training required; personality and attitudinal considerations

(b) **Duties and responsibilities of the job:** physical aspects; mental effort; routine or requiring initiative; difficult and/or disagreeable features; degree of independence or discretion; responsibilities for staff, materials, equipment or cash etc; component tasks (where, when, how frequently, how carried out); standards of output and/or accuracy required; relative value of tasks and how they fit together

(c) **Environment and conditions of the job:** physical surroundings, with notable features such as temperature or noise; hazards; remuneration; other conditions such as hours, shifts, benefits, holidays; career prospects; provision of employee services – canteens, protective clothing etc

(d) **Social factors of the job:** size of the department; teamwork or isolation; sort of people dealt with – senior management, the public; amount of supervision; job status.

2.3 Methods of job analysis

Opportunities for analyses occur when jobs fall vacant, when salaries are reviewed, or when targets are being set, and the HR department should take advantage of such opportunities to review and revise existing jobs.

Job analysis can be carried out by:

(a) **Observation of working practice**, where jobs are relatively routine and repetitive. The analyst watches and records the job holder's activity, task times and performance standards, working conditions and so on. A proforma question sheet listing the factors to be recorded would normally be used, incorporating range statements (circumstances in which each task is carried out and standards to which competence is required) and rating scales.

(b) **Questionnaires and interviews**, for jobs with longer task cycles and invisible work (planning, problem solving and so on). The job holder would be asked to explain, describe and quantify (as far as possible) the job. His or her manager, and other third parties, may be asked to complete the same exercise.

(c) **Diaries, time sheets and other self-recording techniques.** The job holder may be asked periodically to record activity, or may include **critical incidents** highlighting key aspects of the job.

ACTIVITY 1 — 15 mins

The fact that a job analysis is being carried out may cause some concern among employees: they may fear that standards will be raised, rates cut, or that the job may be found to be redundant or require rationalisation

How might the analyst need to carry out his or her work in order to gain their confidence?

3 Job description

A **job description** is a broad description of a job or position at a given time (since jobs are dynamic, subject to change and variation). 'It is a written statement of those facts which are important regarding the duties, responsibilities, and their organisational and operational interrelationships.' (Livy, 1988)

3.1 Purposes and uses of job descriptions

In **recruitment**, a job description can be used:

(a) To decide which skills (for example, technical, human, conceptual, design) and qualifications are required of the job holder. When formulating recruitment advertisements, and interviewing an applicant for the job, the interviewer can use the resulting job description to match the candidate against the job.

(b) To assess whether the job will efficiently utilise the abilities and provide scope for the aspirations of the prospective job holder.

(c) To determine a rate of pay which is fair for the job, if this has not already been decided by some other means.

3.2 The contents of a job description

A job description should be clear and to the point, and so ought not to be lengthy. A standard format for a job description would provide the information shown below.

(a) **Job title** and department and job code number; the person to whom the job holder is responsible; possibly, the grading of the job.

(b) **Job summary** – showing in a few paragraphs the major functions and any tools, machinery and special equipment used; possibly also a small organisation chart.

(c) **Job scope and content** – for manual work, a list of the sequence of operations that constitute the job, noting main levels of difficulty. In the case of management work there should be a list of the main duties and responsibilities of the job, indicating frequency of performance – typically between 5 and 15 main duties should be listed. This includes the degree of initiative involved, and the nature of responsibility (for other people, machinery and/or other resources).

(d) The extent (and limits) of the jobholder's authority and responsibility.

(e) Statement showing relation of job to other closely associated jobs, including superior and subordinate positions and liaison required with other departments.

(f) Working hours, basis of pay and benefits, and conditions of employment, including location, special pressures, social isolation, physical conditions, or health hazards.

(g) Opportunities for training, transfer and promotion.

(h) Possibly, also, objectives and expected results, which will be compared against actual performance during employee appraisal – although this may be done as a separate exercise, as part of the appraisal process.

(i) Any formal qualifications required.

SPECIMEN JOB DESCRIPTION

MIDWEST BANK PLC.

1 *Job title*: Clerk (Grade 2)

2 *Branch*: All branches and administrative offices

3 *Job summary*: To provide clerical support to activities within the bank

4 *Job content*: Typical duties will include:

- (a) Cashier's duties
- (b) Processing of branch clearing
- (c) Processing of standing orders
- (d) Support to branch management

5 *Reporting structure*:

Administrative officer/assistant manager

Supervisor (Grade 3)

Clerk (Grade 2)

6 *Experience/Education*: Experience not required; minimum 3 GCSEs or equivalent.

7 *Training to be provided*: Initial on-the-job training plus regular formal courses and training.

8 *Hours*: 38 hours per week

9 *Objectives and appraisal*: Annual appraisal in line with objectives above.

10 *Salary*: Refer to separate standard salary structure.

Job description prepared by: Head office HR department (October 2009)

3.3 Limitations of job descriptions

(a) They are only suited for jobs where the work is largely repetitive and therefore performed by low-grade employees.

(b) Jobs are likely to be constantly changing as turbulent business environments impact upon them, so a job description is constantly out of date or limiting.

(c) Job descriptions stifle flexibility and encourage demarcation disputes, where people adhere strictly to the contents of the job description, rather than responding flexibly to task or organisational requirements.

3.4 Alternatives to job description

Marchington and Wilkinson (2008) argue that job descriptions go against the concept of high performance working. The focus on the definitions of what is expected and 'working to contract' are counter to initiatives to add value and 'work beyond contract' where the individual is expected to use their own initiative to deliver at and beyond what is expected within the role. To counter the highly descriptive job description has seen the emergence of **role definitions** or **accountability statements**.

Where job descriptions are used, it should be remembered that:

(a) A job description is like a photograph, an image 'frozen' at one point in time, they fail to reflect the potential changes to come

(b) A job description needs constant and negotiated revision

(c) A job description should be secondary in importance to a customer requirement, quality improvement or problems solved.

Completing a job description is also a useful way to identify what is important in a role and help prioritise what is being sought from future candidates. They also serve to provide the basis by which to measure whether someone is performing in the role.

To overcome some of these problems some organisations are therefore moving towards:

(a) **Goal, competence or accountability statements**, setting out the outputs and performance levels expected of the individual (or team). We will look at competence profiles in section 4.3.

Example of a job description in contrast to an accountability profile for a doctor's receptionist. (Taylor 2010)

Job description	Accountability profile
Main duties	Key result areas
• Opening and closing the premises	• Ensures that the premises are opened on time and secured at the end of surgery hours
• Checking heating	• Checks the heating equipment is in working order and that the correct temperature is maintained
• Reconnecting the regular telephone service	• Reconnects the regular telephone service at the start of surgery hours
• Opening and distributing the mail	• Opens all mail on receipt and takes responsibility for its prompt distribution to each doctor
• Answering general enquiries	• Ensures that all enquiries are dealt with promptly and courteously
• Registering patients	• Completes all procedures associated with the registration of new patients
• Making appointments	
• Filing and extracting patient records	
• Receiving and logging samples	

Example of a job description in contrast to an accountability profile for a doctor's receptionist. (Taylor 2010)	
	• Accurately maintains appointment records • Ensures the accurate extraction and filing of patient records • Receives and logs all samples received promptly and accurately

(b) **Role definitions**, defining the part played by the job holder in meeting organisational and departmental objectives. A role definition is therefore wider than a job description, focusing less on 'content' than on how the job holder contributes to business processes and results through competent and flexible performances.

A role profile or definition will therefore specify: the overall purpose of the role; what role holders are expected to achieve (key results) and what they will be accountable for; and the behavioural/technical competences required to achieve the defined level of contribution.

Think about an organisation you are familiar with; do they use job descriptions, accountability statements or role definitions? Why has it adopted that practice?

4 Person Specification and Competencies

A **person specification** profiles the type of person the organisation should be trying to recruit for a given position: that is, the 'ideal' candidate.

Professor Alec Rodger was a pioneer of the systematic approach to recruitment and selection in the UK. He suggested that:

> If matching *[ie of demands of the job and the person who is to perform it]* is to be done satisfactorily, the requirements of an occupation (or job) must be described in the same terms as the aptitudes of the people who are being considered for it.

This was the basis for the formulation of person specification as a way of matching people to jobs on the basis of comparative sets of data: defining job requirements and personal suitability along the same lines.

4.1 Models for person specification

Two influential models were adopted as the basis of person specification.

The Seven Point Plan (Rodger, 1970)	Five Point Pattern of Personality (Munro Fraser 1971)
Physical attributes (such as neat appearance, ability to speak clearly and without impediment) Attainment (including educational qualifications and experience) General intelligence (intellectual capacity) Special aptitudes (manual dexterity, speed and accuracy) Interests (practical and social) Disposition (or manner: friendly, helpful, dependable and so on) Background circumstances	Impact on others, including physical attributes, speech and manner Acquired knowledge or qualifications, including education, training and work experience Innate ability, including mental agility, aptitude for learning Motivation: individual goals, demonstrated effort and success at achieving them Adjustment: emotional stability, tolerance of stress, human relations skills

Each feature in the specification may be classified as:

(a) **Essential –** for instance, honesty in a cashier is essential whilst a special aptitude for conceptual thought is not

(b) **Desirable** – for instance, a reasonably pleasant manner should ensure satisfactory standards in a person dealing with the public

(c) **Contra-indicated** – some features are actively disadvantageous, such as an inability to work in a team when acting as project leader.

PERSON SPECIFICATION: PERSONNEL ADMINISTRATOR FOR HIGH STREET CHAIN STORE

	Essential	Desirable	Contra indicators
Physical attributes	Clear speech Well groomed and presentable to external customers Good health		Chronic ill health and history of (non- disability related) absence
Attainments	2 'A' levels GCSE Maths and English Previous experience working in retail minimum 18 months	Degree (any subject) HR qualification Experience of multi locations	No retail experience
Aptitudes	Attention to detail and accuracy Social skills for dealing with external and internal queries	IT skills, especially Oracle Analytical abilities especially problem solving	Poor attention to detail No IT skills
Disposition	Team player Goal orientated Tolerant of pressure and change	Initiative	Unsocial Low tolerance for responsibility

4.2 Limitations of person specifications

As our example suggests, a wide number of variables may be included in a person specification. If it is not used flexibly, however, and the specification fails to evolve as external environment and employment conditions change, it may swiftly lose its relevance. For example:

(a) Attainments are often focused on educational achievements, since there has traditionally been a strong correlation between management potential and higher education. However, this does not necessarily reflect the range of learning and experience available, nor the increasing diversity of educational backgrounds and qualification standards in a global labour market.

(b) 'Physical attributes' and 'background circumstances' may suggest criteria which can now be interpreted as discriminatory, to the disabled (in the case of a speech impairment, say) or to women (for example, the ability of women with family responsibilities to undertake full-time employment).

(c) The category of 'general intelligence' has traditionally been based on 'IQ', a narrow definition of intelligence as mental dexterity. It is now accepted that there are at least seven different intelligences, not least of which are emotional, intuitive, practical and interpersonal intelligence, which are key factors in the new fluid, horizontal business world.

'Forget loyalty and conformity. We can't afford narrow-skill people' (Rosabeth Moss Kanter). What does this say about the concept of the desirable disposition for an employee? What kind of characteristics may now take the place of loyalty and conformity as desirable attributes for success and contribution in today's business environment (or in an industry or occupation of your choice)?.

4.3 Competence profiles

Competence may be defined as 'the set of behaviour patterns that the incumbent needs to bring to a position in order to perform its tasks and functions with competence'. (Woodruffe, 1992)

Competences are the critical skills, knowledge and attitude that a jobholder must have to perform effectively. Typically competences are defined across four categories:

(a) What the role encompasses - ie what does the incumbent need to be competent to do.

Examples of competence include:

(i) exercise of judgement and discretion
(ii) communication skills
(iii) cost consciousness
(iv) personal planning and time management
(v) capacity to meet deadlines or work under pressure
(vi) developing teamwork.

(b) The knowledge, skills and attitude that make up that competence.

(c) What level of competence is required – e.g. whether a basic knowledge of the subject is adequate, or expert knowledge?

(d) What evidence proves the competence – i.e. what evidence will be sought from candidates to demonstrate the competency.

Roberts (1997) differentiates between four types of competency:

(a) **Natural competences** – made up of the 'big five' dimensions: extraversion/introversion, emotional stability, agreeableness, conscientiousness and openness to experience

(b) **Acquired competences** – knowledge and skills acquired through work or other avenues

(c) **Adapting competences** – the ability to adapt natural talents and acquire skills to a new situation

(d) **Performing competences** – comprising observable behaviours and outputs

Competence frameworks, definitions or profiles are based on **key success factors** in a given business or sector (through benchmarking exercises or definitions formulated by standard-setting lead bodies). They may also be developed within organisations, linked to their specific strategic objectives, cultural values and task requirements.

The advantage of competence-based profiles include the following.

(a) They can be linked directly to the strategic objectives of an organisation.

(b) They reflect best practice in the relevant occupation or profession (if defined by standard-setting bodies).

(c) They are flexible in the face of changing conditions and requirements, as they are menu-driven and non-prescriptive about job/organisational specifics.

(d) They can be applied at all levels of the organisation (although the behaviours expected will obviously vary), which helps to foster core values and consistent practice in the organisation.

(e) They directly relate candidates' attainments and attributes to the demands of the job, and should therefore be both accurate (in predicting job performance) and non-discriminatory.

To be able to fit the wide diversity of many organisations, most competency frameworks simply produce the same sets of words and phrases, and so lose their purpose and any meaningful application in the recruitment process.

Advantages of competency-based recruitment

1 The process of developing and defining competences helps an organisation understand what is needed from its human resources and clarifies the how recruitment and selection will contribute to embedding these.

2 The use of competences during recruitment and selection leads to a more informed and rigorous process.

3 Where competences are used for more than recruitment and selection, the visible set of agreed standards across an organisation leads to fairer, more effective and valid processes.

ACTIVITY 2 — 15 mins

Think of an example of competences that are (a) likely to have been demonstrated in candidates' academic or working life; (b) likely to predict successful job performance; and (c) readily assessable in an interview or other selection test.

5 Recruitment methods and media

5.1 External recruitment

A number of methods are available to organisations to contact (and attract) potential candidates. These can be summarised as follows.

Method	Evaluation
Unsolicited requests: Write-ins or walk-ins (Media: word-of mouth, recommendation, previous recruitment advertising, general employer branding)	*Advantages:* Inexpensive Pre-selected for enthusiasm, initiative Open walk-in policy may encourage application where job difficult to fill *Disadvantage:* Needs control and systematic application handling
Existing contacts: Previous (re-employable) employees; retirees; career break; previous applicants of suitable general quality held on file	*Advantages:* Work behaviour/attributes known; may be amenable to part-time, temporary or flexible working *Disadvantage:* Needs systematic database management
Referrals: Registers of members seeking employment, kept e.g. by trade unions and professional bodies	*Advantages:* Pre-selection at low cost *Disadvantage:* Indirectly discriminative
JobCentre Plus: Network of agencies provided by central government: particularly for manual and junior positions in admin/clerical/retail	*Advantages:* Free Local and national Socially responsible (not-for-profit) *Disadvantage:* Register limited to unemployed Require relationship/selection management
Resettlement services: Finding civilian positions for armed forces personnel at end of service	*Advantages:* Can be highly trained/experienced *Disadvantage:* Inexperience in civilian culture?
Careers services: Placing graduates of schools and training institutions	*Advantages:* Potential for young unsocialised recruits Potential for preview through work placements Financial incentives (government schemes such as YT, Apex) Potential for strong relationship – selection preference, curriculum influence *Disadvantage:* Recruits may lack experience Administration of work-experience Possible indirect discrimination
Employment agencies: Wide range of specialising agencies; temporary agencies for one-off requirements and short-term cover	*Advantages:* May undertake pre-screening *Disadvantage:* Temp agencies facilitate flexible working Quality can vary Cost

Method	Evaluation
Selection consultants: Recruit and select for positions; may cover clerical/admin staff, specialist staff (media, financial etc), or managerial	*Advantages:* Reduces administration for employer Specialist selection skills Wide-ranging contacts *Disadvantage:* Cost May lack awareness of organisation's culture, values, detailed criteria Excludes internal applicants Lack of accountability
Outplacement consultants: Registers, retraining etc to help redundant and early-retired employees	*Advantages:* Perceived socially responsible Provide some training *Disadvantage:* Quality varies
Search consultants: 'Head hunters'. Networking to track highly employable individuals: candidates proactively approached	*Advantages:* Selects for high employability net-working, exploration opportunity Cost *Disadvantage:* Limited range Organisation may be victim as well as beneficiary!
Direct to source: Schools, colleges, universities (Media: advertisement, 'milk-round' presentation)	*Advantages* Networking relationships Opportunities to preview via work placement, 'gap' year etc Access to graduates in desirable (scarce) disciplines Local catchment area *Disadvantage:* Tends to be annual 'season' Recruits lack experience Potential for indirect discrimination
Alumni Former employees of the organisation with whom an ongoing communications is maintained	*Advantage* Low cost Known to the organisation Already has the required perquisite skills Even if not employed could become a future client or customer *Disadvantages:* Organisation may have no wish to reemploy individual Effort to manage the scheme Skills become out of date, as does knowledge of the organisation

Method	Evaluation
Recruitment advertising: Hard copy media such as newspapers, trade magazines and professional publications	*Advantages:* Trade and professional journals direct target suitable candidates Newspapers receive distribution to a wide range of potential applicants Allow scope for branding and conveying employer branding information and images Ensures compliance with Equal Opportunities requirements due to wide readership *Disadvantages;* Often highly expensive May attract high volumes of applications from unsuitable applicants
The Internet: Wide range of recruitment databases, plus web advertising/ application	*Advantages:* IT-literate users Pre-selection by database, low cost World-wide catchment *Disadvantages:* Difficulty of verification Competition

USE OF RECOMMENDATIONS

A survey reported in People Management (31 May 2007) showed that only 18% of employers use recommendations from employees as a recruiting tool – and thereby 'throw away millions of pounds on recruitment advertising'.

A company hiring 250 people a year could save £80,000 if 10% of hires came from referrals by employees of people they know – even if a £250 reward was offered for a successful referral!

ACTIVITY 3 20 mins

We have already mentioned some of the 'media' by which an organisation can advertise or make known its staffing needs by the methods listed above. Brainstorm as full a list as you can of advertising/information media relevant to recruitment. For each of the media you mention, add any advantages or disadvantages you can think of.

CIPD most effective methods for attracting applications (2011)

	All 2010	All 2011
Own corporate website	63	59
Recruitment agencies	60	54
Local newspaper advertisements	36	32
Employee referral scheme	35	29
Commercial job boards	33	27
Specialist journals/trade press	31	27
Encourage speculative applications/word of mouth	24	25

	All 2010	All 2011
Jobcentre Plus	23	25
Professional networking (such as LinkedIn)	14	16
Search consultants	22	15
Links with schools/colleges/universities	18	13
Apprenticeships	12	11
National newspaper advertisements	16	11
Secondments	11	11
Links with other local organisations making redundancies	N/A	7
Alumni (previous employees)	5	5
Social networking sites (such as Facebook)	3	4
Local Employment Partnership (LEP)	6	3
Other	5	5

Conduct a short poll amongst your friends or fellow students as to sources used to seek jobs? Are organisations using the right means to communicate jobs to people like your friends and fellow students (see CIPD table above)? If there is a disparity, why might that be happening?

Virgin Group.

Check out the 'Jobs' section of this (and other corporate sites) for examples of e-recruitment. The Virgin site has helpful information on the recruitment process, equality and diversity policies and so on.

www.virgin.com

5.2 E-recruitment

E- (or Internet or online) recruiting has exploded in recent years, having been used mainly for IT jobs in the early stages of Internet adoption. E-recruitment can be subdivided into organisations' own corporate websites and commercial job boards.

The Internet is a useful tool in a number of ways.

(a) To post or advertise vacancies, either on the employer's own website (or intranet, for internal advertising) or on specialist online recruitment sites.

(b) To provide information about the employer, recruitment policies and jobs (often available on the employer's own website, as well as recruiter databases).

(c) To allow database searches, matching employers' requirements and job seekers' CVs.

(d) To facilitate communication (via e-mail) between enquirers/applicants and employers.

(e) To complete recruitment applications electronically (online application forms, computerised screening of essential matching criteria, online psychometric tests and so on).

As we have seen in the previous section, organisations using their own website to recruit is now predominant; however the use of commercial job boards by organisations has seen a lower take up. The main users of job boards would appear to be recruitment agencies who wish to communicate to the largest possible audience. Research also indicates that recruiting organisations will often supplement their online campaign with other techniques such as recruitment agencies or printed advertising.

Advantages of e-recruitment include:

(a) Its cost-effectiveness, compared to traditional forms of advertising

(b) Its ability to reach a wide and geographically dispersed (even global) audience of potential candidates

(c) The advert may be seen by suitable candidates who may not have considered or even been aware of the recruiting organisation

(d) Its ability to offer more information (for self-selection) about the organisation and the job, potentially in a more attractive (interactive, multi-media) format

(e) Its demonstration of basic computer literacy (where desired) by applicants

(f) Electronic support for application, CV matching, short-listing and so on – more swiftly and cost-effectively than by human agency

(g) The provision of application information for use in Human Resource Information Systems, e.g. to analyse applications received, monitor equal opportunities and so on

(h) The ability to monitor traffic (hits on the site, pages views etc) to derive information on the effectiveness of the site, levels of interest and so on.

Whilst the use of e-recruitment has many advantages, research indicates that these factors are not the only ones driving the adoption, other causes are:

- Industry culture, if both the organisation and workers tend to be online then there will be a greater likelihood of using e-recruitment
- If it is perceived that the industry and type of employees sought are orientated to online working
- Where employers are inundated with unsuitable applicants, the use of online filters will reduce the burden
- HR managers believe that to be seen as current and progressive practitioners they are expected to use e-recruitment, even though they maybe sceptical as to the measurable benefits.

Disadvantages of e-recruitment

(a) Many applications are unsuitable (especially if the organisation only wants to recruit locally or nationally).

(b) Technical problems with the site risks losing suitable candidates.

(c) Insufficient information about the job or the company encourages speculative applications or fails to fully inform and engage potentially suitable applicants.

(d) Screening and short-listing software relies heavily on matching keywords, and can disqualify suitable candidates on this basis.

(e) The impersonal nature of the process does not start the development of the psychological contract on a positive note.

(f) May still screen out otherwise suitable applicants for whom it is not the preferred job-seeking tool.

(g)) Poor quality sites are interpreted by some applicants as representing poor quality organisations and so are deterred from applying.

RECRUITMENT PROCESSES AT SUPERDRUG

Superdrug has streamlined its recruitment process, increased its capacity quickly and efficiently to process large numbers of applications – and reduced its cost per hire by 87 percent

Health and beauty retailer Superdrug has over 700 stores in the UK, employs 12,500 people and serves over 4.5 million customers each week. The company is continually searching for top talent for positions that range from store managers to pharmacists to head-office roles.

In late 2004, it launched its career website and ran several job-board campaigns to help to fill vacancies across the UK. In response, it received an average of around 2,000 CVs a month. However, applications were sent to a central email address and administered using spreadsheets and email. Processing such a large number of CVs became a hugely time-consuming task, particularly for the field recruiters.

The decision was made to automate recruitment by moving the entire process online.

Potential job applicants go to the Superdrug website to view the openings available and to apply for specific vacancies. Candidates are provided with a user profile and can update their profiles, search for jobs and create email alerts for positions matching their criteria. They can also monitor the progress of their application online.

The system makes the first match between the job requirements and the competences and experience of the candidate. It then retains a pool of applicants on file, which ensures Superdrug has a readily available supply of CVs for open positions. Each registered applicant is automatically asked to update his or her CV in order to remain active on the system.

Internal applicants are encouraged to visit the website to view the list of vacancies. Around 85 percent of retail vacancies – store specialists, assistant store managers and store managers – are from internal applicants.

Superdrug will soon use the e-recruitment system to ensure that all vacancies on the website are also automatically posted to the company's intranet. This will enable employees to see a complete list of vacancies and apply directly, which will help to encourage internal mobility further.

Superdrug has recently begun to sell 3 phones in its stores and successfully sourced telephone specialists through the e-recruitment system. These specialists needed to be fun, friendly and passionate people to work in-store, selling the 3 phones to a predominantly female market. Superdrug also used job-boards – such as Handbag.com – aimed at the target candidates, and placed a national advertisement on Totaljobs. Candidates using the job-boards could apply online via Superdrug's careers website. The result was a high number of capable applicants.

Fast, effective recruitment and great cost savings

Superdrug has reduced its cost per hire by 87 percent, and the company now recruits 54 percent of all its store and head-office management and pharmacist vacancies through its website. Superdrug also uses recruitment agencies to find candidates and has provided its suppliers with a unique log-on to the website. This ensures that the agencies are notified of new vacancies, and that candidates who are put forward can be tracked through the process and can be given specific feedback.

Superdrug hopes to use mobile phones as part of application process. This will mean that candidates can text a mobile phone number advertised on in-store posters as the first stage of their application. They will then complete a mini application form on their phone, which will automatically be sent back to be processed.

As well as providing a greater choice of application methods, the text service will be immediate and therefore in keeping with the Superdrug values of being bold and fast in recruitment. Candidates will be able to continue to keep in contact with the website by text, if they choose. However, as the process will be fully integrated with the Superdrug e-recruitment solution, the applicant will still be able to choose to update his or her details using the website.

ACTIVITY 4

1 hour

Use the Internet to appraise the e-recruitment strategies of two or more firms, using the checklist suggested by the benchmarking study cited above.

(a) Start with your own organisation or place of study.

(b) Browse the sites of Amec, or any other top companies you are interested in.

(c) Browse the 'jobs' or 'careers' channels of your preferred Internet search engine (Yahoo! or Google, say), or the specialist careers/jobs agencies/sites advertised.

5.3 The recruitment advertisement

The object of recruitment advertising is to home in on the target market of labour, and to attract interest in the organisation and the job.

In a way, it is already part of the **selection** process. The advertisement will be placed where suitable people are likely to see it (say, internally only – immediately pre-selecting members of the organisation – or in a specialist journal, pre-selecting those specialists). It should be worded in a way that further weeds out people who would not be suitable for the job (or for whom the job would not be suitable).

The way in which a job is advertised will depend on the type of organisation and the type of job.

A factory is likely to advertise a vacancy for an unskilled worker in a different way to a company advertising for a CIPD-qualified person for a senior HR position. Managerial jobs may merit national advertisement, whereas semi- or un-skilled jobs may only warrant local coverage, depending on the supply of suitable candidates in the local area. Specific skills may be most appropriately reached through trade, technical or professional journals.

The advertisement, based on information set out in the job description, (or variants) and recruitment policy, should contain the following information.

(a) The organisation: its main business and location (at least)

(b) The job: title, main duties and responsibilities and special features

(c) Conditions: special factors affecting the job

(d) Qualifications and experience (required, and preferred); other attributes, aptitudes and/or knowledge required

(e) Rewards: salary and benefits (negotiable, if appropriate), opportunities for training and career development, and so on

(f) Application: how to apply, to whom, and by what date.

The advertisement should encourage a degree of **self-selection**, so that the target population begins to narrow itself down. (The information contained in the advertisement should deter unsuitable applicants as well as encourage potentially suitable ones.) It should also reflect the desired image of the organisation in the outside world: its employer brand.

The aim of the recruitment process is applications by suitably qualified candidates. What form might an application take, in order for it to be fed into the selection process?

5.4 Applications

Applications for a particular advertised (or unadvertised) vacancy, or for employment in the organisation as and when vacancies arise, may be received in various forms.

(a) **Unsolicited letter, e-mail, 'walk-in' or other enquiry**. This would normally be responded to with a request for the following.

(b) **Application form**

(i) For lower-level, relatively standardised jobs, for which a high volume of applicants is expected, this may be a brief, directly targeted form (focusing on qualifications and experience considered essential to the job) in order to facilitate ruthless weeding out of unsuitable applicants, and requiring minimal discretion, self-expression and time in both completion and interpretation.

(ii) For managerial, specialist or culturally-driven jobs, a more complex application form or package may be used, in order to elicit more complex responses: biographical/psychological ('biodata') questionnaires, guided self-expression, samples for hand-writing analysis, preliminary testing (description of previous work-related problem solving, or response to case-study scenarios, say) and so on. Such in-depth tools for pre-selection save time and effort at the interview stage, but are time-consuming to prepare and analyse, and should be subjected to cost-benefit considerations.

(c) **Curriculum vitae (CV)** or **résumé**, usually accompanied by a **covering letter** drawing the recruiter's attention to specific aspects of the applicant's CV which are relevant to the vacancy or organisation. The CV is essentially a brief, systematic summary of the applicant's qualifications, previous work experience and relevant skills/interests/requirements, plus details of individuals willing to vouch for his or her performance, character and employability **(referees)**.

The application form or CV will be used to find out relevant information about the applicant, in order to decide, at the initial sifting stage:

(a) Whether the applicant is obviously unsuitable for the job, or
(b) Whether the applicant might be of the right calibre, and worth inviting to interview.

The application form will be designed by the organisation (or recruitment agency) fulfil the following criteria.

(a) It should elicit information about the applicant which can be directly compared with the requirements of the job.

(b) For managerial, interpersonal and culturally-driven jobs – requiring particular values, orientations and attributes – it should give applicants the opportunity to describe (briefly) their career ambitions, why they want the job, perceived strengths and weaknesses and so on.

(c) It should convey a professional, accurate and favourable impression of the organisation, a public relations and employer branding tool.

(d) It should elicit any information required to enable the organisation subsequently to monitor and evaluate the success of its recruitment procedures (in regard to numbers of female, minority and disabled applicants, number of applications per source and so on).

ACTIVITY 5 — 20 mins

Suggest four ways in which an application form could be badly designed (both in appearance and content). You may be able to do this from personal experience.

5.5 Internal recruitment

Internal advertising of vacancies may be a requirement for some organisations, under agreements negotiated with trade unions. Advertising media include noticeboards (paper and electronic – for example via corporate intranet), in-house journals, memoranda to supervisors/managers soliciting recommendations and observation and word-of-mouth (the **grapevine**).

Methods of **internal recruitment** include:

(a) Advertising for self-applicants
(b) Soliciting recommendations from supervisors/managers and training officers
(c) Soliciting referrals by existing employees to family, friends and contacts
(d) Formal succession, promotion and transfer planning.

Most of these methods incur little extra cost, being based on existing or easily accessible information about the candidate's abilities, attitudes and so on.

6 Evaluating recruitment

An evaluation of recruitment (and selection) procedures will aim to determine whether the procedures succeeded in getting a *suitable* person into a job, at the *time* when the person was required and at an acceptable *cost*. At a more strategic level, it determines whether recruitment is succeeding in achieving the organisation's overall HR plan.

Connock (1991) suggests that the recruitment process can be audited at four levels.

(a) **Performance indicators** should be established and measured at each stage of the process including:

- Total numbers of applications received
- Time taken to locate applicants
- Cost per applicant
- Time taken to process applications/per application
- Number of female/minority/disabled/mature-age applicants
- Number of qualified applicants (matching advertised criteria)
- Number of qualified female/minority/disabled/mature-age applicants.

These metrics basically assess the effectiveness and cost-efficiency of recruitment advertising, equal opportunities policy and recruitment administration. Post-entry criteria – such as number of offers extended per source/method or in relation to applications received, cost and time of training recruits, subsequent job performance and length of service of recruits and so on – may only be applied after the selection process, but still reflect on recruitment.

(b) **Cost-effectiveness** of the various methods used should be measured. It may be that a certain advertising medium is too costly for the number of worthwhile responses it generates, for example.

ACTIVITY 6 — 20 mins

What kind of information would you need to record in order to appraise the cost-effectiveness of a recruitment method/medium? Aim to end up with a meaningful figure for the cost per person appointed (and actually entering employment).

(c) **Monitoring the make up of the workforce** and the impact of new recruits is essential as part of an equal opportunities policy to identify areas where certain groups are under-represented.

(d) An **attitude survey** may be conducted amongst recruits to measure satisfaction and gather feedback: did the job advertisement give a fair idea of the job, were they frustrated by the length of time they had to wait for a decision and so on?

Other methods of evaluating recruitment and selection include **'benchmarking':** comparing the organisation's systems with known example of good practice used in other organisations. Where the HR department has adopted the concept of the **'internal customer'**, it can also gather feedback from internal customers (line managers) and users (job applicants and recruits).

Chapter Roundup

- Recruitment is concerned with defining job requirements and attracting suitable applicants. Selection is concerned with fitting the person to the job.
- A systematic recruitment procedure can be summarised in diagrammatic form shown overleaf.
- Job analysis determines the essential characteristics of a job, this information is then used to inform the job description. The job analysis can be conducted by a variety of methods including observation, interview and diaries.
- A job description is the statement of the duties, responsibilities and reporting lines of a position within an organisation. It is often the primary source of data used when recruiting. However due to the limits of descriptions alternative methods of conveying broader expectations of the job holder can be used e.g. accountability statements.
- A person specification describes the ideal candidate who would match the job description.
- Competence profiles provide an alternative or complementary source of data by which to select, which some argue is superior as it links the requirements of the role with the objectives of the organisation.
- Numerous methods and media are available to the recruiter, each needs to be evaluated to determine whether it is effective for the purpose required. E-recruitment demands individual attention mostly due to its ever-increasing popularity and usage. The cost benefit is the primary attraction although it is not without its problems such as the number of unsuitable applicants that apply and the rudimentary screening methods of some screening software.
- There are a number of recognised methods for evaluating the effectiveness of recruitment. These need to be applied to ensure that the recruiter is providing best value for money to their organisation and is achieving the strategic objectives.

Cont...

Chapter Roundup cont

The Recruitment Process

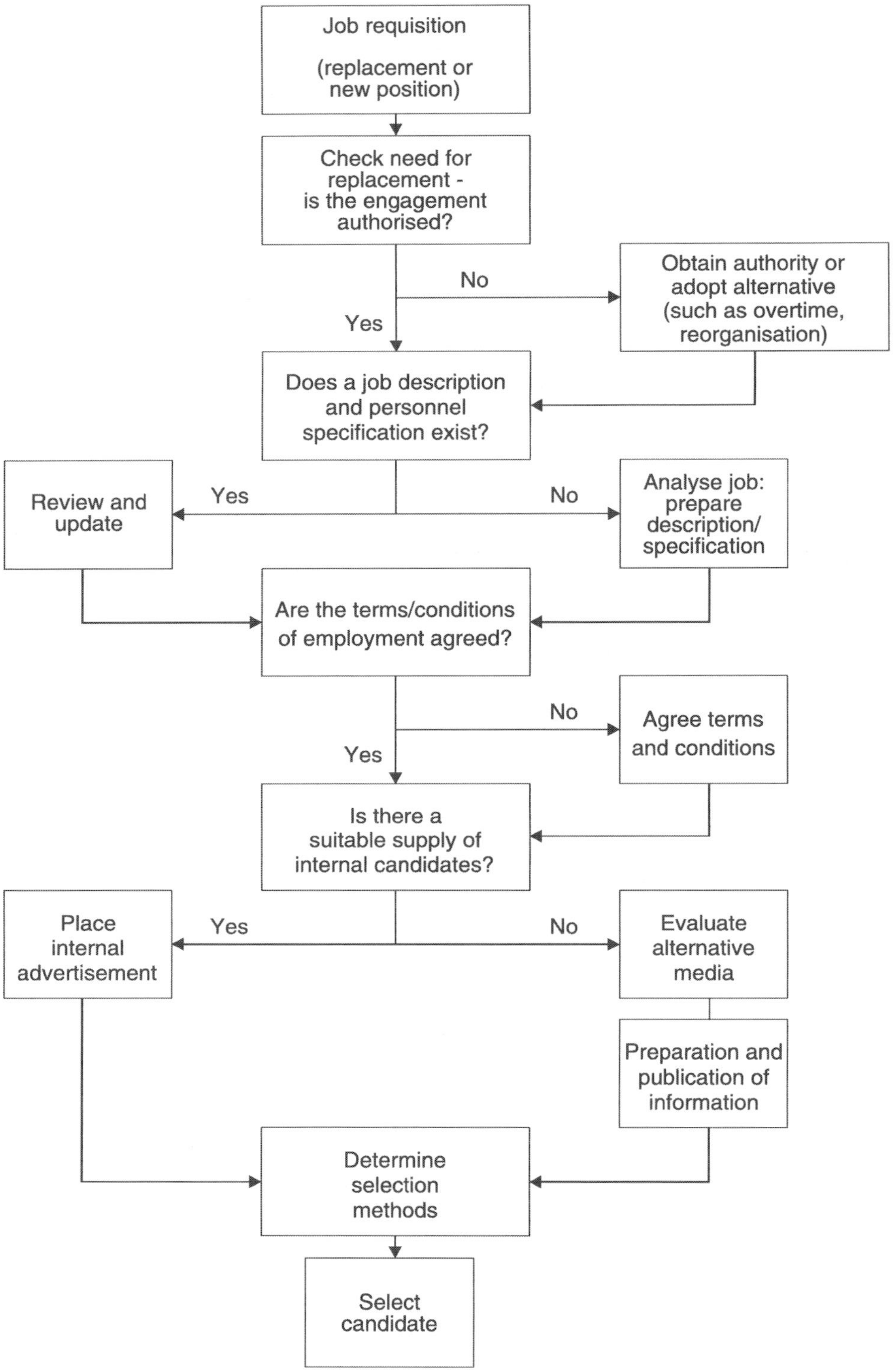

Quick Quiz

1 Which of the following does **not** influence recruitment policy

(a) The organisation's People Plan

(b) Legislation and regulations

(c) Relationships with recruitment agencies

(d) Cultural values

2 List three methods by which job analysis may be carried out.

3 What is a job description?

4 Identify two alternatives to job descriptions

5 Which of the following is **not** a type of competency identified by Roberts?

(a) Acquired
(b) Adapting
(c) Attaining

6 List five methods of recruitment of candidates from the external job market.

7 Identify three drawbacks of e-recruitment

8 List four methods of receiving applications.

9 What does CV stand for?

10 List three methods by which recruitment procedures may be evaluated.

Answers to Quick Quiz

1 C. Relationships with recruitment agencies (para 1.3)

2 Observation, questionnaire/interview, diaries/self-recording (para 2.3)

3 A broad description of the purpose, scope, duties and responsibilities of a particular job. (para 3)

4 Goal, competence or accountability statements or role definitions (para 3.4)

5 Attaining (para 4.3)

6 You could have included: agencies, consultancies, Internet, direct to source, careers services, existing contacts, alumni (para 5.1)

7 Unsuitable applications; Shortlisting software; Impersonal nature of the process; Poor quality sites (para 5.2)

8 CV; application form; unsolicited enquiry; web application. (para 5.4)

9 Curriculum vitae (para 5.4)

10 By determining key performance indicators and monitoring performance against them; by measuring cost-effectiveness; by monitoring the make-up of the workforce; by conducting attitude surveys. (section 6)

Answers to Activities

Activity 1

1 The job analyst will need to gain their confidence by:

(a) Communicating: explaining the process, methods and purpose of the appraisal

(b) Being thorough and competent in carrying out the analysis

(c) Respecting the work flow of the department, which should not be disrupted

(d) Giving feedback on the results of the appraisal, and the achievement of its objectives. If staff are asked to co-operate in developing a framework for office training, and then never hear anything more about it, they are unlikely to be responsive on a later occasion.

Activity 2

- Likely to be demonstrated: eg leadership, initiative, ability to work with others, ability to work under (or without) supervision
- Likely to predict job performance: eg motivation to achieve, specific technical skills related to the job (numeracy, computer use)
- Assessable: eg team building (asking candidates to describe when they have successfully built a team), problem analysis (asking candidates to analyse and suggest solutions to a case study scenario), conflict resolution (asking a candidate to role play a mediator in an industrial conflict scenario)

Activity 3

Some of the media you may have come up with include the following.

Newspapers and journals (trade, professional) – ie 'Press' media	• Journals better targeted, papers offer wider local or national coverage • Wider and more targeted coverage – higher cost: cost-effectiveness must be monitored, controlled • May offer opportunity to produce own artwork – may not (control required)
Cinema, radio, TV – ie 'broadcast' media	• Can offer general marketing opportunity • Powerful all-senses effect • Expensive (especially TV) • Mass coverage (option of local) • Appeal to young audience
LinkedIn, Facebook, Twitter	• May only reach IT savvy audience • Will only reach signed up application users, who may not be target audience • Low cost

Exhibitions, conferences, roadshows, open-days, presentations	• If well targeted location, can reach large number of relevant people • Opportunities for non-committal networking, exploration • Immediacy of face-to-face communication – but also a risk • Can be expensive to organise/delegate
Websites	• Untargeted (except to IT-literate) • Controllable • Relatively low-cost • Opportunity for general marketing

Activity 4

This is a research exercise. You may like to print out some of your findings for your portfolio or assignment bibliography.

Activity 5

(a) Answer spaces too small to contain the information asked for

(b) Forms which are (or look) so lengthy or complicated that prospective applicants either complete them perfunctorily or give up (and apply to another employer instead)

(c) Illegal (eg discriminatory) or offensive questions

(d) Lack of clarity as to what (and how much) information is required

Activity 6

A framework such as that shown below may be used to determine the cost per person appointed for each method.

Source of application	Number of applications	Number of shortlisted candidates	Number offered job	Number commenced employment	Total cost	Cost per head appointed
Local press advert						
National press advert						
Specialist press advert						
Internet job board						
Total						

Chapter 7

Selection

Selection is the part of the employee resourcing process which leads naturally on from recruitment. Selection involves identifying the most suitable of the candidates attracted by recruitment efforts. (In practice, this may be a negative process of weeding out people who are unsuitable for the job or organisation – or people for whom the job or organisation may be unsuitable.)

The selection of the right candidate(s) is of vital importance. No organisation would like to find a 'star' employee for a competing organisation on its rejection list, any more than it wants an employee who can't do the job and doesn't 'fit in' – however perfect they may have seemed in the interview! Various selection methods are used to try to reduce the risks of either event by gathering as much relevant information about the candidate as possible. In this chapter we look at how this can be done.

1 The selection process

1.1 The aims and objectives of selection

The overall aim of the selection process is to identify candidates who are suitable for the vacancy or wider requirements of the People Plan (e.g. in regard to workforce diversity).

Within this aim, there may be a number of subsidiary goals.

(a) To predict, as accurately as possible, the future or potential job performance of candidates.

(b) To compare, as validly as possible, one candidate with another, to find 'best fit' between applicants and the organisation's needs.

(c) To inform candidates, as accurately and attractively as possible, about the organisation, the job, the psychological contract of employment and likely future prospects, in order to:

  (i) Facilitate self-selection by the candidates

  (ii) Facilitate subsequent adjustment by the successful candidate, minimising disappointment and induction crisis and supporting retention.

(d) To give the best possible impression of the organisation as a potential employer: creating a brand as 'employer of choice' in an industry or sector, or in competition with other potential employers.

(e) To comply with legislation, policy and organisational values in regard to equal opportunity, fair treatment and professionalism in dealing with candidates.

(f) To provide information for other HR processes, such as employee induction and development, or the evaluation of the selection process itself.

1.2 A systematic approach to selection

A typical selection system will include the following basic procedures.

(a) Take any **initial steps** required. If the decision to interview or reject cannot be made immediately, a standard email/letter of acknowledgement might be sent, as a courtesy, to each applicant. It may be that the job advertisement required applicants to write to HR with personal details and to request an application form: this would then be sent to applicants for completion and return. It is almost standard practice that this is all completed via email today, although for anti-discrimination reasons an organisation needs to have the capability to send out such information in hard copy for those who are unable to access or use the internet.

(b) Set each application against **key criteria** in the job advertisement and specification. Critical factors may include qualifications, experience or competences.

(c) **Sort applications** into 'possible', 'unsuitable' and 'marginal'.

(d) 'Possibles' will then be more closely scrutinised, and a **shortlist for interview** drawn up. Ideally, this should be done by both the HR specialist and the prospective manager of the successful candidate, who will have more immediate knowledge of the type of person that will fit into the culture and activities of the department.

(e) Invite candidates for **interviews** (requiring them to complete an application form, if this has not been done at an earlier stage).

(f) Interview potentially qualified candidates.

(g) Reinforce interviews with **selection testing** and other mechanisms where required.

(h) Check the **references** of short-listed candidates.

(i) Institute **follow-up procedures** for successful applicants.

(j) Review un-interviewed 'possibles', and 'marginals', and put potential future candidates on **hold** or in reserve.

(k) Send standard correspondence to **unsuccessful applicants**, informing them that they have not been successful. Best practice now also includes the offering of feedback to unsuccessful applicants, on request, as to why their application was unsuccessful.

(l) Keep **records** of criteria and processes used in decision making, both for evaluation – and to provide evidence of fair dealing if required to counter a claim of discrimination.

RISKS ASSOCIATED WITH TESTING EMPLOYEES

A US retailer testing some 2,500 applicants for security jobs required applicants to answer intimate personal questions in a pre-employment psychological examination, but was later forced to pay more than $2 million to settle a lawsuit over the test, which included 'true or false?' questions such as:

- I have never indulged in any unusual sexual practices
- I am very strongly attracted by members of my own sex
- I believe my sins are unpardonable
- I feel sure there is only one true religion

The employer argued in court that the test was necessary to screen out applicants who are emotionally unstable, unreliable, and resistant to established rules, as well as applicants with addictive or violent tendencies who might put customers or other employees at risk...

(From Bulletin to Management, 1993, cited by Shuler, 1995)

Aside from the actual outcome of the case example cited above, how far do you think a test of this kind is:

(a) Useful or effective (and with what intention)?
(b) Ethically reprehensible (and on what grounds)?

To the extent that the employer's concerns are genuine, what other means of screening might or should they employ?

1.3 Selection methods

Various techniques are available, depending on the policy and criteria of selection in each case.

(a) **Interviews**. These may be variously structured (one-to-one, panel, sequential), and using various criteria of job relevance (application details, skills and competences, critical incident/situational questions) and scoring methods (general impressions, criteria ratings). As the most popular of methods, interviews will be considered in detail below.

(b) **Evaluation of education and experience**, comparing application data to job requirements.

(c) **Selection testing**. Written tests of ability and aptitude (cognitive and/or mechanical), personality and so on are increasingly used, alongside work sample tests which simulate job-related activities (such as typing or copywriting tests) and examination of portfolios of work (eg for architects or photographers). Tests are also discussed in more detail below.

(d) **Background and reference checks**, in order to verify application claims as to qualifications, previous employment record and reasons for leaving and so on. References will be discussed in Section 5 of this chapter.

(e) **Biodata analysis**. Biodata (biographical data) is gathered via multiple-choice questions on family background, life experiences, attitudes and preferences. The results are compared against an 'ideal' profile based on correlations with effective job performance.

(f) **Handwriting analysis,** or graphology. Handwriting is said to indicate up to 300 character traits of the individual. There is no scientific evidence of its predictive accuracy, but it is popular in Europe and to a lesser extent in the USA and Australia. (In general, handwritten covering letters are requested as a useful general indicator of orderly thinking, presentation and so on.)

(g) **Group selection methods**, or **assessment centres**, allowing the assessment of team-working, leadership, problem-solving and communication skills through the use of group discussions, role plays, business games and 'in-tray' simulations. These are discussed below.

ACTIVITY 1 — 20 mins

How accurate do you think the above-listed methods are at predicting job performance and suitability?

A number of research studies have attempted to measure how popular and how effective various techniques are.

- **Effectiveness** is measured according to the **'predictive validity'** scale, which ranges from 1 (the technique unfailingly predicts candidates' subsequent job performance) to 0 (the technique is no better than random chance at predicting candidates' subsequent job performance).
- **Popularity** is measured by the % of surveyed companies that use the technique.

(a) Rank the following techniques in order from most popular to least popular, from what you might anticipate.

(b) For each, add a number between 0.00 and 1.00 to indicate what you think their predictive validity might be.

Techniques: Personality tests, references, work sampling, interviews, assessment centres, cognitive tests, graphology, biodata.

SELECTION PRACTICES IN SRI LANKA

A research study of staffing practices in the Sri Lankan private sector for junior level managerial jobs found a number of practices.

The process begins with candidates responding to adverts in newspapers by sending detailed bio-data/CVs together with names of two unrelated referees. When organisations receive high volumes of applications per vacancy, pre-selection devices becomes a necessity and the typical response is to send a company-specific standard official application form to short-listed candidates.

When identifying criteria by which to invite applicants for interview, priority was given to educational qualifications followed by work experience, professional qualifications and personality.

Selection interview (88%) rated as the most frequently used method. Written examination (30%) is the second most used method, followed by psychometric test and assessment centre.

When used, written examinations are designed to ascertain applicants' intelligence, logical thinking, proficiency in languages and general business awareness. Applicants who are successful in the written examination are called for interview. The majority of companies conduct a series of interviews. At each interview stage potential candidates are shortlisted for the next interview stage. The first two interview stages are conducted by line managers with the assistance of HR managers. In certain instances first interviews are conducted by only the line manager. The third and/or final interview is conducted by a board comprising three or four senior line managers and the HR manager. Companies use some method of scoring during the interviews when more than one person assesses a candidate. After the preliminary interview, but before the final interview, references are obtained from previous employers/referees of the shortlisted candidates. HR managers identified conducting reference checks and medical examinations as a norm during the selection process. In some companies, only one interview session is held with the involvement of panel of staff members.

Vathsala Wickramasinghe. Staffing practices in the private sector in Sri Lanka (2007)

We will now look at each of the three major techniques in turn.

2 Selection interviews

2.1 Types of interview

Individual or **one-to-one interviews** are the most common selection method. They offer the advantages of direct face-to-face communication, and opportunity to establish **rapport** between the candidate and interviewer: each has to give their attention solely to the other, and there is potentially a relaxed atmosphere, if the interviewer is willing to establish an informal style.

The disadvantage of a one-to-one interview is the scope it allows for a biased or superficial decision.

(a) The candidate may be able to disguise lack of knowledge in a specialist area of which the interviewer knows little.

(b) The interviewer's perception may be selective or distorted and this lack of objectivity may go unnoticed and unchecked.

(c) The greater opportunity for personal rapport with the candidate may cause a weakening of the interviewer's objective judgement.

Panel interviews are designed to overcome the above disadvantages. A panel may consist of two or three people who together interview a single candidate: most commonly, an HR specialist and the candidate's future boss. This may be more daunting for the candidate (depending on the tone and conduct of the interview) but it has several advantages.

(a) The HR and line specialists can gather the information they each need about the candidate and give him or her the various information(s)he requires from each of them at one sitting.

(b) The interviewers make a joint assessment of the candidate's abilities and behaviour at the interview. Personal bias is more likely to be guarded against, and checked if it does emerge.

However, panel interviews come with disadvantages of their own.

(a) The possibility that the members of the panel may all be biased in the same direction – very likely if they are all from the same organisation – so the impartiality of the selection process is undermined still further.

(b) The possibility of domination of the panel by one or more members, so that the resultant 'panel' decision is actually a reflection of the views of possibly the most senior panel member. This could be especially relevant for candidates who are being rejected for reasons which are unreliable.

(c) The inability of the panel to follow potentially profitable lines of questioning, because of a need to adhere to previously-agreed division of roles among the panel members.

(d) The potentially intimidating nature of the panel interview environment, where one candidate is confronted by three, four or even more panel members.

Large formal panels, or **selection boards,** may also be convened where there are a number of individuals or groups with an interest in the selection. This has the advantage of allowing a number of people to see the candidates, and to share information about them at a single meeting: similarly, they can compare their assessments on the spot, without a subsequent effort at liaison and communication.

Offsetting these administrative advantages, however, there are some drawbacks to selection boards.

(a) There is no evidence that panel interviews are more successful at selecting the right candidate than one-to-one interviews.

(b) Questions tend to be more varied, and more random. Candidates may have trouble switching from one topic to another so quickly, and may not be allowed time to expand their answers in such as way as to do justice to themselves.

(c) Some candidates may not perform well in a formal, artificial situation such as a board interview, and may find such a situation extremely stressful. The interview will thus not show the best qualities of someone who might nevertheless be highly effective in the work context.

(d) Board interviews favour individuals who are confident, and who project an immediate and strong image: those who are articulate, dress well and so on. First impressions of such a candidate may cover underlying faults or shortcomings.

(e) Whilst one of the benefits of panel interviews often cited is that they cancel out the bias of the other members, it is equally plausible that they all share the same bias, and the so the effect is multiplied rather than cancelled out.

(f) Panels can be dominated by an individual member that can have undue influence over the other members.

The most effective approach to cancelling out the disadvantages of panel interview, albeit a time consuming and administratively burdensome one, is to run a series of one-to-one interviews, with would be panel members. Each interviewer has a separate brief and after the interviews the interviewers compare notes and identify the best candidate.

FORMS OF EMPLOYMENT INTERVIEW

Research was conducted across Europe to understand the selection tools used. The research was conducted amongst large recruitment agencies and large employers. While one of the conclusions is that the tools appear astonishingly similar, there are interesting observations regarding interview styles:

- In the UK, the style of employment interview is rather directive. This is the case in large companies like Grand Met and ICI where the interviews are very structured and very focused. The tendency towards directive interviews is strengthening as traditional companies use a semi-structures style, while the modern companies and banks are turning towards structured interviews accompanied by tests. Research has recently demonstrated the greater reliability of structured interviews in which the questions are related to duties.

- In Ireland the employment interview has the appearance of an informal conversation, but among professional recruiters it is very structured in its objectives. All recruiters who follow the contributions of the research in this field have a tendency to orient themselves towards structured or semi-structured employment interviews. The other recruiters who generally have a non-structured approach in interviews. Structured interviews are very friendly in their form, but the recruiter expects answers to questions and precise information on which to base decisions. It is mainly the big companies which practise this form of interview.

- In Austria, the employment interview uses a style which goes from the semi-structured to the structured. The questions are very structured and all the points which the recruiter tries to elucidate are covered and verified. Some make use of the checklist, but discussion is open around each of the items.

- In Germany, the employment interview has a style which is more structured than in France. If the conversation is open-ended, the recruiter is fond of precise questions; the applicant is thus guided. The interview is meticulous and the recruiter expects concrete answers to the series of questions. He shows much rigour in his approach and does not let the applicant speak as freely as does the French recruiter.

- In Luxemburg, the employment interview is conducted in a friendly tone and the recruiter originating from Luxemburg has a reputation for being respectful to the applicant. The foreign recruiter in Luxemburg tends to be more aggressive. Although the interview style is informal, an initial interview has many questions and relatively little real dialogue. The interview may have a structure from the professional recruiter's stance, but this structure is not always apparent to the applicant. Most generally, the interview style is relatively unstructured.

- In Italy, the employment interview is less formal than in France, as is the whole recruitment procedure. The Italian personnel manager has less impact on the decision than in France and therefore exercises less method in his recruitment. The interview in appearance is open, informal, flexible and non-structured. There are no particular schools of thought in Italy, and each recruiter has an individual style which can vary from one situation to another. There is nothing predetermined in the process.
- In Portugal, the employment interview style is largely unstructured, especially with individuals who have high professional status. Today, however, recruiters are oriented towards semi-structured interviews. A framework guides the recruiter, and a few key questions are systematically asked. The relationship is one of equality between the recruiter and the applicant, which in a period when or a region where there is limited unemployment, is a situation which puts the applicant more at ease.

Maud Tixier - Employers' recruitment tools across Europe (1996)

ACTIVITY 2 — 20 mins

In some cases, there may be the option of sequential interviewing: instead of, say, four people on a panel spending an hour with each of four candidates, the members might each spend an hour alone with each candidate. The panel could then take its selection decision in the light of the information obtained at the separate interviews.

What do you think would be the pros and cons of this approach?

2.2 Preparing interviews

In brief, the factors to be considered with regard to conducting selection interviews are:

(a) The impression of the organisation given by the interview arrangements

(b) The psychological effects of the location of the interview, seating arrangements and manner of the interviewer(s)

(c) The extent to which the candidate can be encouraged to talk freely (by asking open questions) and honestly (by asking probing questions), in accordance with the organisation's need for information

(d) The opportunity for the candidate to learn about the job and organisation

(e) The control of bias or hasty judgement by the interviewer.

The interview is a two-way process, but the **interviewer** must have a clear idea of what it is intended to achieve, and must be in sufficient control of the process to cover the required ground.

The **interview** agenda and questions will be based on:

(a) The job description, competence profile and/or person specification setting out the job/role requirements

(b) The information supplied by the candidate in the application form, CV and covering letter.

The interview process should be efficiently run to make a favourable impression on the candidates and to avoid unnecessary stress (unless ability to handle pressure is a selection criterion!).

2.3 Interviewer skills and questioning techniques

> 'Interviews are so common that they are often taken for granted. People view interviews as simply conversations during which information is gathered. While interviews are similar to conversations, there are important differences. An interview is a specialised form of conversation conducted for a specific task-related purpose.' (Whetten & Cameron, 2002)

Whetten & Cameron identify the following key skills for interviewers.

(a) Creating **effective questions**, arising out of a clear purpose and agenda, with the aim of eliciting the information required.

(b) Creating an **appropriate climate** for information sharing, using supportive communication techniques, such as:

 (i) Rapport building, establishing trust and relationship

 (ii) Active listening, using attentive body language and responsive verbal behaviours (eg summarising, clarifying)

 (iii) Introducing the interview in a way that establishes a positive tone and orients the candidate as to how the interview will be conducted.

(c) Using **question types** intentionally, in order to control the pace and direction of the interview, remaining responsive to the replies given by the candidate. (This is discussed further below.)

(d) Using and interpreting **non-verbal cues**, or 'body language' (dress, posture, eye contact, gestures, facial expressions).

(e) Being willing, and able, to identify shallow or unconvincing responses, and to **probe and challenge** when necessary: in other words, critically evaluating the candidate's responses.

(f) Being alert to the influence of first impressions, stereotypes and other forms of potential **bias**.

PEOPLE-ORIENTATED SELECTION INTERVIEW PROCESS

Whetten & Cameron (2002) cite a six-step process used by a major firm (un-named) outlining an effective interview process.

P Prepare
 1 Review application, CV and other background information
 2 Prepare both general and individual-specific questions
 3 Prepare suitable physical arrangements

E Establish Rapport
 1 Try to make applicant comfortable
 2 Convey genuine interest
 3 Communicate supportive attitude with voice and names

O Obtain Information
 1 Ask questions
 2 Probe
 3 Listen carefully
 4 Observe the person (dress, mannerisms, body language)

P Provide Information
 1 Describe current and future job opportunities
 2 Sell positive features of firm
 3 Respond to applicant's questions

L Lead to Close
 1 Clarify responses
 2 Provide an opportunity for final applicant input
 3 Explain what happens next

E Evaluate
 1 Assess match between technical qualifications and job requirements
 2 Judge personal qualities (leadership, maturity, team orientation)
 3 Make a recommendation

A variety of question styles may be used, to different effects.

(a) **Open questions** or open-ended questions ('Who...? What...? Where...? When...? Why...?') force interviewees to put together their own responses in complete sentences. This encourages the interviewee to talk, keeps the interview flowing and is most revealing ('Why do you want to be in HR?')

(b) **Probing questions** are similar to open questions in their phrasing but aim to discover the deeper significance of the candidate's experience or achievements. (If a candidate claimed to have had 'years of relevant experience', in a covering letter, the interviewer might need to ask 'How many years?', or 'Which particular jobs or positions do you consider relevant and how?')

(c) **Closed questions** are the opposite, inviting only 'yes' or 'no' answers: ('Did you...?', 'Have you...?'). A closed question has the following effects:

    (i) It elicits answers only to the question asked by the interviewer. This may be useful where there are small points to be established ('Did you pass your exam?') but there may be other questions and issues that (s)he has not anticipated but will emerge if the interviewee is given the chance to expand ('How did you think your studies went?').

    (ii) It does not allow interviewees to express their personality, so that interaction can take place on a deeper level.

    (iii) It makes it easier for interviewees to conceal things ('You never *asked* me....').

    (iv) It makes the interviewer work very hard!

(d) **Multiple questions** are just that: two or more questions are asked at once. ('Tell me about your last job? How did your knowledge of HR help you there, and do you think you are up-to-date or will you need to spend time studying?') This type of question can be used to encourage the candidate to talk at some length, but not to stray too far from the point. It might also test the candidate's ability to listen and handle large amounts of information, but should be used judiciously in this case.

(e) **Problem-solving or situational questions** present candidates with a situation and ask them to explain how they would deal with it or how they have dealt with it in the past. ('How would you motivate your staff to do a task that they did not want to do?' or 'Can you tell us about a time when you were successful about setting a goal and achieving it?') Such questions are used to establish whether the candidate will be able to deal with the sort of problems that are likely to arise in the job, or whether (s)he has sufficient technical knowledge. Whetten and Cameron (2002) suggest asking negative questions as well as positive ('Now tell us about a time you *failed* to meet a goal you set. How could you have done better?') in order to expose hidden bias.

(f) **Leading questions** lead the interviewee to give a certain reply. ('We are looking for somebody who likes detailed figure work. How much do you enjoy dealing with numbers?', or 'Don't you agree that...?', 'Surely...?')

    The danger with this type of question is that interviewees will give the answer they think the interviewer wants to hear, but it might legitimately be used to deal with highly reticent or nervous candidates, simply to encourage them to talk.

ACTIVITY 3 — 20 mins

Identify the type of question used in the following examples, and discuss the opportunities and constraints they offer the interviewee who must answer them.

(a) 'So you're interested in a business studies degree, are you, Jo?
(b) 'Surely you're not interested in business studies, Jo?'
(c) 'How about a really useful qualification like a Business Studies degree, Jo? Would you consider that?'
(d) 'Why are you interested in a Business Studies degree, Jo?'
(e) 'Why particularly Business Studies, Jo?'

Candidates should also be given the opportunity to **ask questions**. Indeed, well-prepared candidates will go into an interview knowing what questions they want to ask. Their choice of questions might well have some influence on how the interviewers finally assess them. Moreover, there is information that the candidate will need to know about the organisation and the job, and about:

(a) Terms and conditions of employment (although negotiations about detailed terms may not take place until a provisional offer has been made) and

(b) The next step in the selection process – whether there are further interviews, when a decision might be made, or which references might be taken up.

As we know, interviews remain the most popular method for selecting candidates, yet they score poorly predictive validity, why is this?

2.4 Limitations of interviews

Interviews are criticised because they fail to provide accurate predictions of how a person will perform in the job. The main reasons why this might be so are as follows.

(a) **Limited scope**. An interview is necessarily too brief to 'get to know' candidates in the kind of depth required to make an accurate prediction of their behaviour in any given situation.

(b) **Limited relevance**. Interviews that lack structure and focus may fail to elicit information that is relevant to the candidate's likely future performance in the job and compatibility with the organisation.

(c) **Artificiality**. An interview is an artificial situation: candidates may be 'on their best behaviour' or, conversely, so nervous that they do not do themselves justice. Neither situation reflects what the person is 'really like'.

(d) **Errors of judgement** by interviewers. These include:

    (i) The **halo effect** – a tendency for people to make an initial general judgement about a person based on a single obvious attribute, such as being neatly dressed, or well-spoken, which will colour later perceptions.

    (ii) **Contagious bias** – a process whereby an interviewer changes the behaviour or responses of the applicant by suggestion, through the wording of questions or non-verbal cues.

    (iii) **Logical error**. For example, an interviewer might place too much emphasis on isolated strengths or weaknesses, or draw unwarranted conclusions from facts (confusing career mobility with disloyalty, say).

(e) **Lack of skill and experience** by interviewers. For example:

- Inability to take control of the direction and length of the interview
- A reluctance to probe into facts and challenge statements where necessary

3 Selection testing

3.1 Types of tests

In many job selection procedures, an interview is now supplemented by some form of selection test.

Cushway (1994) lists six criteria which such tests should satisfy.

1 A **sensitive** measuring instrument that discriminates between subjects
2 **Standardised**, so that an individual's score can be related to others
3 **Reliable**, in that it always measures the same thing
4 **Valid**, in that the test measures what it is designed to measure

5 **Acceptable** to the candidate
6 **Non-discriminatory**

The science of measuring mental capacities and processes is called 'psychometrics'; hence the term **'psychometric testing'**. There are four types of test commonly used in practice.

Intelligence or cognitive ability tests

These are tests of general cognitive ability which typically test memory, ability to think quickly (perceptual speed, verbal fluency) and logically (inductive reasoning), and problem-solving skills. Reliance on such criteria has shown steady increase, perhaps because of uncertainty in employers' minds about the validity of school exam results, the wide variation in degree classes between higher educational institutions and the difficulties of comparing international qualifications.

Most people have experience of IQ tests, and few would dispute their validity as good measures of general intellectual performance.

Aptitude tests

Aptitude tests are designed to predict an individual's **potential** for performing a job or learning new skills. There are various accepted areas of aptitude, as follows.

(a) **Reasoning** – verbal, numerical and abstract/visual (eg accuracy and speed in arithmetical calculations, naming or making words, identifying shapes)

(b) **Spatio-visual ability** – practical intelligence, non-verbal ability and creative ability (eg ability to solve mechanical puzzles)

(c) **Perceptual speed and accuracy** – eg clerical ability (identifying non-identical pairs of numbers)

(d) **'Psycho-motor' ability** – mechanical, manual, musical and athletic: ability to respond accurately and rapidly to stimuli (eg pressing lighted buttons), using controlled muscular adjustments and/or finger dexterity and so on.

With a few possible exceptions, most of the areas of aptitude mentioned above are fairly easily measurable: so long as it is possible to determine what particular aptitudes are required for a job, such tests are likely to be useful for selection.

Personality tests

Personality tests may measure a variety of characteristics, such as applicants' skill in dealing with other people, ambition, motivation or emotional stability. Probably the best known example is the 16PF, originally developed by Cattell in 1950 and was described (in *People Management*) as follows.

> The 16PF comprises 16 scales, each of which measures a factor that influences the way a person behaves.
>
> The factors are functionally different underlying personality characteristics, and each is associated with not just one single piece of behaviour but rather is the source of a relatively broad range of behaviours. For this reason the factors themselves are referred to as source traits and the behaviours associated with them are called surface traits.
>
> The advantage of measuring source traits, as the 16PF does, is that you end up with a much richer understanding of the person because you are not just describing what can be seen but also the characteristics underlying what can be seen.
>
> The 16PF analyses how a person is likely to behave generally, including, for example, contributions likely to be made to particular work contexts, aspects of the work environment to which the person is likely to be more or less suited, and how best to manage the person.

Other examples include the Myers-Briggs Type Indicator® (mostly intended for self-development purposes), the Minnesota Multiphasic Personality Inventory (MMPI) and the FIRO-B personality profile. The validity of such tests has been much debated, but it seems that some have been shown by research to be valid predictors of job performance, so long as they are used and interpreted properly. A test may indicate that a candidate is introverted, has creative ability and is pragmatic – but this is only of use if this combination of characteristics can be linked to success or failure in the type of work for which the candidate is being considered.

Another area of current interest (which falls somewhere between personality, aptitude and intelligence testing) is the concept of **emotional intelligence**.

The capacity for **emotional intelligence (EQ)** is recognising our own feelings and those of others, for motivating ourselves, and for managing emotions well in ourselves and in our relationships. (Goleman, 1998)

Goleman argues that: 'the more complex the job, the more emotional intelligence matters – if only because a deficiency in these abilities can hinder the use of whatever technical expertise or intellect a person may have'. Emotional competence accounts for some 70% of the competences listed by an organisation as essential for effective performance. They also correlate strongly with managerial success, labour stability, completion of training and promotability (Whetten & Cameron, 2002; Goleman, 1998).

Goleman (and others) have published **Emotional Competence Assessment** questionnaires for each of the five key domains of EQ: self awareness, self regulation, motivation, empathy and social skills.

Proficiency and attainment tests

Proficiency tests are perhaps the most closely related to an assessor's objectives, because they measure ability to do the work involved. An applicant for an audio typist's job, for example, might be given a dictation tape and asked to type it. This is a type of attainment test, in that it is designed to measure abilities or skills already acquired by the candidate.

ACTIVITY 4 — 30 mins

What kind of work sample or proficiency tests would you devise for the following categories of employee? For each, state whether your test is a physical, verbal or mental test

(a) Administrative assistants
(b) Construction supervisors
(c) Airline pilots
(d) Magazine editors
(e) Telephone operators

PSYCHOMETRIC TESTS IN THE PUBLIC SECTOR

'A government agency has adopted innovative recruitment techniques by using psychometric tests to measure how well candidates fit in with the public-sector culture.

'And other public-sector organisations could soon follow suit, after the Environment Agency revealed the move had dramatically reduced staff turnover rates.

'The agency overhauled its recruitment for environmental officers, following retention problems. Candidates are now sent to assessment centres specifically to evaluate whether they have the "personality and qualities to work in the public sector" ...

'Understanding the public-sector ethos is being increasingly recognised as important and as necessary to getting the right skills ... It is certainly harder to train people in those behavioural attributes than it is to train them in the technical side.'

Watkins (2003).

3.2 Limitations of psychometric testing

Psychometric testing has grown in popularity in recent years, but does have a number of drawbacks.

(a) There is not always a direct (let alone predictive) relationship between ability in the test and ability in the job: the job situation is very different from artificial test conditions.

(b) The interpretation of test results is a skilled task, for which training and experience is essential. It is also highly subjective (particularly in the case of personality tests), which belies the apparent scientific nature of the approach.

(c) Additional difficulties are experienced with particular kinds of test. For example:

- (i) An aptitude test measuring arithmetical ability would need to be constantly revised or its content might become known to later applicants.
- (ii) Personality tests can often give misleading results because applicants seem able to guess which answers will be looked at most favourably.
- (iii) It is difficult to design intelligence tests which give a fair chance to people from different cultures and social groups and which test the *kind* of intelligence that the organisation wants from its employees: the ability to score highly in IQ tests does not necessarily correlate with desirable traits such as mature judgement or creativity, merely mental agility. In addition, 'practice makes perfect': most tests are subject to coaching and practice effects.

(d) It is difficult to exclude discrimination and bias from tests. Many tests (including personality tests) are tackled less successfully by women than by men, or by immigrants than by locally-born applicants because of the particular aspects chosen for testing. This may make their use indirectly discriminatory.

The most recent edition of the 16PF test, for example has been scrutinised by expert psychologists 'to exclude certain types of content, such as dated material, content that might lead to bias, material that might be unacceptable in an organisational setting and anything considered to be strongly socially desirable or undesirable'.

> 'Among the qualities which neither the interview nor intelligence tests are able to assess accurately are the candidate's ability to get on with and influence his [or her] colleagues, to display qualities of spontaneous leadership and to produce ideas in a real-life situation.'
>
> (Plumbley)
>
> Why might this be a drawback? What can be done about it?

4 Group selection methods

4.1 Techniques in group selection

Group selection methods or **assessment centres** might be used by an organisation as the final stage of a selection process for high-value jobs (since they are comparatively expensive to run). They consist of a series of tests, interviews and group situations over a period of two days, involving a small number of candidates (typically six to eight).

Group selection methods are appropriate for assessing the following.

(a) **Social skills** such as sensitivity to the views and opinions of others, reaction to disagreement and criticism, and the ability to influence and persuade others.

(b) **Intellectual skills** such as the consideration of the merits and demerits of other arguments put forward and the ability to think clearly (particularly at short notice), situational problem solving and so on.

(c) **Attitudes**, such as political, racial or religious views, attitude to authority, or willingness to take risks (initiative).

Typical techniques used in group selection include:

(a) Group **role-play** exercises, in which candidates can explore (and hopefully display) interpersonal skills and/or work through simulated managerial tasks

(b) **Case studies**, where candidates' analytical and problem-solving abilities are tested in working through described situations/problems, as well as their interpersonal skills, in taking part in (or leading) group discussions of the case study

(c) **'In-tray' exercises,** simulating a typical work-load to be managed

(d) **Leaderless discussion groups** (LDGs), allowing leadership skills and issues to emerge freely.

Often what are termed '**leaderless group activities**' will be conducted. Such activities can be used to assess the leadership potential of job applicants in uncertain situations with no formal power structure. The group is presented with a topic for discussion and given a defined period of time to reach a conclusion. The topic may be related to the job in question, and may either be of a problem-solving nature ('Should product X be developed given the following marketing and financial information?') or more general ('Is capital punishment an effective deterrent?'). The contribution made by individual candidates will be scored according to factors such as assertiveness, quality of thought and expression, analytical skill, and the ability to lead the group towards a decision.

Another method of assessment involves giving candidates a typical job problem to solve individually in a set time, at the end of which each candidate has to present and justify his or her solution to the other members of the group.

SELECTION AT VIRGIN ATLANTIC

The **Virgin Atlantic** careers website outlines its selection methods for prospective candidates as follows.

Assessment Centres

An Assessment Centre is a method of assessing the strengths and development needs of candidates. They generally last for all or part of a day and they're made up of a number of exercises.

For positions in Cabin Crew, In-Flight Beauty Therapist, Airports and Contact Centre there will be some kind of assessment centre, which will contain some of the following elements:

- Group decision
- Role plays
- Analysis presentation
- Ability tests, such as numerical reasoning
- Behavioural/biographical interview

Group discussions

These are useful in assessing candidates who are applying for roles with a strong element of teamwork.

Ability tests

These measure certain abilities or aptitudes and usually involve some kind of scoring that will indicate the level of your ability in the area being tested or your potential to lean more.

Behavioural/biographical interviews

In a behavioural interview you will be asked to give specific examples of situations that you have dealt with and what the outcomes were.

At a biographical interview you will be asked to discuss your CV and employent history, outlining what you have done, what your achievements are and how/why you have made your career choices.

4.2 Purposes of group selection

Group sessions might be useful because:

(a) They give selectors a longer opportunity to study the candidates.

(b) They reveal more than application forms, interviews and tests alone about the ability of candidates to persuade others, negotiate with others, and explain ideas to others and also to investigate problems efficiently. These are typical management skills.

(c) They reveal more about how candidates' personalities and attributes will affect the work team and their own performance.

(d) They achieve some measure of comparability between candidates.

(e) The pooled judgement of the panel of assessors is likely to be more accurate than the judgement of a single interviewer.

5 Follow up procedures

5.1 Reference checking

References provide further confidential information about the prospective employee, although it may be of varying value: the reliability of all but the most factual information must be questioned. A reference should contain:

(a) Straightforward factual information confirming the nature of the applicant's previous job(s), period of employment, pay, and circumstances of leaving.

(b) Opinions about the applicant's personality and other attributes. These should obviously be treated with some caution. Allowances should be made for prejudice (favourable or unfavourable), charity (withholding detrimental remarks), and possibly fear of being actionable for libel (although references are privileged, as long as they are factually correct and devoid of malice).

At least two **employer** references are desirable, providing necessary factual information, and comparison of personal views. (**Personal** references tell the prospective employer little more than that the applicant has a friend or two.)

If a judgement of character and suitability is desired, it might be most tellingly formulated as the question: 'Would you re-employ this individual? (If not, why not?)'

Telephone references may be time-saving, if standard reference letters or forms are not available. They may also elicit a more honest opinion than a carefully prepared written statement. For this reason, a telephone call may also be made to check a very glowing or very reluctant reference...

(Note that when **giving** references, caution is also required. A landmark legal judgement in *Spring v Guardian Assurance plc 1995*, decided that an employer owes a duty of care to employees in relation to giving a reference, and in obtaining the information upon which the reference is based. On the other hand, an employer could face civil liability from a company which suffered economic loss as a result of hiring an employee on the basis of a false complimentary reference!)

ACTIVITY 5 — 10 mins

At the end of a recent selection process one candidate was, in the view of everyone involved, outstanding. However, you have just received a very bad reference from her current employer. What do you do?

6 Evaluating the process

6.1 Evaluating selection

Evaluating the selection process falls into two approaches, one that validates the methodology, the other that looks at effectiveness of the outcomes.

The methodology review considers four criteria:

Practicality	The method has to be both acceptable to those conducting it, those being assessed, the legal and professional bodies. Additionally it has to be practical in terms of the cost, both time and financial relative to the outcome being sought. Also the method has to be within the capabilities of those conducting it.
Sensitivity	Does the method being used actually differentiate between the candidates in terms of their ability to do the job.
Reliability	Is the method used proven to be robust and able to consistently produce the same results, regardless of whoever who may be conducting it. The method should be reliable regardless of the person conducting the method, the sequence in which it is used relative to other tests and over a duration of time.
Validity	Do the criteria employed accurately predict the job performance? The issue of validity is the key question for selection. Many organisations have developed competences which they use as part of the process. However many competences are described at a fairly generic level in order to make them applicable to every position in the organisation, and also they are often based on the behaviours that have been effective to date. Very few competences are based on future expectations. In addition to identifying the criteria that need to be identified the issue then arises as to how to assess these, which returns to the questions of practicality, sensitivity and reliability.

Marchington and Wilkinson (2008) include an analysis of the accuracy of selection methods. As can be seen combining methods produces the most reliable outcome.

1.00	Perfect selection	0.40	Personality tests
0.65	Intelligence tests and integrity tests	0.37	Assessment centres
0.63	Intelligence tests and structured interviews	0.35	Biodata
0.60	Intelligence tests and work sampling	0.26	References
0.54	Work sample tests	0.18	Years of job experience
0.51	Intelligence tests	0.10	Years of education
0.51	Structured interviews	0.02	Graphology
0.41	Integrity tests	0.00	Selection with a pin

Selection procedures can further be evaluated by determining whether selection decisions seem to have been 'correct' in the light of subsequent job performance, cultural impact and service longevity of the successful candidate.

(a) If tests were used to assess likely potential to perform certain tasks, the retained test results can be compared against actual performance in the job. Regular discrepancies may suggest that the tests are flawed.

(b) Similar comparisons may be made using interview ratings and notes. Interviewers who consistently fall short in the accuracy of their judgements should be trained accordingly.

Other performance criteria for evaluating selection procedures include:

(a) Number of candidates (and/or minority/female/disabled candidates) interviewed in relation to applications

(b) Number of offers made in relation to number of interviews (especially to minority/female/disabled candidates)

(c) Number of acceptances in relation to offers made

(d) Number of successful applicants subsequently appraised as competent in the job

(e) Lead time for successful applicants to be trained to competence

(f) Number of starters still employed after one year (two years or an appropriate period of measurement)

(g) Cost of selection methods per starter employed one year later.

Chapter Roundup

- The primary purpose of selection is to identify suitable candidates.
- The most effective method to achieving this is to follow a systematic approach. This will also withstand scrutiny in terms of discrimination and fairness.
- There are many selection methods available; those chosen will reflect national, organisational and individual preferences. However the validity and reliability of these can vary enormously. The best method is to use a number of methods, this is the approach typically adopted for assessment centres.
- Interviews can be conducted in a variety of forms including one-to-one and panel. Interviews are a highly popular method but not a valid or reliable method.
- Selection tests have better validity and predictability, but needs to be administered by qualified testers and are relatively more expensive to conduct. Different tests can be used to predict different qualities e.g. intelligence, aptitude, personality.
- Group selection methods can used to test for different abilities such as social skills and attitude. Different techniques can be used to test these, they are often conducted during assessment centres.
- References should be taken for all successful candidates if only to validate the facts they have stated on their CV, however little reliability can be placed on any opinions stated.
- The contents of this chapter may be summarised in diagrammatic form.

Cont...

Chapter Roundup cont

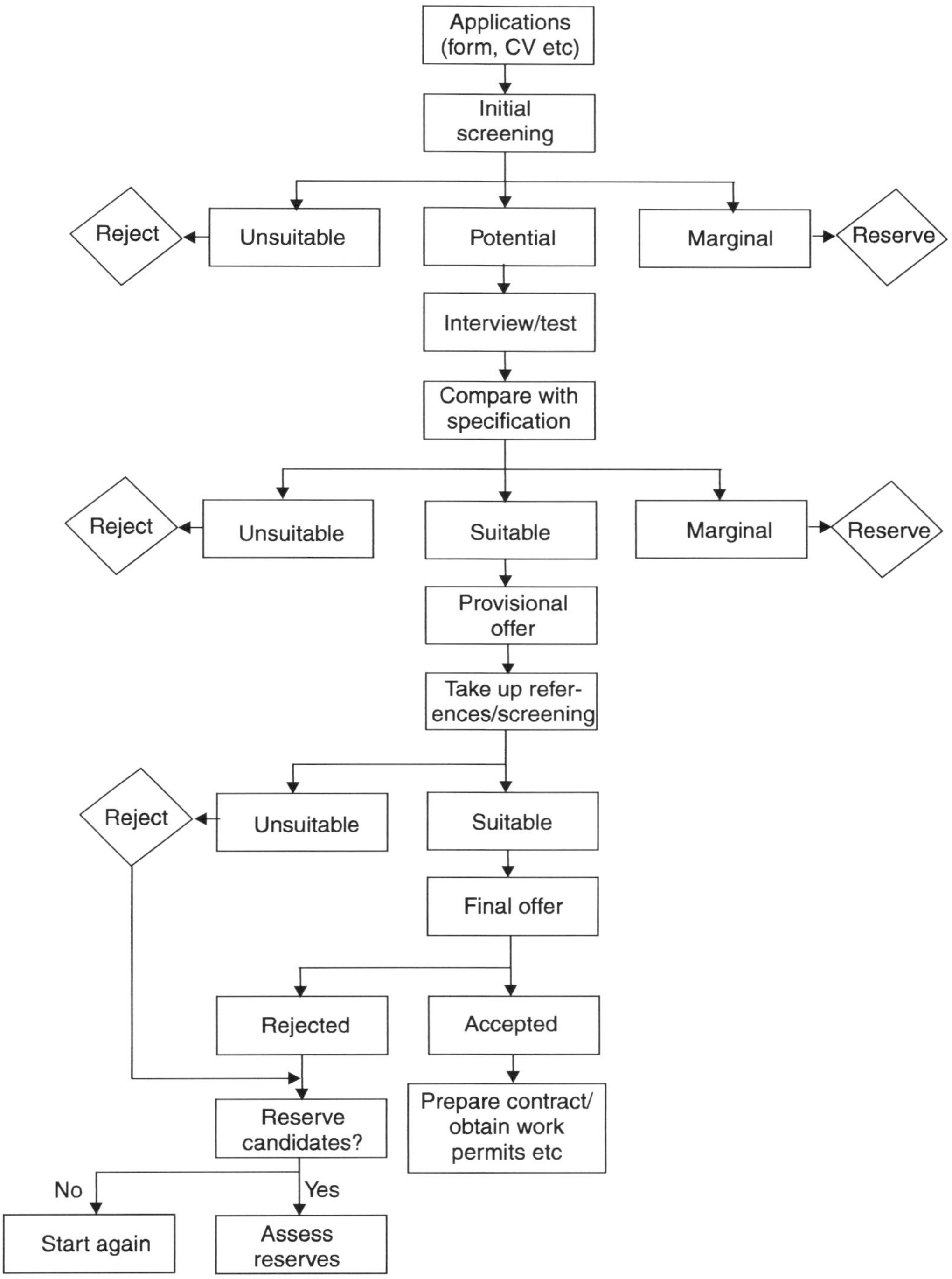

Quick Quiz

1 What are the aims of selection?

2 What are the stages of the systematic approach to selection?

3 What is another name for a large formal panel interview?

4 A job selection interview has several aims. If you were conducting one, though, you should **not** be concerned with:

(a) Comparing the application against the job/person specification
(b) Getting as much information as possible about the applicant
(c) Giving the applicant information about the job and organisation
(d) Making the applicant feel he has been treated fairly

5 What can be done to improve the effectiveness of selection interviews?

6 Amon Leigh-Hewman is interviewing a candidate for a vacancy in his firm. He asks a question about the candidate's views on a work-related issue. The candidate starts to answer, and sees to his horror that Amon in pursing his lips and shaking his head slightly to himself. 'Of course, that's what some people say', continues the candidate, 'but I myself...' Amon smiles. His next question is 'Don't you think that...?

Amon is getting a distorted view of the candidate because of:

(a) The halo effect
(b) Contagious bias
(c) Stereotyping
(d) Logical error

7 Selection tests such as IQ tests and personality tests may not be effective in getting the right person for the job for several reasons. Which of the following criticisms is false, though?

(a) Test results can be influenced by practice and coaching rather than genuine ability
(b) Subjects are able (and tend) to deliberately falsify results
(c) Tests do not eliminate bias and subjectivity
(d) Test are generally less accurate predictors of success than interviews

8 List the four main types of selection testing.

9 What is an 'assessment centre'?

10 What types of information should an employer reference contain about the candidate?

Answers to Quick Quiz

1 Filling vacancies with best person; informing applicants (to facilitate self-selection and adjustment); creating employer brand; upholding values of fairness and professionalism. (para 1.1)

2 Set key criteria; compare applications (forms, CV) against criteria; sort and shortlist; acknowledge all responses; invite candidates to interview/selection testing or other methods; check references; send standard letters to 'rejects' and 'reserves'. (para 1.2)

3 Selection Board (para 2.1)

4 B. Information needs to be relevant (para 2.1)

5 Planning; relevant criteria; interviewer training and appraisal; structured style of questioning; awareness of potential for bias. (paras 2.2-2.3)

6 B Contagious bias (para 2.4)

7 D Interviews are generally less accurate. (para 3.1)

8 (a) Intelligence or Cognitive
(b) Aptitude
(c) Personality
(d) Proficiency

(para 3.1)

9 A group selection process, using a series of tests, interviews and group situations and exercises over a period of two days, typically involving 6-8 candidates for a job. (para 4.1)

10 Factual information confirming the nature of the applicant's previous job, period of employment, pay and circumstances of leaving. Opinions about the applicant's attributes and employability should be treated with caution. (para 5.1)

Answers to Activities

Activity 1

Influential research by Smith & Abrahamsen (1994) showed the following results.

Method	% use	Predictive validity
Interviews	92	0.17
References	74	0.13
Work sampling	18	0.57
Assessment centres	14	0.40
Personality tests	13	0.40
Cognitive tests	11	0.54
Biodata	4	0.40
Graphology	3	0.00

Employers appear to rely *most* heavily on the least *valid* selection methods! Interviews, in particular, seem not much better than tossing a coin...

Activity 2

Rees (1991) suggested the following points. You may not agree with all of them.

(a) The method need take no more time for the organisation: in fact single interviews may turn out to take less than an hour.

(b) Candidates would have to spend more time being interviewed but 'might not mind this if they felt it was a more effective method of selection'.

(c) It is normally easier to create rapport and coax information out of a person when you are seeing him or her alone.

(d) However, inexperienced interviewers will be far more 'exposed' than they would have been in a panel interview. They may prefer merely to observe.

(e) The method is liable to create more argument about the final decision: the interviewee may be flagging by the end of the session and give a totally different impression to later interviewers.

Activity 3

(a) Closed. (The only answer is 'yes' or 'no', unless Jo is prepared to expand on it, at his or her own initiative.)

(b) Leading. (Even if Jo was interested, (s)he would get the message that 'yes' would not be what the interviewer wanted, or expected, to hear.)

(c) Leading closed multiple! ('Really useful' leads Jo to think that the 'correct' answer will be 'yes': there is not much opportunity for any other answer, without expanding on it unasked.)

(d) Open. (Jo has to explain, in his or her own words.)

(e) Probing. (Jo has to defend his or her decision.)

Activity 4

Here are some suggestions.

(a)	Admin assistants	Test Use of specific software or equipment (physical) Dictation (physical) Filing (physical) Letter proof-reading/correction (mental) Telephone answering (verbal)
(b)	Construction supervisors	Plan error recognition (mental) Role play dealing with worker problems (verbal)
(c)	Airline pilots	Rudder control, direction control (physical) Navigational reading (mental) Radio procedures (verbal)
(d)	Magazine editors	Writing headlines (mental) Proof-reading/correction (mental) Page layout (mental/physical)
(e)	Telephone operators	Switchboard handling (physical/mental) Role play in coming calls (verbal)

Activity 5

It is quite possible that her current employer is desperate to retain her. Disregard the reference, or question the referee by telephone, and seek another reference from a previous employer if possible.

Chapter 8

Employee engagement

In Chapter 2 we looked at employee turnover, the causes and the cost. In this chapter we will consider how best to create an environment that valued employees do not wish to leave.

In this chapter we will consider the concept of employee engagement, the idea of employees who are both committed to their employing organisation, who are prepared to make additional effort to help it succeed and so result in the organisation enjoying greater productivity. Unsurprisingly this combination is sought by many organisations; however, as we shall see, the component parts of the required mix are unclear as there is no single formula that will ensure success. The result is that we will consider a range of concepts, you will need to use your judgement as to which model or parts of models will be most applicable to your organisation or situation.

TOPIC LIST		LEARNING OUTCOMES
1	Employee retention	
2	Developing an engaged workforce	2.3, 2.4, 2.5
3	The role and responsibilities of line managers	2.4, 2.5
4	Employee involvement	2.4, 2.5
5	Employee communications – 'employee voice'	2.4, 2.5
6	Employee development	2.4, 2.5
7	On-the-job training and development	2.4, 2.5
8	Off-the-job training and development	2.4, 2.5
9	Measuring engagement	

1 Employee retention

1.1 Retention planning

In Chapter 2 we looked at indicative turnover rates for industry sectors; some organisations may take Comfort from these and conclude that the attrition rates they are experiencing are 'normal'. Other organisations may wish to dig deeper and will need to embark on a **benchmarking** exercise to understand how they compare to their peers. However, some organisations are not prepared to accept that even though within their frame of reference organisations they reflect the median, they may wish to excel.

An organisation faced with unacceptable levels of employee turnover will need to conduct a systematic **investigation** into the causes, using various methods.

(a) Information given at **exit interviews** should be the first step. (It must be recognised, however, that the reasons given for leaving may not be complete, true, or those that would be most useful to the organisation. People may say they are 'going to a better job', for example while the real reason for the move is dissatisfaction with the style of management.)

Exit interviews typically will consider:

- Why is the person leaving?
- What motivated them to look outside the organisation?
- Before working for the organisation, what were the individual's preconceptions of the employer brand; how have they contrasted with reality?
- Was the induction useful?
- What were the working relationships like within their team?
- Did they receive the training they needed?
- What are the pay and benefits at the new employer, how do they compare to the current organisation?
- What are their thoughts about the leadership team at their current organisation?
- Did they get the support they needed/wanted?
- How would they improve internal communications?
- What would they change?

To create statistics that can then prove of value, it is usual to categorise the answers, eg

Reasons for leaving:

1 Career development
2 Pay and benefits
3 Job content
4 Travel to work
5 To attend full time education
6 To go travelling
7 Personal reasons
8 Other

By categorising the answers, this enables comparisons for leaving with employee demographics and departments; over time a picture may develop of why people leave certain departments and certain jobs. This may well take a couple of years, however.

Exit interviews never really get to the truth about why people leave, and so are effectively useless. People are always careful about what they say even when leaving, in case they need a reference or a job back one day!.

Discuss

(b) **Attitude surveys**, to gauge the general climate of the organisation, and the response of the workforce as a whole to working conditions, management style and so on.

Surveys of employee opinions are a useful source of feedback (especially if there are no other direct avenues for employees to express their satisfactions and dissatisfactions). Attitude surveys may be carried out via:

(a) **Questionnaires**, whether standardised or tailored to the particular organisation or issues concerned. These may be paper-based or (increasingly) posted online on a company intranet. Questionnaires have the advantage of being quick and relatively cost-effective to administer, although they must be carefully designed if they are to elicit honest, meaningful and comparable responses.

(b) **Interviews**, either completely free-flowing or structured to a specific agenda of issues. Interviews are time-consuming and costly, but may also be more revealing, allowing a skilled interviewer to probe.

(c) **Focus groups**, allowing a structured response to interview questions by a representative sample of employees on specific issues.

The CIPD has produced the following checklist for conducting an employee attitude survey.

(a) Gain the commitment of senior management, clarify objectives and define areas where the company is prepared to take action.

(b) Decide between a census of employees – probably paper-based – and a random sample – maybe face-to-face interviews.

(c) Conduct a pilot survey.

(d) Design a questionnaire – this needs experienced help.

(e) Tell employees what is being done: the more internal publicity, the greater the chances of success.

(f) Guarantee confidentiality.

(g) Consider measures to improve the response rate, for example by holding supervised completion sessions in company time.

(h) If the survey involves face-to-face interviews, conduct them with one or two employees at a time. Avoid group discussions – it is difficult to maintain confidentiality in groups and to enable everyone to have a say.

(i) Produce the final report. Distil the evidence, reach conclusions and put forward recommendations. Present the report to top management.

(j) Report back to employees with a summary of the main findings.

(k) An individual or a group should be made responsible for action following the survey findings; progress should be monitored.

(c) Information gathered on the number of (interrelated) **variables** which can be assumed to **correlate** with labour turnover – such as an ageing workforce, higher rates of pay outside the organisation and so on.

EMPLOYEE RETENTION IN SOUTHEAST ASIA

An article in the Financial Times (December 2010), considered some of the challenges facing employers in East Asia.

The article identified that a new generation of employees, particularly graduates in such countries as Thailand, Cambodia, Vietnam and the Philippines, no longer had the expectation of working for a single employer for their entire career. They are now expecting to move jobs to secure better pay and career prospects. Indeed for them career development was more important than work-life balance.

Voluntary turnover in the region was now running at double digits.

Vietnam 15%

Malaysia 13%

Singapore 10%

Employers were also beginning to question the traditional method of investing heavily in training employees, realising that many of the new larger employers who were entering their markets for the first time would simply lure away employees with increased salaries. They are also questioning the value of creating schemes rewarding longevity of employment such a pension schemes.

However some of the established employers were able to identify facets of their employment that enabled them to attract and retain staff. For a Cambodian bank these are, desirable industry sector, strong local corporate brand and career planning including the opportunity to work overseas. For an insurance company, these include a policy of internal promotions from middle managers to senior managers.

Consultants observing the market as a whole recommend that employers spend more time understanding what motivates applicants before employing them, tailoring their development programmes to individuals, rather than a 'one fit programmes for all', and policies that prioritise internal candidates for more vacancies before looking externally.

2 Developing an engaged workforce

2.1 Introduction

Engagement '..a combination of commitment to the organisation and its values and a willingness to help out colleagues (organisational citizenship). It goes beyond job satisfaction and is not simply motivation. Engagement is something the employee has to offer: it cannot be 'required' as part of the employment contract.' CIPD (2010)

Naturally the appeal of engaged employees sits in the benefits that the organisation derives e.g. increased customer satisfaction and loyalty, productivity and reduced employee turnover. Therefore organisations are prepared to invest time and expense to achieving the goal.

Human Resource writers and consultants are often in search of the formula to achieve exceptional organisational performance. At one time the discussion was about High Performance Working (HPW)

2.2 High Performance Working

The objective of High Performance Work Systems is to create and harness and sustain HPW. According to the Institute of Work Psychology (2001), one of the required components is resourcing and development practices that are designed to attract and retain the right people with the right motivation.

To achieve this will require some guarantee of job security, an emphasis on internal selection, sophisticated selection techniques and employee attitude surveys with feedback to those involved.

Probably the most recognised work on what is required to achieve HPW is the work of Pfeffer (1998), He identified seven factors that are required. He argued that it was the **combination** of the factors or the **'bundle'** that was key.

1 **Employment security.** If employees are working in fear of losing their job, they will be constantly evaluating their potential actions to see if they increase or decrease their likelihood of losing their job; they will be circumspect in their actions. Organisations should ensure that employees feel secure in their jobs and future employment. There should be an emphasis on internal career development.

2 **Selective hiring**. Selecting the right people, who are a good organisational fit, and ensuring they are in the right place in the organisation, is a key requirement. Pfeffer proposed the use of competency-based criteria as the means of selection.

3 **Extensive training**, learning and development. The organisation should regard employee development as an investment and not a cost. Employees with high skills and knowledge levels are better able to create greater value in the organisation. The return on investment will be demonstrated through improved performance and lower attrition.

4 **Self-managed teams** and decentralisation of decision making. Employees should be grouped into teams. The teams should be without a supervisor and therefore self-managing. The self-managed team will have greater awareness of everyone's contribution and in turn accept responsibility and accountability.

5 **High compensation** contingent on organisational performance. If reward design is linked to organisational performance and seen to be structured fairly, employees are more likely to show commitment.

6 **Reduction of status differences**. Employee terms and conditions and benefits should be as homogeneous as possible; through creating an equitable environment, employees will have a greater sense of common purpose.

7 **Sharing information and employee involvement.** By sharing information and informing employees of the organisation's position will create an environment of trust and commitment. Additionally, informed with information as to the organisation's performance will enable employees to make better decisions.

HPW has somewhat fallen out of favour as there was little evidence to demonstrate that the 'bundle' did have the anticipated impact on the organisation, and identifying the 'right' bundle was problematic. In fact certain commentators began to conclude that High Performing Organisations produced the bundle of factors more as a by-product in their efforts to gain high performance, rather than being the primary purpose of their activities.

2.3 Employee commitment

While seeking the ideal 'bundle' may be appealing to an organisation, the enthusiasm for identifying the perfect 'bundle' has somewhat dissipated with the lack of concrete evidence of a link. The attention has instead turned more towards **employee attitudes**. The theory being that if the attitudes of employees can be positively influenced, this will lead to positive behaviour and, in turn, enhanced performance.

The most important attitude to consider is that of **commitment**.

Organisations strive to have engaged employees as such employees are likely to display higher levels of commitment. However it is worth noting that not all committed employees are necessarily actively engaged. Meyer and Allen (1991) identified three types of commitment.

Normative (or moral)	The individual feels they ought to be committed to the organisation regardless of whether or not they actually believe in the values of the organisation
Continuance	Where the individual chooses to remain with the organisation as long as they consider the benefits of doing so outweigh the costs of leaving
Affective	The individual feels an emotional connection to the organisation

The final 'affective' commitment is that most sought by employers. The employee who feels such an emotional connection to their organisation is likely to go the extra mile and display other positive behaviours.

2.4 Employee engagement

The Institute of Employment Studies found the following areas to be the key to engagement:

Good quality line management	Managers who care about their employees, treat them fairly, encourage them to perform well, take an interest in their career aspirations and provide opportunities for development
Two-way open communication	Allows employees to voice ideas and suggestions and keeps employees informed about things that are relevant to them
Effective co-operation	Between different departments and between management and trade unions
Focus on employee development	Providing training that employees need for their current role and fair access to development opportunities
Commitment to employee well-being	Taking health and safety seriously, working to minimise accidents, injuries, violence and harassment, and taking effective action should a problem occur
Clear, accessible HR policies and practices	Senior management and line management commitment to appraisals, equal opportunities and family friendliness
Fair pay and benefits	In terms of comparison inside and outside the organisation
Harmonious working environment	Encouraging employees to respect and help one another

The CIPD following a study identified the most popular steps taken specifically to address staff retention.

- Improved line managers' people skills
- Increased learning and development opportunities
- Improved induction process
- Improved employee involvement
- Improved selection techniques
- Improved pay
- Offered coaching/mentoring/ buddy systems
- Improved benefits
- Better promotion to employees of the employer brand
- Created clearer career paths
- Revised the way staff are rewarded so their efforts are better recognised
- Made changes to improve work– life balance
- Improved physical working conditions
- Redesigned jobs to make them more satisfying
- Increased our use of counteroffers
- No specific initiatives undertaken

When reviewing the information above, the same three factors occur in the top four reasons:

1 The quality and skills of line managers
2 Employee involvement and communications
3 Employee development

3 The role and responsibilities of line managers

The responsibility of line managers for delivering HR outcomes is a distinctive feature of the Human Resource Management approach, but even in a traditional personnel management model, line managers would often have responsibility for activities immediately concerned with the manager-team relationship: team selection, interviewing, and timekeeping management, performance appraisal, team motivation and so on.

Not only for reasons of cost, over the last two decades many duties of HR have been transferred to line managers. They have become responsible for recruitment, induction, training, performance appraisals, pay reviews and exit interviews. In some organisations the HR database allows the line manager to input employee changes. This has generally been seen as a good thing:

1 It empowers the line manager to manage their own staff and take responsibility.
2 It can reduce the overhead cost of HR.
3 Enables HR to focus on greater value-adding activities.

However it is not only for these reasons such changes have been occurring. There has been a growing recognition that line managers have a greater influence over their own employees both in terms of motivation and retention than the actions of the organisation. Hutchinson and Purcell (2004) found that the line manager is

> '..the most important factor explaining the variation in both job satisfaction and job discretion, or the choice that people have over how they do their jobs. It is also one of the most important factors in developing organizational commitment'

Torrington (2011) states

> '...a bad relationship with their immediate supervisor... was by far the most commonly mentioned (reason for leaving)...lending support to the often-stated point that people leave their managers and not their organisations'

Is Torrington correct, do people leave their managers and not their organisations? Think of people you know who have left an organisation and their reason(s) for doing so. Does that lead you to agree or disagree with Torrington?.

The line manager has a direct influence on:

- How much feedback and coaching is given
- How development opportunities are identified and discussed
- Whether the individual feels recognised and valued
- Whether their workload is manageable.

The importance of the line manager cannot be underestimated. The 12 Engagement Questions (conducted by Gallup) is an analysis tool dedicated to evaluating employee engagement which is biased towards the impact of the line manager. It is proposed that the survey is conducted regularly (twice a year) and used more as a barometer of feeling within a supervisor's team, than an absolute measure.

It should be noted that the 12 Engagement Questions is copyrighted to Gallup and no attempts should be made to replicate this tool using the table in this study text.

The survey consisted of 12 questions in which employees were asked to rate their responses to each question on a low to high scale of 1 to 5					
	1	2	3	4	5
Did my supervisor make me fully aware of what was needed from me at work?					
Did I have all the supplies I needed to do my work?					
Whilst at work, did I have the chance to do what I excel at every day?					
Was I acknowledged or praised for good work regularly?					
Did my supervisor appear to care for me as a person?					
Was my supervisor supportive of my development?					
Were my ideas and views taken seriously at work?					
Did the organisation's direction, focus and goals make me feel that my work is important?					
Are the people I work with dedicated to producing quality?					
Is there someone at work who is a close friend?					
Did my supervisor review progress with me regularly?					
Has my work offered me the chance to develop both my skills and as a person?					

Organisations that invest in the selection of line managers and developing the skills of line managers can expect a greater level of engagement from their employees. The challenge when considering supervisor development is that the skills are often highly interpersonal and dependent upon the organisational context and particular set of circumstances, Taylor (2010) cites six 'golden rules' for supervisors:

1 Give praise where praise is due
2 Avoid the perception of favouritism
3 Talk to every team member regularly
4 Act when you suspect there are problems
5 Give people as much autonomy as you can
6 Involve people in decision-making

4 Employee involvement

4.1 Employee involvement

Employee involvement describes a wide range of policies and techniques for 'informing and consulting employees about, or associating them with, one or more aspects of running an organisation.'
(Gennard & Judge, 2005)

Employee involvement concentrates mainly on individual employees and the degree to which they can be encouraged to identify with the goals of the organisation. It can be distinguished from employee participation, which concerns the extent to which employees are involved (via their representatives) in management decision making.

The aims of involvement may be:

(a) To generate commitment to the organisation

(b) To help the organisation improve performance, especially in the face of change

(c) To enable the organisation to better meet changing customer requirements

(d) To improve the challenge and satisfaction of the work experience

(e) To aid the organisation in attracting and retaining skilled workers

(f) To develop the business awareness of workers at all levels

(g) To increase employee incentives and accountabilities through tying reward to company performance and profitability

(h) To make the employer/employee bond primary and the trade union bond secondary.

Guest (2001) describes five ways to get employees involved.

1 By improving the provision of information to employees
2 By improving the provision of information from employees
3 By changing the structure and arrangement of work
4 By changing the incentives
5 By changing relationships, through more participative leadership and informality.

Marchington *et al* (1992) similarly divide employee involvement schemes into four categories.

(a) **Downwards communications:** from managers to other employees and soon. This includes house journals, employee reports and briefings.

(b) **Upwards problem-solving forms:** designed to tap into individual and team knowledge and expertise. This includes suggestion schemes, attitude surveys, quality circles, customer care programmes and so on.

(c) **Financial participation:** linking rewards of individuals to the performance of the unit or business. This includes profit sharing, employee share ownership and factory-wide or value-added bonus schemes.

(d) **Representative participation:** employees are involved in decision-making through their representatives on Joint Consultative Committee JCCs, advisory councils, works councils, or collective bargaining. (This may operate at different levels of involvement, from consultation and dialogue to co-determination and even to control, e.g. in worker-managed teams or co-operatives.)

In addition, involvement may be encouraged by:

(a) **Empowerment**: the devolving of control and responsibility to individuals or teams at the workplace or 'front line' customer-service level. Empowerment may be 'soft' (providing enhanced opportunities for involvement in decision making, fewer status barriers, more open communication, greater flexibility) or 'hard' (devolution of responsibility and accountability: standards and targets, monitoring and control)

(b) **Inclusion in the cultural and strategic priorities of the business**. Employees are invited and encouraged to share in commitment to quality, customer care, continuous improvement, learning and so on. This is frequently linked to empowerment as a set of guiding values and objectives within which teams can be more or less self-managing.

We will now look briefly at some of these techniques in more detail.

4.2 Downward communication

Downward communication is usually well-established in an organisation in the form of instructions, job briefings, rules and policies and announcement of plans by managers to staff.

There may, however, be potential for more empowering downward information flow about a wider range of matters, including: company strategy and future plans; positive performance feedback, celebrating individual, team and company achievements; competitor and other environmental factors that may influence work (or stimulating problem-solving); and so on.

Examples of mechanisms for downward communication of this type include:

(a) **In-house journals**, bulletins and new sheets (and their electronic equivalents by e-mail or intranet pages). This is commonly used to foster a sense of involvement and belonging, but may be made a tool for greater participation by including various mechanisms for feedback and interaction: suggestion schemes, 'letter' pages, discussion forums, notice boards and so on.

(b) **Team briefings**, where management pass information face-to-face to team members, on a regular basis. This enables people to feel that they know what is going on, and have access to the information required to do their work. Briefing meetings can also be used for interactive question-and-answer and problem solving, however, for a more participative element.

(c) **Management by walking around**. The managerial culture of some organisations will need to be changed in order to increase information flow to employees. The hoarding of information as a source of power by managers, or the withholding of information on a 'need to know' basis are a feature of command-and-control cultures rather than facilitate-and-empower organisations.

Is there too much information flowing around organisations – or does keeping employees 'in the loop' meaningfully contribute to employee relations?

4.3 Upward communication

Upward communication is rarer than downward – but vital to many modern organisations in:

(a) Providing feedback on progress and performance, so that plans can be adjusted where necessary

(b) Harnessing the experience and know-how of employees for innovation, problem solving and decision making

(c) Giving management insight into employees' needs, interests and problems, to help them manage better

(d) Demonstrating the value management places on employees, establishing the mutual trust and commitment that underpins constructive employee relations.

Suggestion schemes are a way of offering performance rewards and incentives. They are also an important mechanism for upward communication.

ACTIVITY 1 — 15 mins

How would you respond to the following objections from a management traditionalist to employee surveys?

(a) Good managers already know their staff's opinions.
(b) Surveys are superficial, impersonal and bureaucratic.
(c) Surveys open cans of worms and raise false hopes.
(d) Surveys contain built-in bias because of the unknown opinions of the many who do not respond.

4.4 Empowerment

Empowerment has two key aspects. It involves giving workers discretion to make decisions about how to organise work in order to achieve task goals *and* making workers responsible for achieving production and quality targets. (The French word for empowerment is '*responsibilisation*'.)

The purpose of empowerment is:

(a) To free employees from rigorous control by instructions and orders, which contributes to job satisfaction *and* learning and flexibility.

(b) To give employees opportunities for growth and job satisfaction through taking responsibility for their ideas and actions.

(c) To release and develop resources in the workforce that would otherwise remain inaccessible, including creativity and initiative.

(d) To harness employee commitment by allowing them to share in the process of target-setting and work organisation.

(e) To decentralise decision-making and problem-solving initiative to 'frontline' customer-facing roles, to enhance the flexibility and responsiveness of customer service.

Empowerment goes hand in hand with:

(a) **Delayering**, or a cut in the number of levels in the organisation hierarchy: responsibility previously held by managers is, in effect, being given to operational workers

(b) **Flexibility**, since giving responsibility to the people closest to the product or customer encourages responsiveness

(c) **New technology**, since skilled knowledge workers need less supervision, being better equipped to identify and control the means to clearly understood ends

(d) **Employee development**, since the personal and interpersonal skills needed to meet the challenges of responsibility and participation in decision making need to be developed.

Empowerment implies a shift in the role of both **line managers** (who effectively become 'coaches' and 'facilitators' in team decision-making processes, setting parameters and providing information and guidance where required) and **HR practitioners** (who increasingly share responsibility for delivering HR policy outcomes not only with line managers but with employees themselves).

4.5 Self-managed teams

Self-managed teams are the most highly-developed form of team working. They are permanent structures in which team members collaboratively decide all the major issues affecting their work: work processes and schedules, task allocation, the selection and development of team members, the distribution of rewards and the management of group processes (problem solving, conflict management, internal discipline and so on).

The team leader is a member of the team, acting in the role of coach and facilitator: leadership roles may be shared or rotated as appropriate.

Self-managed teams generally have the following features (Harrington-Mackin, 1994).

(a) They contract with management to assume various degrees of **managerial responsibility** for planning, organising, directing and monitoring (which may increase as the team develops). Team members learn and share the jobs usually performed by a manager: no 'visible' immediate manager is present. They often report to 'absentee' managers with broad responsibilities for several functions, whose role is to act as integrators/facilitators.

(b) They perform **day-to-day planning and control functions**: scheduling and co-ordinating the daily and occasional tasks of the team and individuals; setting performance goals and standards; formulating and adopting budgets; collecting performance data and reviewing results.

(c) They perform **internal people management functions**: screening and interviewing candidates to join the team, and contributing to selection/hiring decisions; providing orientation for new members; coaching and providing feedback on member performance; designing and conducting cross-training on all tasks.

(d) Team members **cross-train** in all the tasks necessary for a particular process, and members rotate flexibly from job to job.

(e) **Weekly team meetings** are used to identify, analyse and solve task and relationship problems within the team: reviewing team working and progress; getting team members to research and present team issues and soon.

ACTIVITY 2 — 20 mins

What do you think are likely to be the advantages of self-managed team working for the organisation?

On a scale from 'no voice' through involvement and participation to full empowerment or democracy, where would you place the organisation you currently work for, or one you know well?

5 Employee communications – 'employee voice'

5.1 What is employee voice?

Unitary ideology. All members of the organisation, despite their different roles, have common objectives and values which unite their efforts. Workers are loyal, and the prerogative of management is accepted as paternal, and in everyone's best interests.

Pluralist ideology. Organisations are political coalitions of individuals and groups which have their own interests. Management has to create a workable structure for collaboration, taking into account the objectives of all the various interest groups or stakeholders in the organisation. A mutual survival strategy, involving the control of conflict through compromise, can be made acceptable in varying degrees to all concerned.

Armstrong (2009) summarises 'employee voice' as 'the say employees have in matters of concern to them in their organisation'. He suggests that this is closer to **participation** ('ensuring that employees are given the opportunity to influence management decisions and to contribute to the improvement of the organisation's performance') than to **involvement** (where 'management allows employees to discuss with it issues that affect them, but management retains the right to manage'). However, employee voice may be seen as a framework for both processes.

Employee voice is both an individual concept and a collective concept: it includes, for example, individual grievances and suggestions as well as collective bargaining and industrial democracy agreements made with trade unions and/or other employee representatives.

Marchington *et al* (2001) model the territory of employee voice as follows:

(a) Involvement may be **direct** (where management deal with individuals/teams) or **indirect** (where management deal with trade unions or other representative groups)

(b) Involvement may be based on a **shared agenda** (directed at improving organisational performance and the quality of working life) or on a **contested agenda** (directed at addressing areas of conflict, dissatisfaction or competition).

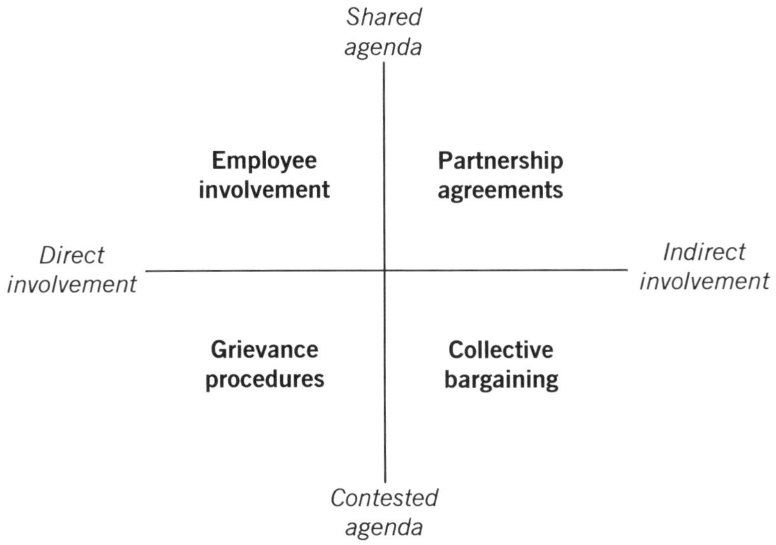

Figure 8.1: Employee voice matrix

In practice, an organisation's approach will be a mixture of direct and indirect, and focus on both shared and contested agendas (weighted according to whether HRM policies take a **pluralistic** or **unitarist** viewpoint). If there is an anti-union culture of management, the balance will shift towards direct involvement. If there is a co-operative or unitarist culture of management, the balance will shift towards shared agenda.

5.2 Purposes of employee voice

Marchington *et al* (2001) suggest that employee voice offers:

(a) The ability for individual employees to express dissatisfaction, solve problems with management and preserve working relationships

(b) The ability for employees collectively to express their needs and wishes in matters that affect them, providing a counterbalance to managerial power

(c) The ability for employees to contribute to management decisions, allowing the organisation to harness the expertise and commitment of workers to improve quality, productivity and work organisation

(d) The ability for employers and employees to demonstrate their intention to focus on shared goals, mutual interests and co-operative working relations, for the long-term benefit of the organisation and its people.

Employee voice thus involves both 'soft' HRM elements (fairness, relationship, mutual commitment) and 'hard' HRM elements (problem solving, conflict/grievance management and performance improvement).

5.2.1 Mechanisms of employee voice

Marchington *et al* (1992, 2001) classify the main approaches to implementing employee voice as 'representative participation' and 'upward problem-solving' (which is included among techniques for 'involvement').

(a) Representative participation includes:

   (i) **Collective representation**: grievance procedures, collective bargaining, collective dispute resolution and other settings in which trade unions, staff associations or elected employee representatives represent the interests of individual employees or groups of employees.

   (ii) **Joint consultation**: formal non-negotiatory meetings between management and employee representatives to discuss matters of shared interest or concern.

   (iii) **European Works Councils**: joint consultation machinery for organisations with sites in two or more member states of the European Union.

   (iv) **Partnership schemes**: formal agreements between management and employee representatives to work together for mutual benefit, in a non-adversarial climate.

(b) Upward problem solving includes:

   (i) **Two-way communication**: encouraging upward communication (from employees to management) as well as downward, e.g. through briefing groups, team meetings and corporate intranets.

   (ii) **Upward communication**: seeking employee feedback, opinions and suggestions, e.g. through attitude surveys, suggestion schemes and employee intranet discussion groups.

   (iii) **Project teams**: getting employees and management together to solve problems, discuss issues or generate ideas (e.g. quality circles, customer care task forces).

> 'What institution embodying the employee voice might be appropriate? Is it a trade union? A works council? Or should employee voice not be viewed any longer in terms of collective representation?' (Gennard & Judge, 2003)
>
> What do you think?

To make employee voice effective will often involve sharing information; it is interesting to note what Marchington (2008) has to say about sharing information.

1 Sharing information about financial performance, strategy and operational matters not only ensures that employees are informed and understand such matters; it also 'conveys a symbolic and substantive message that they are to be trusted and treated in an open and positive manner'.

2 For team working to be effective it requires the team members to have information available to them in order that they develop ideas and suggest improvements to increase organisational performance.

3 Through sharing information with employees and hearing their thoughts and responses, management can claim that the workforce has been involved in the process, which goes some way to validating the decisions made.

6 Employee development

6.1 Introduction

When considering the most effective ways in which to retain and engage employees, investing in employee development often promotes differing opinions:

For: Career development is a primary cause of people leaving, if people are to be encouraged to stay, investing in their development must be **visible**, otherwise ambitious individuals will look for other organisations that will provide this.

Against: Developing employees skills will make them **more sought after** in the market and enables them to apply for a greater diversity of roles. The investment is only to the benefit of the employee, whose salary demands can increase, and the new employer who recruits already-trained employees.

There is however very little of the research undertaken to indicate that employees who receive training are more likely to leave; the results suggest at best it encourages employees to stay and at worst it is a neutral factor in employees' considerations.

It is also worth considering the type of development that individuals value. Too often the employee expectation of development is being sent on a specific off-site course, preferably in a nice location. Today, cost and management thinking has changed regarding these considerations; today the focus is on cost and the direct applicability of skills, value in other words.

Organisations however need to make a decision as to whether to invest in employee development or not; in the next section will we consider the process that can be followed and options available.

6.2 Training programmes and learning plans

The options available fall into two categories: training and learning.

(a) **Training programmes** – a menu or 'core curriculum' of training initiatives. Examples (Hargreaves and Jarvis, 2000) include:

- Finance training for project managers
- Management skills for all management employees
- Presentation and interpersonal skills for trainers, interviewers and customer service staff
- Teambuilding and team working for all departments
- Basic health and safety training for all employees
- Intra-departmental seminars and in-house discussion groups.

(b) **Learning plans** – individual or team plans for accessing training courses/ resources and/or for taking advantage of learning opportunities at work. These may be more flexibly adapted to individual and team needs. Coaching, mentoring, reading and e-learning, for example, would not require formally designed programmes: learning targets, timescales and monitoring/ evaluation procedures would still need to be planned.

6.3 Type of learning

Learning experiences may be of different types, which will variously suit particular learning needs.

(a) **Formal and informal learning**

Formal learning often takes place **away from the work** setting, and involves techniques such as classroom teaching and instruction. It is driven by the teacher or trainer, often to a pre-set curriculum or agenda which may or may not be adapted to all members of the learning group. Transfer of learning may be difficult, although theorists may prefer this method.

Informal learning occurs **in the workplace**, in response to immediate, job-relevant needs. The learner essentially drives the process by asking questions and accessing opportunities for coaching, advice and instruction. Since it is largely unplanned, it may not systematically meet training needs.

However, some learners will find this method more relevant, more suited to their learning style and easier to apply in practice.

(b) **On-the-job and off-the-job learning**

On-the-job or workplace learning may use the workplace as a training environment (e.g. for briefings, demonstrations or site visits) or may use actual work processes and tasks as learning events. On-the-job training methods include: systematic job instruction; working with experienced colleagues or trainers; coaching or mentoring; and various guided challenges such as project or committee work.

Off-the-job learning methods include: formal taught or self-administered courses (e.g. by computer-based training); outdoor training; research assignments and so on.

(c) **Self-managed learning**

Individuals are encouraged to define their own learning objectives and create action plans (or Personal Development Plans) to meet them. Managers, mentors or trainers may jointly agree learning objectives, in the form of a **learning contract**. They may also guide the learner in accessing resources and learning opportunities, provide coaching, offer feedback as part of the evaluation process and so on.

(d) **Programmed learning**

The trainee works at his or her own pace through a carefully ordered sequence of learning modules and assessments. This is a feature of many distance learning and computer-based training programmes.

(e) **Blended learning**

Blended learning is a recognition that a mix of learning types, styles and technologies may be most effective in order to meet individual needs and learning preferences. This might be applied to a training course or programme: for example, using instruction on basic principles, group exercises for practice, e-learning for consolidation and coaching and mentoring for follow-up back in the workplace. Similarly, an individual's personal development plan might include a blend of reading, e-learning, experiential learning (using mentor feedback), coaching where required, and formal courses for certification.

ACTIVITY 3 — 20 mins

What methods of learning and training have you encountered in your job? What methods are you using now to study for your qualification? What do you think are the advantages and disadvantages of this 'blend' for you as a learner?

Training falls into two types: on–the-job and off-the-job.

7 On-the-job training and development

7.1 'Sitting with Nellie'

This is the traditional method of skill training. The trainee is placed beside an experienced worker (Nellie) and learns by observing her work and by imitating her operations and methods under close instruction and supervision, working with the actual materials and equipment that are involved in the job.

Advantages	Disadvantages
• High transfer of learning (because learning is in context) • Effective and economical (where the task is amenable to observation imitation) • Immediate feedback and adjustment • Establishes working relationships as well as skills	• Ineffective if 'Nellie' uses poor work technique, or the skill is not amenable to observation • Ineffective if 'Nellie' lacks training/instruction skills and the job requires explanation • Trainee is socialised into shop floor culture of work: not necessarily the methods or attitudes desired by management

7.2 Job instruction training

This is a technique which can be added to the 'sitting with Nellie' approach to minimise the disadvantages cited above. It was developed as a guide to systematic on-the-job training, involving:

(a) Careful selection and preparation of trainer/'Nellie' and trainee: goals and objectives of learning outlined etc

(b) Full explanation and demonstration of skill/task by the trainer/'Nellie'

(c) Trial on-the-job practice/performance by the trainee

(d) Thorough feedback session between trainer/'Nellie' and trainee to appraise and adjust trainee's performance and set further improvement goals. (Repeat (b) – (d) as required.)

7.3 Coaching

Coaching is one element of the 'sitting with Nellie' approach, but may be used flexibly in a wide range of training situations, and at any time during performance on an on-going basis. Coaching is on-the-job guidance, advice, correction and feedback-giving with a view to improving performance in specific skill areas. A coach should:

(a) Demonstrate how areas of a job are performed, and guide the trainee's own performance of the same tasks, by advice and correction

(b) Help the trainee to identify and resolve problems in his or her work

(c) Seek out or identify opportunities for the trainee to develop, through doing new things at work

(d) Give feedback on progress and results, to guide learning

(e) Encourage the trainee to assess his or her own progress and performance, and to formulate further plans for improvement in an ongoing cycle.

Essentially, coaching is a **collaboration** between the coach and the trainee, in which the coach's special role is encouragement and guidance as the trainee develops on the job.

Advantages	Disadvantages
• Flexible and interactive: the pace and content of learning can be suited to trainee needs and trainer analysis • Collaborative: involves trainee in problem solving • High transfer of learning (connected to live job performance)	• Requires coaching skills • Learning is limited to the abilities of the coach

Coaching is often associated with executive or accelerated development programmes. However it is possible for employees at all levels in an organisation to have a coach.

7.4 Mentoring

A **mentor** is a guide, ideally both more experienced and more powerful in the organisation, whose concern is the trainee's long-term personal development. The role is varied: counsellor, role model, champion/sponsor, spur to action or improvement, critical friend, encourager and so on.

While coaching is directed at short-term, skill-based development, mentoring is a longer-term relationship focused on broader career and personal development. A mentor should assist as follows.

(a) Help the trainee to greater self-awareness, by listening to, questioning and challenging his or her ideas, and feeding back on his or her behaviour.

(b) Help the trainee to formulate and clarify his or her needs and ambitions in life, and to identify where events and opportunities at work fit into those plans.

(c) Encourage the trainee to take responsibility for his or her development, while offering support – personally and within the organisation – if required.

(d) Help the trainee to reconcile his or her non-work needs, interests and circumstances with the demands of work (or vice versa).

(e) Help the trainee to plan specific development and career paths or directions, offering opportunities where appropriate and possible.

ACTIVITY 4 — 20 mins

Would you recommend coaching or mentoring for the following types of employees and why?

(a) Graduate trainee
(b) Newly promoted supervisor
(c) Employee put on the fast-track talent programme
(d) Newly appointed director

7.5 Action learning

Action learning is described (Pedler *et al,* 2003) as a method for individual and organisational development in which 'working in small groups, people tackle important organisational issues or problems and learn from their attempts to change things'.

The key elements of action learning programmes are as follows.

(a) A small group of four or five people (usually managers) meet together regularly, on a wholly voluntary basis, for the programme period (perhaps several months).

(b) Each participant brings a managerial or organisational problem they want to deal with.

(c) Group members support and learn from one another, acting as a mentoring, consulting and problem-solving network. (An external advisor may sit in and facilitate.)

(d) The group both generates and examines options in response to member issues/problems *and* learns about the interpersonal and managerial processes involved as they do so.

(e) Group members take action – and the group learns further from feedback on that action (in a learning cycle).

Pedlar *et al* note that many project teams, self-help groups, productivity improvement meetings and quality circles offer action learning processes.

So far we have looked at ways in which employees can acquire and improve skills in a particular job or task through guided imitation and practice. A slightly different approach is to give employees a 'taste' of different jobs and functions. This is still development and demonstrates the organisation investing in them.

7.6 Training by switching or 'shadowing ' roles

This may be accomplished by a number of methods.

(a) **Job rotation** or **'shadowing'**: the trainee is given several jobs in succession, to gain experience of a wide range of activities and departments. (Even experienced managers may rotate their jobs to gain wider experience; this method is commonly applied in the Civil Service.)

(b) **Temporary promotion:** an individual is promoted into a superior's position while the superior is absent. This gives the individual a chance to experience the demands of a more senior position.

(c) **'Assistant to' positions:** an individual with management potential may be appointed as assistant to a manager. In this way, the individual gains experience of management, without a risky level of responsibility.

(d) **Project or committee work:** trainees might be included in the membership of a project team or committee, to obtain an understanding of interdepartmental relationships, problem solving and particular areas of the organisation's activity.

(e) **Assignments:** trainees may be delegated to a particular task or project by a superior.

Advantages	Disadvantages
• Employees gain experience without risking immediate responsibility • Task/role variety may increase job satisfaction and awareness of organisational processes • Aids career/management/succession planning	• May be perceived as perpetual traineeship: not real work • May be perceived as a 'nuisance' in departments having to 'carry' trainees

7.7 Advantages and disadvantages of on-the-job training and development

On-the-job training is very common, especially when the work involved is not complex, but will only be successful under the following circumstances.

(a) **Assignments must have a specific purpose** from which the trainee can learn and gain experience; otherwise, it can be unfocused and overwhelming.

(b) **It works best where the trainee is a practical type,** who prefers to learn by doing and can tolerate the process of trial and error.

(c) **Trainers are themselves trained** in instruction and coaching techniques (as well as modelling efficient and effective work practices).

(d) **The organisation is tolerant of mistakes.** Mistakes are an inevitable part of on-the-job learning, and if they are punished or frowned on, the trainee will be reluctant to take further risks and will be de-motivated to learn.

There may be real risks involved in throwing people in at the deep-end: the cost of mistakes or inefficiencies may be high and the pressure on learners great. (Would you want medical procedures, or air traffic control procedures to be learned on-the-job?)

The key **advantage** of on-the-job training, however, is that it takes place in the environment of the job itself, and in the context of the work group in which the trainee will have to operate. The style of supervision, personal relations with colleagues, working conditions and pressures, the culture of the office/shop floor and so on will be absorbed as part of the training process.

ACTIVITY 5 — 20 mins

Using your work experience, list the advantages of on-the-job training as they applied to you.

7.8 Self-development approaches

There are various methods for self development.

(a) **Personal Development Plans** and **learning contracts** formulated with line managers or mentors: formal commitment to work towards specified learning goals, with action plans.

(b) **Personal Development Journals** or **learning logs**: a structured approach to the learning cycle. The learner selects a critical incident at work which illustrates a learning need: (s)he describes what happened, reflects on the event and its consequences, draws conclusions, and identifies future actions to reinforce successful behaviours and/or change unsuccessful behaviours.

(c) **Self-development groups**: groups which meet to discuss personal development and work issues, give each other feedback and information and so on – like a flexible action learning group.

8 Off-the-job training and development

8.1 Training providers

Off-the-job training providers include:

(a) Universities and colleges

(b) Private-sector colleges and training organisations, including assessment centres for group training exercises, and on-line or e-learning providers

(c) Training consultancies, which may help the organisation locate or develop courses to meet its needs

(d) Publishers of training materials (texts and workbooks, videos, computer-based training packages)

(e) The in-house education and training department of the organisation itself (in large organisations).

Internal courses are sometimes run by the training departments of larger organisations. Skills may be taught at a technical level, related to the organisation's particular product and market, or to aspects such as marketing, teambuilding, interviewing or information technology management. Some organisations also encourage the wider development of staff by offering opportunities to learn languages or other skills.

One convenient and popular method of in-house education is **computer-based training** (CBT), **Interactive Video** (IV) or **e-learning** (Internet-based) using equipment in offices or even trainees' homes. Training programmes may be developed by the organisation or by outside consultants – or bought 'off the shelf': the software (or 'courseware') can then be distributed, so that large numbers of dispersed staff can learn about new products or procedures quickly and simultaneously.

8.2 Training methods

Some methods of off-the-job training include the following.

(a) **Training room instruction.** Similar to on-the-job instruction training, but in a dedicated training environment. Instruction is given using presentation techniques and/or a simulation of workplace equipment and methods.

(b) **Lectures** or **taught classes.** These are useful for knowledge or theory/principle-based learning. They may incorporate elements of instruction, case-study, role-play and other techniques to overcome the limitations of passive learning. They suit large numbers of trainees requiring the same basic body of knowledge. Drawbacks include their passivity and the difficulty of absorbing more than three or four key points per session, and their relative inflexibility to individual trainees' learning styles and needs.

(c) **Case study**. Using a description of a real-life scenario or example for analysis, providing insights and opportunities to exercise problem-solving skills, which can be transferred to the work context. Case studies are a kind of on-paper simulation of work scenarios, allowing experimentation and exploration without risk. They are particularly useful for problem solving and decision making in a wide range of specific contexts.

(d) **Role play.** The simulation of an interpersonal scenario, allowing trainees to experiment with learned behaviours and skills and to observe their effects in interpersonal encounters. This is particularly helpful in training for customer service, interviewing, conflict resolution and so on. It suits small groups, allowing for all-member participation.

(e) **Simulation.** In technical training, this may involve the mocking-up of equipment and environments so that trainees can experiment with technical skills and observe results in a safe, progressively-staged and controlled manner. (Flight simulators for pilots is one example.) In other forms of training, simulation may involve case studies, role plays, assignments of 'intray' exercises, which mock up typical tasks and scenarios to test trainees' organisational and problem-solving skills.

(f) **Open** or **distance learning.** Employees access technology-assisted instruction where and when it suits them, using training manuals, workbooks, video (and video conferencing for group sessions), tapes, computer-based packages and so on. Some face-to-face tuition may be used periodically to assess or reinforce learning, or to add more interactive and group work. This can be a highly economical method, especially where trainees are geographically dispersed.

(g) **Discovery learning.** A method by which trainees explore a task or concept for themselves, with relatively little initial instruction or demonstration. Trainees are thus encouraged to find out the key principles, constraints and methods of the task, and to ask the questions that are relevant to them. This is a highly trainee-centred technique which is tailored to the learning styles and needs of the trainees and fosters problem-solving and learning skills alongside specific technical competencies. It is, however, time-, labour– and cost-intensive.

(h) **Programmed learning.** A structure of learning by which a trainee, working at his or her own pace, works through a carefully ordered sequence of units or operations, each with objectives, instruction, testing and consolidation which allow the trainee to master one unit before progressing to the next. This is a feature of many distance learning and computer-based learning programmes.

(i) **Visits and tours**. Trainees are given opportunities to observe other sites, departments, operations and so on. This may be helpful in demonstrating: how skills learned in the classroom are applied in practice; different types of machinery and work organisation; stages of operation before and after that in which the trainee will be involved; application of products/services by customers or end users; and so on.

(j) **Outdoor training**. Physical tasks and activities in challenging environments, designed to help trainees learn about themselves and their motivations, leadership skills, group dynamics and co-operation and so on. This is increasingly used in team-building and leadership training. Another growth area is corporate social responsibility (Allen, 2003), with teams being sent to renovate inner-city residential hostels and similar experiences, to encourage awareness of the wider community's needs. Learning takes place through the process of working out a group solution to a problem or challenge, with a facilitator aiding reflection and analysis afterwards. Outdoor training specialists are increasingly looking to target their offering more accurately, keeping courses short and making sure that they are useful (and clear) metaphors for the workplace.

(k) **Computer-based training.** Using computer software for instruction and assessment

(l) **E-learning**: learning or training delivered by electronic technology, particularly ICT developments such as the Internet and company intranets – in support of (rather than instead of) traditional training methods.

ACTIVITY 6 — 20 mins

Suggest a suitable training method for each of the following situations.

(a) A worker is transferred onto a new machine and needs to learn its operation.

(b) An accounts clerk wishes to work towards becoming qualified with the relevant professional body.

(c) An organisation decides that its supervisors would benefit from 'picking up some ideas' on participative management and democratic leadership.

(d) A new member of staff is about to join the organisation.

(e) A supervisor allows himself to be intimidated by his work team and ends up carrying most of the workload himself. Occasionally, he tries to throw his weight around, but this never lasts.

8.3 Advantages and disadvantages of off-the-job training

Advantages	Disadvantages
• It allows exploration and experimentation by inexperienced employees without risking negative consequences for live performance.	• If the subject matter of the training course is not felt to relate directly to the individual's job and organisation culture, the learning will not be applied afterwards, and will quickly be forgotten.
• It allows trainees to be away from the work environment where interruptions, distractions and performance pressure may interfere with learning.	• Individuals may feel that courses are, in general, a waste of time. They will not benefit from the training unless they are motivated to learn.
• It allows training to be standardised and distributed across a geographically dispersed workforce (eg via video, CBT or distance learning).	• Immediate and relevant feedback on performance and progress may not be available from the learning process, especially if knowledge is tested by unrealistic methods (such as exams) or at wide intervals. This will lower the learner's incentive and sense of direction.
• It allows for self-study at the trainee's own pace (e.g. via distance learning).	• It does not suit some people, who may not have much experience of (or taste for) classroom learning since school. Some people simply prefer a 'hands-on' type of learning: learning by doing.
• It may have organisational status as a reward or peak: being sent on a course is a sign of potential.	• Some organisational cultures encourage fear and insecurity around training courses, with the perception that a person sent on a course must be performing inadequately.

8.4 E-learning

Armstrong (2003) calls e-learning 'perhaps the most important recent development in approaches to the delivery and support of learning'. Surveys suggest that it is showing fast growth worldwide, with the UK becoming a major European market.

E-learning is: 'Learning that is delivered, enabled or mediated by electronic technology for the explicit purposes of training in organisations. It does not include stand-alone technology-based training such as the use of CD-ROMs in isolation.' (CIPD)

This places e-learning firmly in the context of ICT networks, including:

(a) Networked computers forming a corporate intranet
(b) The Internet and World Wide Web.

E-learning systems typically include:

(a) **Software packages** – purchased 'off-the-shelf' from providers, or designed and developed in-house – which provide e-learning programmes and facilities: course content, navigation tools, interactive testing and feedback mechanisms and so on

(b) **Learning support** from online tutors and/or 'e-moderators', who track participation, co-ordinate information-sharing and interactions with other learners (discussion boards, chat sessions, student blogs, web seminars and so on) and provide guidance as appropriate.

In addition, **informal e-learning** may take place through everyday information-sharing and interaction over the Internet or intranet in the course of work.

Advantages	Disadvantages
• Learning at the learner's pace and convenience • Flexible delivery, with access from home, work, libraries etc • Reduction in delivery costs • Potential for collaborative learning in 'virtual learning groups' for employees (and others) spread over wide geographical distances: chat, web conferencing and other technologies allow real time support and interaction • High degree of interactivity, for immediate feedback (e.g. test scoring), question and answer and so on • Potential for multi-media, high-interest presentation of learning material (not just 'e-reading') for enhanced learning motivation	• The need for Internet or network connection, which may not be available to all employees – and may be complex and expensive to set up • The need for culture and attitude change to support e-learning, since it represents (for many people) a radically new way to work and learn • The poor quality or relevance of some off-the-shelf e-learning programmes • Limitations in the applications for which e-learning is suited, notably in the area of interpersonal skills. Over-reliance on e-learning alone has led to disappointed expectations

Applications of e-learning

There are several areas in which e-learning might be particularly appropriate, because there are easily identifiable knowledge/learning needs which can be effectively met by electronic means.

(a) **Training in IT skills**. Learners can be led through relevant programmes, shown what to do, given opportunities to practise, tested and given competence feedback and records with little need for interpersonal or face-to-face support. Online support usually takes the form of e-mail contact and response.

(b) **Information/awareness-based learning**: induction briefings, health and safety awareness programmes, job-related information briefings/updates, new product/service information, company policy/rule changes and so on. E-learning does information transfer efficiently and with potential for greater creativity, interest and user-friendliness than oral briefings or printed manuals.

9 Measuring engagement

Most employee engagement measurement has focused on statistical analysis of the workforce. One such analysis identified correlation between traits and performance, for example 'ability to take initiative' is a better predictor for high performance than academic record. However some organisations claimed to have refined this to identifying that a 0.1% increase in engagement among employees at a particular store is worth more than $100,000 in the store's annual operating income.

In a similar fashion, the Sunday Times Best Companies to Work for survey asks employees to evaluate their employer across eight predetermined categories. Whilst the survey endeavours to ensure that organisations that are credited as a 'Best Company' are not about to embark on redundancy programmes, the organisation's financial health or delivery excellence are not taken into consideration. Consequently the survey is not attempting to establish a link between employee satisfaction and performance, but simply identify employee happiness. Whilst there may be a link between employee engagement and organisational performance, and indeed this study text has made many references to such links, the survey providers do not claim to have identified any points of cause and effect. The study looks at:

1 **Leadership** How employees feel about the head of the company and its senior managers

2 **Wellbeing** How staff feel about stress, pressure and the balance between their work and home duties

3 **Giving back** How much companies are thought by their staff to put back into society in general and the local community in particular

4 **Personal growth** To what extent staff feel they are stretched and challenged by their job

5 **My manager** How staff feel towards their immediate boss and day-to-day managers

6 **My company** Feelings about the company people work for as opposed to the people they work with

7 **My team** How staff feel about their immediate colleagues

8 **Fair deal** Ranks how happy the workforce is with their pay and benefits

Do you know an organisation that has won an award for being an exemplary employer? In your mind did they deserve it, if yes, why?

Share with your study group or friend that you know and understand why some employers are able to be better employers.

In a report by Davenport *et al* the authors identified different types of data that were used to analyse the people in an organisation.

1 Whilst 'hard HR data' e.g. headcount, attrition and recruitment is typically used by many organisations, some expanded their measurement. They also included the answers to particular questions in their employees surveys to assess how employees were engaged with their employer. This idea is similar to the 12 Questions tool discussed at the beginning of this Chapter.

2 Another option is cause and effect statistics: one of the organisations in the study identified that its most successful business units, measured by revenue, costs, employee attrition and customer loyalty, were more densely populated with highly satisfied employees. It was able to identify the actions that line managers were able to take with employees to increase their satisfaction. The targeted action reduced employee attrition by 20% over a 6-year period.

3 The next data type was the answer to the question 'what keeps employees here?', the example from one high-profile IT company was: the vision, the quality of the people and the chance to develop skills.

Using the knowledge of what keeps people in the organisation, the organisation is then able to tailor its initiatives to more accurately resonate with the workforce. The idea is not markedly different from the argument that flexible benefit schemes enable employee to tailor their benefits to their own need at a particular time, rather than being subject to a 'one solution for all' provision. However in this instance the interventions could be the provision of tailored training to assist employees who were not performing to the maximum of their ability

The authors noted that to be successful required supportive senior management, an acceptance that the data was never going to be complete or provide a perfect indicator, and a willingness and commitment to implement an action plan.

Adapted from Davenport *et al* (2010) in the Harvard Business Review

SUNDAY TIMES BEST COMPANY MID COMPANY PARTICIPANT

St Ann's Hospice.

The hospice aims to improve the quality of life for people with life-threatening illnesses while supporting their families and carers. Having a job that matters in a broader sense than just paying the bills motivates 88% of staff, who say the organisation they work for makes a positive difference to the world (the top score for this among all 100 best companies), while 85% feel their contribution to its success is valuable (and the second-best score here). Staff respect and get on with each other, united by their common aim of caring. "We're all working to the same goal," says in-patient services manager Sue Taylor, "We're fortunate as an organisation that we don't have diametrically opposed views. We're supported by a vast array of volunteers and administrative staff, who all share the same goal." Teams score high marks across the board: 82% claim team-mates go out of their way to be helpful and 87% that they have confidence in their team-mates' abilities

Chapter Roundup

- For organisations to understand their employee attrition they need to conduct systematic analysis.
- Employee engagement offers the prospect of productivity, customer satisfaction and lower employee attrition.
- High Performance Working is the achievement of higher levels of organisational performance achieved through installing a combination of human resources practices that in combination drive greater levels of achievement.
- The role of the line manager has been brought to the fore in Human Resources Management practices and they are a key factor in driving employee commitment.
- Employee communications are a key factor, including both upwards and downwards communications, financial awareness and participation.
- Employee Voice is a method of enabling employees to voice opinions and contribute to decision making in an organisation, this is typically achieved through employee bodies e.g. employee forums, formal non-negotiation mechanisms, works councils and partnership schemes.
- Employee development is the third factor for creating greater engagement; this can involve on and off the job training, learning programmes and e-learning.

Quick Quiz

1. Name two ways an organisation can conduct an attitude survey
2. What is another way of expressing moral commitment?
3. In the CIPD 2011 survey what is considered the most effective method of addressing staff retention?
4. The responsibility of line managers for delivering HR outcomes is a distinctive feature of Human Resource Management. True or false?
5. Identify two of the ways to get employees involved as described by Guest
6. What are the two key aspects to empowerment?
7. What is the role of the team leader in self-managed teams?
8. Name two types of learning
9. Identify two disadvantages of coaching
10. Name three methods that can deliver training by switching or shadowing roles

Answers to Quick Quiz

1 Questionnaires & interviews (para 1.1)

2 Normative (para 2.3)

3 Increased learning and development opportunities – 34% (para 2.4)

4 True (para 3)

5 You could have chosen from:

By improving the provision of information to employees
By changing the structure and arrangement of work
By changing relationships, through more participative leadership and informality. (para 4.1)

6 Gives workers discretion to make decisions about how to organise work *and* making workers responsible for achieving production and quality targets (para 4.4)

7 Acting in the role of coach and facilitator (para 4.5)

8 You could have chosen from formal and informal; on-the-job and off-the-job; self-managed; programmed; blended (para 6.3)

9 Requires coaching skills and learning is limited to the abilities of the coach (para 7.3)

10 You could have chosen from job rotation; temporary promotion; 'assistant to' positions; project or committee work; assignments (para 7.6)

Answers to Activities

Activity 1

Nigel Nicholson (*Financial Times*, January 1993) gave the following answers (briefly summarised).

(a) How do managers know if their reading of opinions is correct?

(b) Yes, they are no substitute for good personal communications, but' Thanks for asking us' is a common response.

(c) Cans of worms probably should be opened. 'Management's commitment, clearly communicated at the outset, should be not only to take action where feasible, but also to be frank about reasons for not acting when this would be unreasonably difficult, contentious or costly.

(d) Bias is modest when return rates of over 50% are achieved, and a well-designed and carefully introduced survey can expect returns of 65% or more.

Activity 2

Self-managed team working is said to have advantages in:

- Savings in managerial costs
- Gains in quality and productivity, by harnessing the commitment of those who perform work
- Encouraging individual initiative and responsibility, enhancing organisational responsiveness (particularly in front-line customer service units)
- Gains in efficiency, through multi-skilling, the involvement of fewer functions in decision-making and co-ordinating work, and (often) the streamlining of working methods by groups.

However, self-managed teams are a comparatively recent (and rare) phenomenon, and require skilled leadership and culture change (particularly in former 'command and control' organisations) in order to be effective.

Activity 3

Your own experience. Note particularly how the *blend* of approaches gives you variety, suits your learning style and so on. Disadvantages may include inconsistent messages, extra time/cost and so on.

Activity 4

Every individual and every situation needs to be assessed and evaluated before a decision can be made as to whether a coach or mentor is the correct choice. However on a general level, the following would probably be correct:

(a) Graduate trainee may need both. The graduate trainee will need instruction in both how to undertake tasks and manage their day-to-day duties. These will be very practical and hands-on, hence the need for a coach. A graduate trainee however has often been recruited as future talent within the organisation and so they need to manage their assignments and progress through the organisation carefully. This advice would best come from a mentor who can discuss career progression etc in detached manner and not whilst involved in the day-to-day duties of managing a department.

(b) Newly promoted supervisor will need a coach. This person would benefit most from a coach, they need to learn the skills and requirements both of managing a team and the duties that are part of the role.

(c) The employee put on the fast-track talent programme needs a mentor. The purpose of putting an employee on a fast track programme is to enable them to progress up through the organisation quicker. Whilst they need to learn new skills and competences the primary focus is to help them navigate their way around the organisation. An experienced senior manager who knows the organisation and help the employee manage their own progress.

(d) Newly appointed director will need a mentor. Whilst everyone continues to learn and develop, someone at director level is assumed to have the skills necessary to do the job. They need assistance on how to manage their way around the organisation, engage key stakeholders and manage their own behaviour. They need a mentor although it maybe more advisable that the mentor is external to the organisation and so is able to observe the issues from a detached perspective and so only able to facilitate the director's learning rather becoming directly involved.

Activity 5

This answer is personal to you.

Activity 6

Training methods for the various workers indicated are as follows.

(a) Worker on a new machine: on-the-job training, coaching.

(b) Accounts clerk working for professional qualification: external course – evening class or day-release.

(c) Supervisors wishing to benefit from participative management and democratic leadership: internal or external seminar, or group training exercise. Careful attention will need to be given to how these 'ideas' will be integrated into practice on the job.

(d) New staff: induction training.

(e) Intimidated supervisor: assertiveness training.

Chapter 9

Performance management

As we have explored in detail during the previous chapters, organisations can expend large amounts of time and resources ensuring the correct people are selected to join the organisation. However, it cannot be assumed that simply because someone interviewed well and received satisfactorily test scores that they are the right person for the job. Once in place their performance needs to be monitored and a decision taken as to whether the right choice was made. However performance management is not limited to the initial period of employment: it should be woven into the fabric of how people are managed. Previously in this study text we have considered the need for organisations to monitor their own performance, this principle applies equally to the individuals within it.

Assessing performance brings us to the topic of performance management. In this chapter we will review how performance can be assessed and what to do if the individual is not performing as expected or required. Employees can also respond to a poor selection choice through their own actions. In this chapter we will also focus on absence: the types, causes and remedies.

1 Performance management

1.1 What is performance management?

Performance management is an approach in which there is a dual emphasis: on setting key accountabilities, objectives, measures, priorities and time scales for the following review period *and* monitoring, appraising and adjusting performance on an on-going basis.

Torrington *et al* (2002) summarise a typical performance management system as follows:

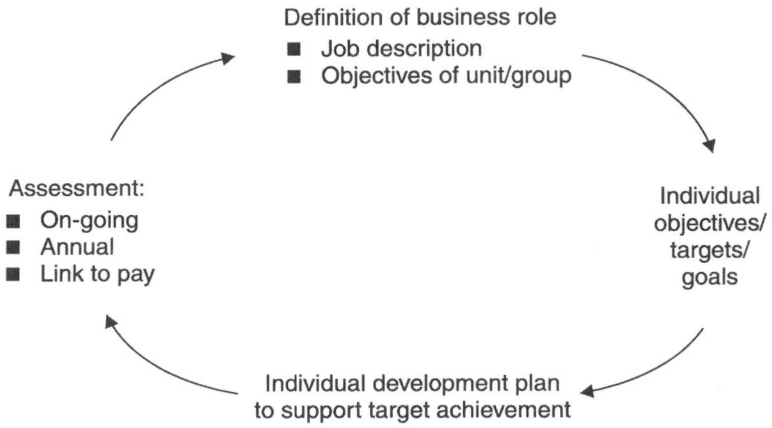

Figure 9.1: Typical performance management system

1.1.1 What performance management is not

(a) It is not another name for a discipline-based approach for managing poor performance among individual employees and taking remedial action to bring the employee's performance up to the expected standard.

(b) It is not another name for 'performance appraisal'. Properly conceived, performance appraisal is an essential component of performance management, but it is only a part and not the whole thing. Another way of putting it is that appraisal is essential to effective performance management, but performance management isn't essential to performance appraisal (especially if the appraisal system is principally geared to the personal development of the person being appraised).

1.2 Why performance management?

There are a number of advantages to a performance management orientation.

(a) Objective-setting gives employees the security and satisfaction of both understanding their jobs and knowing exactly what is expected of them. (A report by the Audit Commission, entitled '*Calling the Tune*', showed that local authorities who operated a comprehensive performance management system scored highly in staff attitude surveys on 'know how' and 'feel good' factors. In other words, objective-setting and appraisal help staff to feel that they understand more about their work, and 'feel good' about it.)

(b) Joint-objective setting and a developmental approach are positive and participatory, encouraging regular and frequent dialogue, a shared results focus; helping employees to own and commit to change and improvement.

(c) Performance management focuses on future performance planning and improvement rather than retrospective performance appraisal, so it contributes to an output, customer flexibility and continuous improvement focus.

However, it should also be noted that such a system depends on the integration of goal-setting, development planning, appraisal and reward planning activities – and this appears (Torrington *et al*, 2002) not to be widespread in organisations using it. Performance management is also not immune to the problems of appraisal: inconsistent use of ratings, appraiser bias, lack of training for line managers implementing the scheme and so on.

1.3 The use of goals and objectives

An understanding of the organisation's strategy is invaluable for setting and controlling the overall functioning and progress of the organisation. However, it is possible for an organisation to operate reasonably effectively even if most of the people within it have only an intuitive or vague understanding of its purpose. Most individual's work is defined in terms of far more specific and immediate things to be achieved: if these things are related in some way to the wider purpose, the organisation will function. Loosely speaking, these 'things to be achieved' are the goals, objectives and targets of the various departments, offices, and individuals that make up the organisation. In more effective organisations, goal congruence will be achieved: all these disparate goals, objectives and targets will be consistent with one another and will operate together to support progress with the mission.

Goals can be related in several ways:

- Hierarchically, as in the pyramid structure
- Functionally, as when colleagues collaborate on a project
- Logistically, as when resources must be shared or used in sequence and in wider organisational senses, as when senior management make decisions about their operational priorities.

A good example of the last category is the tension between long- and short-term priorities in such matters as the need to contain costs while at the same time increasing productivity by investing in improved plant.

A hierarchy of objectives

A simple model of the relationship between the various goals, objectives and targets is a pyramid analogous to the traditional organisational hierarchy. At the top is the overall mission; this is supported by a small number of wide-ranging goals, which may correspond to overall departmental or functional responsibilities. For a business, a primary, corporate objective will be the return offered to shareholders, however this is measured. There may be other primary objectives and there will certainly be supporting objectives for costs, innovation, markets, products and so on.

Each of the high-level goals is supported in turn by more detailed, subordinate goals. These may correspond, perhaps, to the responsibilities of the senior managers in the function concerned. The pattern is continued downwards until we reach the work targets of individual members of the organisation.

We owe the concept of a hierarchy or cascade of objectives to the great management thinker and writer Peter Drucker, who outlined the system now known as management by objectives (MbO) in the middle of the twentieth century. MbO is still in use as a management tool, though no longer promoted as a universal solution. Its importance for this discussion of goals and objectives is that Drucker was the first to suggest that objectives should be SMART. This acronym originally stood for the qualities listed below.

Specific **M**easurable **A**chievable **R**ealistic **T**ime-related

Today, *realistic* is often replaced with *results-focused*, for two reasons.

(a) The pursuit of innovation as a route to competitive advantage makes it very important that managerial attention is directed towards **achieving results** rather than just **administering established processes**.

(b) Realistic means much the same thing as achievable, anyway.

There are other variants: *achievable* may be replaced with *attainable*, which has an almost identical meaning, and *relevant* (meaning appropriate to the group or individual concerned) has been proposed as a third option for *R*.

Finally the SMART objective can have a 'Stretch' aspect to it. The idea behind this is that the SMART objective describes what needs to done to achieve satisfactory performance. To answer the question 'what does exceptional performance look like?' an additional Stretch version is created. Achieving Stretch performance would often be accompanied by a greater reward.

1.4 Performance management activities

There are four key performance management activities.

- Preparation of performance agreements
- Preparation of performance and development plans
- Management of performance throughout the year
- Performance reviews

Preparation of performance agreements or contracts

These set out individual or team objectives; how performance will be measured; the knowledge, skills and behaviour needed to achieve the objectives; and the organisation's core values.

Objectives may be either:

(a) Work/operational (results to be achieved or contribution to be made to the accomplishment of team, departmental and/or organisational objectives) or

(b) Developmental (personal or learning objectives).

Objectives and their wider role in the organisation are discussed further below.

Performance measures should be objective and capable of being assessed: relevant data should be readily available. They should relate to results (not to effort) and those results should be within the individual's control.

Some typical areas for the setting of performance targets are listed below.

(a) Sales (for sales representatives)

(b) Growth in turnover, profitability or shareholder value (for the most senior executives)

(c) Waiting times (for hospital executives)

(d) Pass rates (for teachers and lecturers)

(e) Punctuality and attendance (for junior workers)

Discussions should ensure that individuals fully understand what is expected of them and that if they fulfil those expectations they will be regarded as having performed well.

Preparation of performance and development plans

These set out detailed performance and personal development needs, and action plans to address them, in order to meet individual objectives.

Management of performance throughout the year

This involves the continuous process of providing feedback on performance, conducting informal progress reviews and dealing with performance problems as necessary. This may include the planning and implementation of:

(a) Learning, coaching or training interventions, to address competence gaps or other shortfalls (or opportunities)

(b) Disciplinary action, to improve individual behaviours and attitudes

(c) Counselling interventions, to guide individuals in defining and solving problems

(d) Managerial intervention to improve resources, systems, work organisation or other barriers to performance.

It is worth noting that 'performance management' has become associated with the management of 'problem' performers and situations: disciplinary and performance counselling interventions and so on. We will discuss these in the following sections of this chapter – but there is also a strong overlap with the topic of 'employee welfare', since performance problems may be caused by the illness, stress or difficulties of an employee.

Performance reviews

Performance reviews involve both taking a view of an individual's progress to date *and* reaching an agreement about what should be done in the future. The performance review provides the means by which:

(a) Results can be **measured** against targets
(b) The employee can be given **feedback**
(c) An **agreement can be reached** on on-going development needs and future performance targets.

2 The purpose of appraisal

Performance appraisal is the process whereby an individual's performance is reviewed against previously agreed goals, and whereby new goals are agreed which will develop the individual and improve performance over the forthcoming review period.

2.1 Role of performance appraisal

Monitoring and evaluating the performance of individuals and groups is an essential part of human resource management. It has several key aims.

(a) To identify individuals' learning/development and performance improvement needs.

(b) To identify problems or barriers to performance which require intervention.

(c) To identify people with potential for future promotion, supporting succession planning.

(d) To provide a basis for reward decisions: eligibility for results-related bonuses, competence-related increments, merit awards and so on.

(e) To improve communication about work issues, performance and development opportunities between managers and team members.

Armstrong (2003) describes the purpose of performance management as follows.

Performance management is a means of getting better results from the organisation, teams and individuals by understanding and managing performance within an agreed framework of planned goals, standards and competence requirements. It is a process for establishing shared understanding about what is to be achieved, and an approach to managing and developing people in a way which increases the probability that it will be achieved in the short and long term. It is owned and driven by line management

How is this different from performance appraisal?

Some of these purposes conflict with each other: for instance, if the principal purpose of a given system is to justify the payment of performance bonuses and other financial rewards, then it is not possible for the same system to be used as a platform for the personal development of the person appraised. If appraisees know that the appraisal process will determine their remuneration levels, they are not going to take part constructively in any dispassionate review of their strengths and weaknesses.

2.2 Why have a formal appraisal system?

It must be recognised that, if no system of formal appraisal is in place:

(a) Managers may obtain random impressions of subordinates' performance (perhaps from their more noticeable successes and failures), but not a coherent, complete and objective picture

(b) Managers may have a fair idea of their subordinates' shortcomings – but may not have devoted time and attention to the matter of improvement and development

(c) Different managers may be applying a different set of criteria, and varying standards of objectivity and judgement, undermining the value and credibility of appraisal

(d) Managers rarely give their subordinates systematic or constructive feedback on their performance.

Common practice is to provide for formal appraisal at least annually. Appraisal at six-monthly intervals is not unusual. It will be normal for supervision to be closer and appraisal more frequent during the initial phase of employment, especially where satisfactory completion of a period of probation is required.

ACTIVITY 1 — 15 mins

List four disadvantages to the employee of not having an appraisal system.

2.3 The systematic approach to appraisal

A typical appraisal system would involve:

(a) Identification of **criteria** for assessment

(b) The preparation of an **appraisal report**

(c) An **appraisal interview**, for an exchange of views about the results of the assessment, targets for improvement, solutions to problems and so on

(d) The preparation and implementation of **action plans** to achieve improvements and changes agreed

(e) **Follow-up:** monitoring the progress of the action plan.

3 Appraisal procedures and techniques

3.1 What should be monitored and assessed?

Assessments must be related to a common set of standards, so that comparisons can be made between individuals. On the other hand, they should be related to meaningful and specific performance criteria, which take account of the critical variables in each job.

Personal qualities like reliability or outgoingness have often been used as criteria for assessing people. However, they are not necessarily relevant to job performance: you can be naturally outgoing, but still not good at communicating with customers, if your product knowledge or attitude is poor. Also, personality judgements are notoriously vague and unreliable: words like 'loyalty' and 'ambition' are full of ambiguity and moral connotations.

In practical terms, this has encouraged the use of **competence or results-based appraisals**, where performance is measured against specific, job-related performance criteria.

Most large organisations have pre-printed assessment forms setting out all the relevant criteria and the range of possible judgements. (We reproduce such a form overleaf.) Even so, a manager should critically evaluate such schemes to ensure that the criteria for assessment are relevant to his or her team and task – and that they remain so over time, as the team and task change.

Relevant criteria for assessment might be based on the following.

(a) **Job, role or competence descriptions** as a guide to what competences, responsibilities and results might be monitored and assessed.

(b) **Departmental or team plans, performance standards and targets**. If the plan specifies completion of a certain number of tasks, or production of a certain number of units, to a particular quality standard, assessment can be focused on whether (or how far) those targets have been achieved.

(c) **Individually negotiated goals and standards** for performance and/or improvement. This is a feature of 'performance management', discussed in Section 3 of this Chapter.

Let us now look at some of the performance monitoring and reporting methods used in organisations.

3.2 Reporting methods

Overall assessment

The manager writes in narrative form his or her judgements about the appraisee. There will be no guaranteed consistency of the criteria and areas of assessment, and managers may not be able to convey clear, effective judgements in writing.

Guided assessment

Assessors are required to comment on a number of specified characteristics and performance elements, with guidelines as to how terms such as 'application', 'integrity' and 'adaptability' are to be interpreted in the work context. This is a more precise, but still rather vague method.

Grading

Grading adds a comparative frame of reference to the general guidelines, whereby managers are asked to select one of a number of defined levels or degrees to which an individual displays a given characteristic. These are also known as rating scales, and have been much used in standard appraisal forms.

Numerical values may be added to gradings to give rating scores. Alternatively a less precise graphic scale may be used to indicate general position on a plus/minus scale, as shown here.

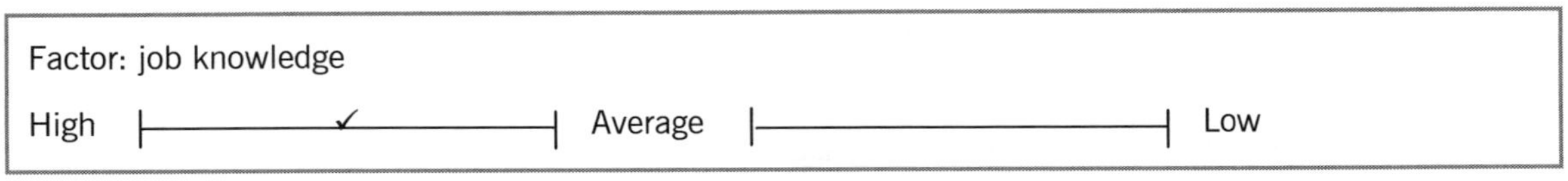

Figure 9.2: Graphic scale

Personnel Appraisal: Employees in Salary Grades 5-8

Date of review	Time in position Yrs Mths	S.G.	Age Yrs	Name
Period of Review	Position Title			Area

Important : Read guidance notes carefully before proceeding with the following sections

Section One	N/A	U	M	SP	E	O	Section Two	1	2	3	4	5
Performance Factors							Personal Characteristics					
Administrative Skills							Initiative					
Communications - Written							Persistence					
Communications - Oral							Ability to work with others					
Problem Analysis							Adaptability					
Decision making							Persuasiveness					
Delegation							Self-confidence					
Quantity of Work							Judgement					
Development of Personnel							Leadership					
Development of Quality Improvements							Creativity					

Section Three Highlight Performance Factors and particular strengths/weaknesses of employee which significantly affect Job Performance

Overall Performance Rating (Taking into account ratings given)

Prepared by: Signature ____________ Date ________ Position Title ____________

Section Four Comments by reviewing authority

HR Review Initial

Signature ____________ Date ________ Position Title ____________ Date

Section Five Supervisor's Notes on Counselling Interview

Signature ____________ Date ________ Position Title ____________

Section Six Employee's Reactions and Comment

Signature ____________ Date ________

Performance Classification

Outstanding performance is characterised by high ability which leaves little or nothing to be desired.

Personnel rated as such are those who regularly make significant contributions to the organisation which are above the requirements of their position. Unusual and challenging assignments are consistently well handled.

Excellent performance is marked by above-average ability, with little supervision required.

Satisfactory Plus performance indicates fully adequate ability, without the need for excessive supervision.

Personnel with this rating are able to give proper consideration to normal assignments, which are generally well-handled. They will meet the requirements of the position. '**Satisfactory plus**' performers may include those who lack the experience at their current level to demonstrate above-average ability.

Marginal performance is in instances where the ability demonstrated does not fully meet the requirements of the position, with excessive supervision and direction normally required.

Employees rated as such will show specific deficiencies in their performance which prevent them from performing at an acceptable level.

Unsatisfactory performance indicates an ability which falls clearly below the minimum requirements of the position.

'**Unsatisfactory**' performers will demonstrate marked deficiencies in most of the major aspects of their responsibilities, and considerable improvement is required to permit retention of the employee in the current position.

Personal Characteristic Ratings

1.- Needs considerable improvement - substantial improvement required to meet acceptable standards
2.- Needs improvement - some improvement required to meet acceptable standards
3.- Normal - meets acceptable standards
4.- Above normal - exceeds normally acceptable standards in most instances
5.- Exceptional - displays rare and unusual personal characteristics

4168B/1

Figure 9.3: Standard appraisal form

Behavioural incident methods

These concentrate on employee behaviour, which is measured against typical behaviour in each job, as defined by common **'critical incidents'** of successful and unsuccessful job behaviour reported by managers. The analysis is carried out for **key tasks**, which are identified as critical to success in the job and for which specific standards of performance *must* be reached. This makes scales highly relevant to job performance, and facilitates objective assessment because ratings are described in behavioural terms.

The behavioural equivalent of the graphic scale for a manager's key task of 'marketing initiative' might appear as follows.

Produces no new ideas for marketing. Appears apathetic to competitive challenge	Produces ideas when urged by head office. Ideas not clearly thought out nor enthusiastically applied	Produces ideas when urged by head office and gives full commitment to new programmes	Spontaneously generates new ideas for marketing and champions them through head office approval. Ideas related to identified needs and effective in practice

Figure 9.4: Critical incident scale

Results-orientated schemes

All the above techniques may be used with more or less results-orientated criteria. A wholly results-orientated approach sets out to review performance against specific targets and standards of performance, which are agreed in advance by a manager and subordinate together.

Key advantages of such an approach include the following.

(a) The subordinate is more involved in appraisal, and performance, because (s)he is able to evaluate progress in achieving clear, jointly-agreed measures.

(b) The manager is relieved of the 'critic' role and becomes more of a 'counsellor', jointly defining solutions to performance issues.

(c) Clear and known targets are beneficial in motivation, especially in maximising the effectiveness of financial incentives.

(d) The emphasis of appraisal becomes forward-looking (focusing on improvements and incentives), rather than purely retrospective.

Which of the above reporting methods would you consider:

(a) Fairest
(b) Most easily justified to the person being appraised
(c) Most suitable for determining performance pay awards?

We have raised the possibility that an employee might be involved in monitoring and evaluating his or her own performance. Let's look at some of the sources of assessment feedback other than the appraisee's immediate manager.

3.3 Sources of performance feedback

Organisations have begun to recognise that the employee's immediate manager is not the only (or necessarily the best) person to assess his or her performance. Other options include:

(a) The employee him or herself (self appraisal)
(b) Peers and co-workers (peer appraisal)
(c) Subordinates (upwards appraisal)
(d) A combination of sources (360 degree feedback).

Self-appraisal

Self-appraisal allows individuals to carry out a self-evaluation as a major input to the appraisal process.

The advantages of such an approach include the following.

(a) It **saves the manager time**, as employees identify the areas which are most relevant to the job and their relative strengths.

(b) It offers **increased responsibility** to the individual, which may improve motivation.

(c) It helps to integrate the goals of the individual with those of the organisation.

On the other hand, of course, people are often not the best judges of their own performance! They may deliberately over- (or under-)estimate their performance, in order to gain approval or reward – or to conform to group norms, say.

Upward appraisal

This is a notable modern trend, adopted in the UK by companies such as BP and British Airways, whereby the subordinates/team appraise their manager/leader.

The advantages of such an approach might be as follows.

(a) Subordinates tend to know their superior (particularly in the area of leadership skills) better than anyone.

(b) Multiple ratings (from a group of subordinates) have greater statistical validity than a single view.

(c) Upward appraisal encourages subordinates to give feedback and raise problems they may have with their boss, which otherwise would be too difficult or risky for them.

(d) It supports upward communication in general, which may have knock-on benefits for creativity, problem-solving and employee relations.

ACTIVITY 2 — 15 mins

Imagine you had to do an upward appraisal on your boss, parent or lecturer. Suggest the two major problems that might be experienced with upward appraisal

Customer appraisal

In some companies, part of the appraisal process may take the form of feedback from 'customers' (internal or external). This may be taken further into an influence on remuneration: at Rank-Xerox, for example, 30% of a manager's annual bonus is conditional upon satisfactory levels of customer feedback.

Feedback from customers (external and internal) is particularly valuable in:

(a) Encouraging and monitoring the customer care orientation of the organisation as a whole – in line with modern thinking about business processes, quality management and so on

(b) Showing a commitment to respond meaningfully to customer feedback

(c) Focusing on areas of an employee's performance that are recognised to have real impact on the business

(d) Encouraging the 'internal customer' concept within the organisation, as an aid to co-ordination.

360 degree feedback

360 degree feedback (also known as 'multi-rater instruments' and 'multi-source assessment') is the most radical recognition of multiple **stakeholders** in an individual's performance. As described by Peter Ward (who introduced the system at Tesco):

> Traditional performance measurement systems have rarely operated on more than one or two dimensions. However, 360-degree feedback is designed to enable all the stakeholders in a person's performance to comment and give feedback. This includes the current (and perhaps previous) boss (including temporary supervisors), peers and co-workers, subordinates and even external customers. Finally, the employee's own self-assessment is added and compared.

Information is usually collected (anonymously) through questionnaires, either on paper or online.

The advantages of 360 degree feedback are as follows.

(a) It offers the opportunity to build up a rounded picture of an employee's performance: the more relevant parties contribute, the more complete the picture.

(b) Multiple appraisers may reduce or at least balance the element of subjectivity which inevitably enters appraisal of one individual by another.

(c) 360 degree feedback increases the amount and openness of multi-directional task and performance-related communication in the organisation. This is particularly beneficial in the case of cross-functional communication, creating opportunities for improved integration, co-ordination and knowledge/ideas sharing.

(d) The extensive information-gathering process, and feedback from key performance areas and contacts (including customers and suppliers, where relevant), signals the seriousness with which appraisal is regarded by the organisation, reinforcing commitment to performance management and improvement.

The approach has a number of disadvantages, however.

(a) Subjectivity is not eliminated by the process: a number of subjective viewpoints is arguably no fairer than just one!

(b) There are still difficulties in gathering feedback from peers (fear of being 'disloyal' and subordinates (fear of reprisals).

(c) It is not easy to define performance criteria that will be meaningful and measurable for each appraiser, nor to weight the evaluations of the different appraisers, nor to reconcile or prioritise contradictory evaluations by different appraisers.

(d) There is extra organisation, paperwork and evaluation to be done, although this is now minimised by a range of software packages for the process, allowing computer or online 'form' filling, integration and reporting.

360 DEGREE APPRAISAL

W H Smith is often used as a case study for 360 degree appraisal. The company had operated upwards appraisal (covering some 1,200 managers) since 1990, but in 1996 it trialed a 360 degree system in its HR function.

Between eight and fifteen people filled in forms covering each manager's competences and personal objectives. The appraisers were asked to rate them on a scale of one to five and give anecdotal examples to support the marks (ie 'critical incidents'). The forms were sent to an independent third party for collating.

The company found that the system sharpened the developmental aspects of its appraisal meetings, but that it also caused a significant administration load. Many appraisers found it hard to comment on the individual manager's performance objectives, and to come up with anecdotal evidence for ratings.

When the system was rolled out to the IT function, the processing was done in-house (to save costs). When it was extended to the rest of the organisation, a computerised system was developed to reduce bureaucracy.

Having reported on an individual's performance – whether in a written narrative comment, or on a prepared appraisal form – a manager must discuss the content of the report with the individual concerned.

3.4 The appraisal interview

There are basically three ways of approaching appraisal interviews (Maier, 1958).

(a) The **tell and sell** method. The manager tells the subordinate how (s)he has been assessed, and then tries to 'sell' (gain acceptance of) the evaluation and any improvement plans. This requires unusual human relations skills, in order to convey feedback in a constructive manner, and to motivate behavioural change.

(b) The **tell and listen** method. The manager tells the subordinate how (s)he has been assessed, and then invites comments. The manager therefore no longer dominates the interview throughout, and there is greater opportunity for counselling as opposed to pure direction. The employee is encouraged to participate in the assessment and the development of improvement targets and methods. Change in the employee may not be the sole key to improvement, and the manager may receive helpful feedback about job design, methods, environment or supervision.

(c) The **problem-solving** approach. The manager abandons the role of critic altogether, and becomes a counsellor and helper. The discussion is centred not on assessment of past performance, but on future solutions to the employee's work problems. The employee is encouraged to recognise the problems, think solutions through, and commit to improvement. This approach is more involving and satisfying to the employee and may also stimulate creative problem-solving.

Many organisations waste the opportunity represented by appraisal for **upward communication**. If an organisation is development-focused, it should harness the aspirations and abilities of its employees by asking positive and thought-provoking questions such as: Could any changes be made in your job which might result in improved performance? Have you any skills, knowledge, or aptitudes which could be made better use of in the organisation?

3.5 Follow-up

After the appraisal interview, the manager may complete his or her report with an overall assessment and/or the jointly-reached conclusion of the interview, with recommendations for follow-up action. This may take the following forms.

(a) Informing appraisees of the results of the appraisal, if this has not been central to the review interview.

(b) Carrying out agreed actions on reward, training, problem-solving and so on.

(c) Monitoring the appraisee's progress and checking that (s)he has carried out agreed actions or improvements.

(d) Taking necessary steps to help the appraisee to attain improvement objectives, by guidance, providing feedback, upgrading equipment, altering work methods or whatever.

Some key cultural issues are involved in appraisal and its uses. Budhwar & Mellahi (2006), for example, highlight the inequitable application of promotion criteria in some Middle Eastern countries.

Nepotism, known usually as wasta, is perceived to be widespread in Saudi Arabia. Anecdotal evidence suggests that the promotion of people with tribal or family connections is very common. This is especially true in large and public sector organisations. This is a result of the tribal-based collectivist culture, where an individual's loyalty to the tribe, family and friends is valued over and above that to the organisation.

In theory, systematic appraisal schemes may seem fair to the individual and worthwhile for the organisation, but in practice the system often goes wrong. Let's see how, and what can be done.

4 Problems with appraisal schemes

4.1 Problems in practice

Lockett (1992) lists a number of reasons why appraisal may not always be effective in practice.

Appraisal barriers	Comment
Appraisal as confrontation	Many people use appraisals 'as a sort of show down, a good sorting out or a clearing of the air.' In this kind of climate: • There is little collaboration in problem solving. • The feedback is subjective (often hostile). • The feedback is badly delivered. • Appraisals are 'based on yesterday's performance not on the whole year'. • There is lack of attention to positive development potential.
Appraisal as judgement	The appraisal 'is seen as a one-sided process in which the manager acts as judge, jury and counsel for the prosecution'. This puts the subordinate on the defensive. Instead, the process of performance management 'needs to be jointly operated in order to retain the commitment and develop the self-awareness of the individual.'
Appraisal as chat	The appraisal is conducted as if it were a friendly chat 'without ... purpose or outcome ... Many managers, embarrassed by the need to give feedback and set stretching targets, reduce the appraisal to a few mumbled "well dones!" and leave the interview with a briefcase of unresolved issues.'
Appraisal as bureaucracy	Appraisal is a form-filling exercise, to satisfy the HR department. Its underlying purpose, improving individual and organisational performance, is forgotten.
Appraisal as unfinished business	Appraisal should be part of a continuing future-focused process of performance management, not a way of 'wrapping up' the past year's performance issues.

ACTIVITY 3 — 15 mins

What would you anticipate the effects of appraisal on employee motivation to be?

One of the problems with performance appraisal, viewed globally, is the extent to which 'subordinates' in some countries are prepared to participate actively in the exercise and especially in any face-to-face component for appraisal. In countries with strong hierarchical beliefs and a culture of deference to authority, an appraisal system designed more principally for more senior-subordinate relationships is likely to founder or become informally 'adapted' to fit the prevailing values. Many American companies have fallen foul of this difficulty when seeking to impose their appraisal processes worldwide – not just in the Asia Pacific region and Africa, but also in France and Germany.

4.2 Evaluating appraisal

The appraisal scheme should itself be assessed (and regularly re-assessed), according to the following general criteria.

(a) **Relevance**

- ☐ Does the system have a useful purpose, relevant to the needs of the organisation and the individual?
- ☐ Is the purpose clearly expressed and widely understood by all concerned, both appraisers and appraisees?
- ☐ Are the appraisal criteria relevant to the purposes of the system?

(b) **Fairness**

- ☐ Is there reasonable standardisation of criteria and objectivity throughout the organisation?
- ☐ Has attention been given to the potential for direct or indirect discrimination in the criteria and methods of appraisal?

(c) **Serious intent**

- ☐ Are managers committed to the system – or is it just something the HR department thrusts upon them?
- ☐ Who does the interviewing, and are they properly trained in interviewing and assessment techniques?
- ☐ Is reasonable time and attention given to the interviews – or is it a question of 'getting them over with'?
- ☐ Is there a genuine demonstrable link between performance and reward or opportunity for development?

(d) **Co-operation**

- ☐ Is the appraisal a participative, problem-solving activity – or a tool of management control?
- ☐ Is the appraisee given time and encouragement to prepare for the appraisal, so that (s)he can make a constructive contribution?
- ☐ Does a jointly-agreed, concrete conclusion emerge from the process?

(e) **Efficiency**

- ☐ Is all the above achieved with a justifiable investment of time and cost?

ACTIVITY 4 — 15 mins

Look up the procedures manual of your organisation, and read through the appraisal procedures – or ask someone about their organisation.

How effective are these appraisal procedures? Measure them against the criteria given above.

If you can get hold of an appraisal report form, have a go at filling one out for yourself – a good exercise in self-awareness!

In certain instances feedback and counselling are insufficient means to change an employee's performance, the first step is usually Performance Counselling.

5 Performance counselling

Where problems are identified in an individual's performance – whether through annual appraisal or on-going monitoring – a line manager may need to intervene.

5.1 Reasons for poor performance

Factors the manager may need to consider include:

(a) Job changes which have left the job-holder less suited for the work

(b) Personality factors or clashes with team members

(c) Factors outside the work situation (eg marital or financial problems)

(d) Problems with job design, work layout, management style and other factors outside the individual's own control.

5.2 Performance counselling process

In order to deal with the issue, the following four-step process could be implemented.

(a) Counsel the individual through a basic problem-solving process.

- (i) **The facts.** The manager should help the individual to accept and define the problem, through constructive feedback and supportive questioning.
- (ii) **The causes.** The individual and the manager should explore and agree on the causes of the problem. A collaborative, problem-solving orientation is needed.
- (iii) **The remedies.** The individual and the manager should explore and agree on the remedies to the problem.

(b) Ensure the individual understands the consequences of persistent poor performance, where relevant; this might involve invoking the firm's disciplinary procedures.

(c) Set and agree clear improvement targets and action plans and agree a period of time over which performance is expected to improve.

(d) Support the individual with agreed follow-up action: training, coaching, specialist counselling and so on.

Where performance counselling fails it maybe necessary to start disciplinary procedures. In these circumstances they would be for reasons of capability (as opposed to conduct). Ideally the instigation of disciplinary measures will have an immediate effect and the result will be improved employee performance. However where there is no improvement, starting disciplinary procedures will be necessary to eventually fairly terminate an employee's employment.

6 Discipline

Discipline can be considered as: 'a condition in an enterprise in which there is orderliness, in which the members of the enterprise behave sensibly and conduct themselves according to the standards of acceptable behaviour as related to the goals of the organisation'.

Discipline is often imposed in organisations through the definition of rules and standards of capability or conduct, and through the threat of sanctions for non-conformance (this is sometimes called 'negative' discipline, although it need not be applied in a negative way.) Disciplinary action may be **punitive** (punishing an offence), **deterrent** (warning people not to behave in that way) or **reformative** (ensuring that the behaviour will not happen again). Its goal is nevertheless always to improve the future performance or behaviour of the employee concerned, and other members of the organisation.

6.1 Types of disciplinary situations

There are many types of disciplinary situations which may require intervention. The most frequently occurring are:

(a) Defective and/or inadequate work performance
(b) Excessive absenteeism
(c) Repeated poor timekeeping
(d) Poor attitudes which influence the work of others or which reflect on the public image of the firm.

ACTIVITY 5 — 20 mins

Suggest five more reasons for management taking disciplinary action. (You might be able to draw on your own experience at work, school or college.)

In addition, managers might be confronted with disciplinary problems stemming from employee behaviour off the job: abuse of alcohol or drugs, or involvement in some form of law-breaking activity. If off-the-job conduct has an impact upon performance on the job, the manager must be prepared to deal with it

6.2 Model disciplinary procedure

Many enterprises have accepted the idea of **progressive discipline**, which provides for increasing severity of the penalty with each repeated offence: a bit like the yellow card (warning), red card (sent off) system used in football. The following are the suggested steps of progressive disciplinary action.

(a) **The informal talk**

The manager simply discusses with the employee his or her behaviour or performance in relation to the standards expected by the organisation, and tries to get a recognition that such behaviour or performance is unacceptable, with a commitment that it will not be repeated.

(b) **Oral warning or reprimand**

The manager emphasises the undesirability of repeated violations, and warns the offender that it could lead to more serious penalties.

(c) **Written or official warning**

A written warning is a formal matter, and becomes a permanent part of the employee's record. (It may also serve as evidence in case of protest against the later dismissal of a repeated offender.)

(d) **Suspension without pay**

Disciplinary lay-offs may extend over several days or weeks, and may only be used if provided for in the contract of employment.

(e) **Dismissal**

This should be reserved for the most serious offences. For the organisation it involves waste of a labour resource, and potential loss of morale in the work team.

Employers are required by Employment Tribunals to observe the non-statutory *ACAS* (Advisory, Conciliation and Arbitration Service) Code of Practice *Disciplinary & Grievance Procedures* 2009.

- Fairness and transparency are promoted by developing and using rules and procedures for handling disciplinary and grievance situations. These should be set down in writing, be specific and clear.
- Employment tribunals will take the size and resources of an employer into account, in deciding what measures are practicable. However, it is important to deal with issues fairly.
  - Employers and employees should raise and deal with issues promptly, without unreasonable delay.
  - Employers and employees should act consistently.
  - Employers should carry out any necessary investigations to establish the facts of the case.

- Employers should inform employees of the basis of the problem and give them an opportunity to put their case in response before any decisions are made.
- Employers should also allow employees to be accompanied at any formal disciplinary or grievance meeting.
- Employers should allow an employee to appeal against any formal decision made.

(ACAS, 2009)

How (a) accessible and (b) clear are the rules and policies of your college: do people really know what they are and are not supposed to do? Have a look at the student regulations. How easy is it to see them – or were you referred elsewhere? Are they well-indexed and cross-referenced, and in language that all students will understand?.

How (a) accessible and (b) clear are the disciplinary procedures? Who is responsible for discipline?

While the focus so far has been on management expressing their dissatisfaction with employee performance, employees are also able to express their dissatisfaction. One of the most common practices is absence from work. Short-term and frequent absence is a cause for concern. It maybe for entirely legitimate reasons, and so should always be handled sensitively, however its occurrence needs to be monitored and, where necessary, investigated.

7 Employee absence

7.1 Introduction

Employee absence is a significant concern to the employer, for a number of reasons:

1. The financial cost to an organisation. According to ACAS (the Advisory, Conciliation and Arbitration service in the UK), the average UK worker is absent from work for 8.4 days a year. This figure varies from one workplace to another but it adds up to an annual cost of £598 per employee.
2. The causes for sickness may indicate deeper problems within the organisation. Short-term sickness can often be an indicator of morale or stress problems within an organisation. Such problems can grow and lead to employee attrition which will in turn have a knock-on effect on an organisation being able to achieve its objectives.

Absence is normally identified as:

Short-term vs long-term

Aurthorised vs unauthorised

This chapter will focus on the **unauthorised** causes of absence, and both **short** and **long-term** absence.

Authorised absence is often covered by employment protection legislation, such as pregnancy, parental leave, redundancy preparation, trade union activities and time off for jury service etc, and so whilst it can impact an organisation's performance it can usually be prepared for and managed.

7.2 The cost of absence

Concern about organisational performance can be detrimentally affected by employee absence. The impact can occur as:

- Hiring, and paying for, **temporary replacement staff**
- **Missed deadlines** due to a lack of trained, experienced employees
- **Customer satisfaction levels** – service levels drop due to insufficient personnel to answer calls or meet requests
- **Low morale** among colleagues expected to take on extra responsibilities
- **Diminished reputation** with customers and potential employees, and even lost business.

7.3 Causes of absence

Rhodes and Steers (1990) developed a model for understanding absence behaviour and attendance motivation.

Attendance motivation	
Satisfaction with the job Factors that influence job satisfaction: • Job scope and level of responsibility and decision making • Role stress e.g. workload, hours • Size of work group • Immediate managers' work style • Strength of relationship with co-workers • Opportunity for promotion	**Pressure to attend** Factors that influence pressure to attend: • Likelihood of redundancies and ability to find new job • Incentives to attend e.g. attendance bonus • Group norms and impact on group if absent • Personal work ethic • Commitment to the organisation and level of engagement
Personal values and expectations However, job satisfaction is moderated by personal values and expectations. These are influenced by personality, personal characteristics and previous experience. These can change during the working lifetime. How well and closely the job matches the persons values and expectations. • Age • Sex • Length of service	**Ability to attend** However, pressure to attend maybe moderated by the employee's ability to attend. The employee maybe highly motivated to attend yet faces overwhelming barriers to do so. • Lack of transport • Family or domestic commitments • Illness

The Rhodes and Steers (1990) model focuses on the psychological factors that influence someone's desire to attend work. A CIPD study in 2007 identified the following causes of short and long-term absence. As can be seen the primary causes for manual workers are physical, whilst for non-manual these are attributed to a wider variety of causes.

Main causes of short-term absence	Main causes of long-term absence (more than 20 days)
Manual workers	
• Minor illnesses (cold, upset stomach) • Back pain • Musculo–skeletal injury • Home/family responsibilities • Stress • Recurring medical conditions	• Back pain • Musculo–skeletal injury • Acute medical condition • Stress • Operations and recovery • Mental health problem

Non-manual workers	
• Minor illnesses (cold, upset stomach) • Stress • Home/family responsibilities • Recurring medical conditions • Back pain • Musculo–skeletal injury	• Stress • Acute medical condition • Mental health problem • Operations and recovery • Minor illnesses (cold, upset stomach) • Recurring medical conditions

7.4 Managing absence

All organisations when faced with managing absence have to ensure that matters are treated fairly and without discrimination. It is also important that assumptions are not made as to the reasons or causes of absence. Many organisations therefore follow established procedures.

Absence procedure

An absence procedure should do the following.

(a) Require all employees to **notify their manager** as soon as possible on the first day of absence, giving as much information as possible about the nature and likely duration of the absence.

(b) Require all employees absent with prior consent to **complete an absence form** on their return to work.

(c) Require a **medical certificate** to be provided (where relevant) for absences of seven days or more.

In the UK, the Statement of Fitness for work 'or FIT' note is a medical statement issued by GPs since April 2010 - replacing the sick note. It aims to focus on what an employees is able to do at work, rather than what they cannot do.

(d) **Discuss absences** with employees and keep in touch with them, alerting them to the possibility of disciplinary action where appropriate.

(e) Ensure **access to medical information** and check this is up to date, prior to any disciplinary action being considered.

(f) Require the employee to notify management in the event of **infectious or dangerous illness** (so that other staff can be checked or warned).

(g) Look for **suitable alternative work** within the organisation for employees no longer able to perform their duties, and consider requests for flexible working where this might help.

(h) Check employees' **entitlements** to relevant benefits.

Where absence is found to be persistent or occurring more frequently than would normally be expected, organisations can instigate further procedures.

The CIPD identified the following tools for short-term absence:

Top six tools used	Top six most effective tools
• Return-to-work interviews • Disciplinary procedures • Line managers provided with sickness absence information • Trigger mechanisms to review absence • Line managers to take primary responsibility • Leave for family circumstances	• Return-to-work interviews • Trigger mechanisms to review absence • Disciplinary procedures • Restricting sick pay • Line managers to take primary responsibility • Line managers trained in absence management

And the following tools for long-term absence:

Top six tools used	Top six most effective tools
• Return-to-work interviews • Occupational Health involvement • Risk assessment to aid return to work after long-term absence • Line managers provided with sickness absence information • Trigger mechanisms to review absence • Flexible working	• Occupational Health involvement • Rehabilitation programmes • Flexible working • Return-to-work interviews • Restricting sick pay • Changing to working patterns or environment

The most popular of these is the return-to-work interview. The interview demonstrates:

- The organisation is actively monitoring sickness
- The organisation cares about its employees and when acceptable absence levels are breached it will seek to understand why
- Provides an opportunity to understand whether there are more deep-rooted causes for the employee's absence and whether the organisation can hep to resolve these .

Such interviews also serve as useful method of:

- Highlights to the employee that the employer is aware of when they have not been to work
- Convey messages as to how their absence impacts others i.e. sharing their workload
- Spell out future actions if current levels of absence continue.

ACAS in the publication Managing Attendance and Employee Turnover, include the following flow chart.

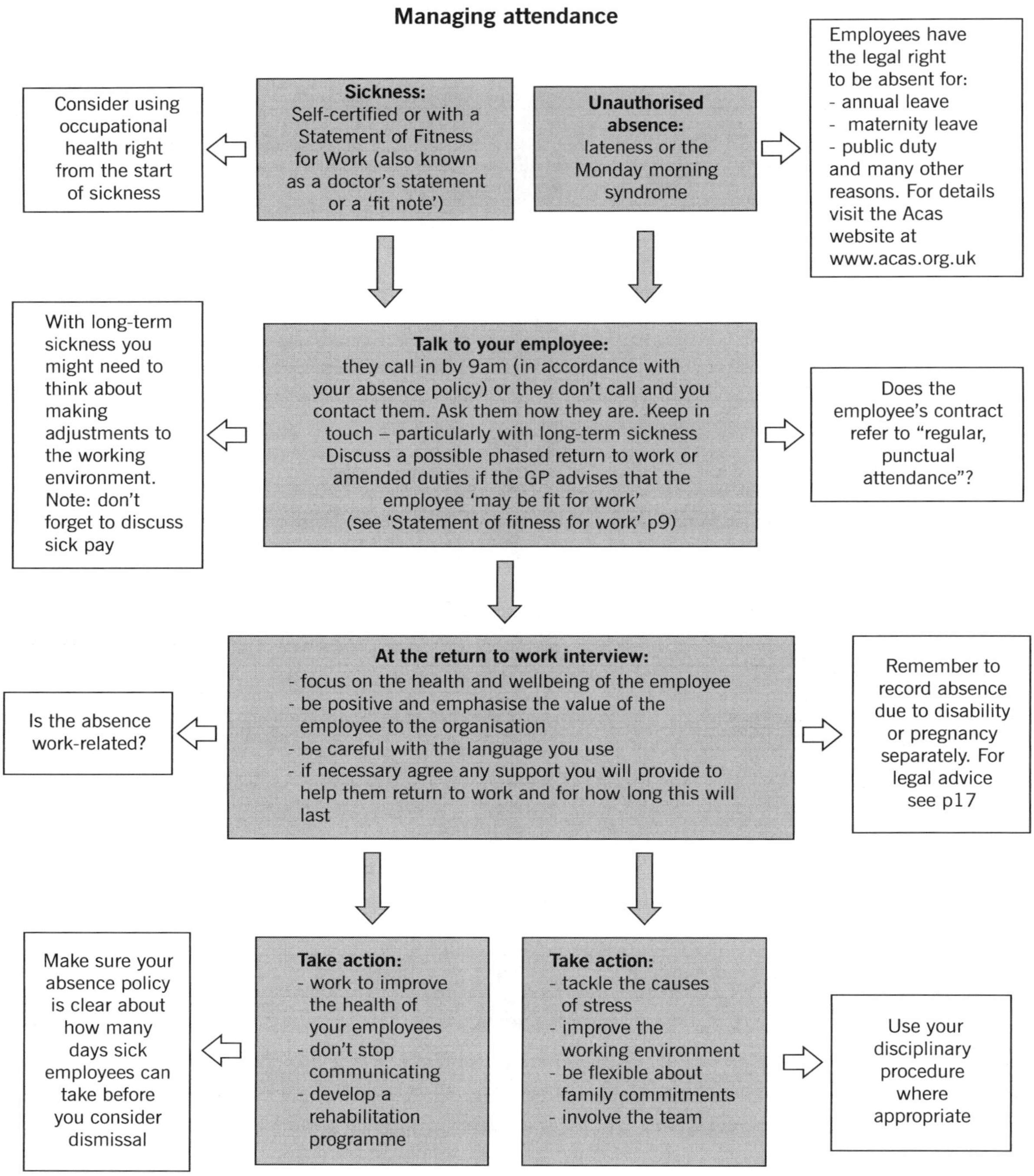

Figure 9.6: Managing attendance flow chart

What do you believe would be the most effective method of reducing absence at your place of work, or maybe for reducing absence amongst people attending your study course?

Do you believe it is better to incentivise people to attend with a reward for full attendance, or punish people when their absence is too high?.

ACTIVITY 6 20 mins

Mr P has been away sick for 4 weeks with stress. Given he has been away, and in order to make sure that no deadlines are missed or customer inquiries go unanswered, you have had to read his emails and look at his computer files. While doing this you have realised that work that he said was near completion is far from it; you have also realised that he is spending much of his day emailing colleagues and friends, in fact you wonder when he actually got any work done.

When he returned to work, considering his medical condition you decided not tackle him on day one. On the first day of his return he asked if he could take two weeks' holiday the following week. You refused saying that his work had built up a backlog and that other people were away and the office needed to be covered.

It's Monday morning of the following week and Mr P has just rung in sick. In order to distribute his work you go into his computer. You discover that he has bought tickets to go to Greece for the next two weeks.

What do you do?

IMPROVING ATTENDANCE IN AUSTRALIA

The State government of New South Wales, Australia, found a radical way of cutting 'sickies' (sick days) among ferry deckhands, with a deal which obliged fellow team members to work extra shifts – unpaid – to cover for absent colleagues! Introduced as part of a wages package, the agreement was based on the 'mateship concept', applying peer pressure within the team. A report by Morgan and Banks revealed that most Australians took an average of six days' sick leave a year – with 12.4% admitting none of their 'sickies' were genuine! The new State Transit deal, however, saw the average number of sick days per employee per year plunge from 13.13 to 5.56....

(Australian Daily Telegraph)

8 Medical information

8.1 Medical information when first hiring a new employee

Many employers when hiring new employees rely on a **self-completed questionnaire**, or **a brief examination** by the organisation's doctor or nurse in order to verify the individual's state of health.

They will often also want to submit existing employees to medical examination if the individual has been **absent for a long period** or has been **absent for short but frequent periods**. A validation process will not only help ascertain their fitness for future work, but help to make decisions in respect of transfer to less demanding work, to retire the employee on ill-health grounds (where often a pension entitlement is triggered), or where there are grounds for dismissal because of incapacity. Although it may be deemed reasonable for the employer to request the employee to undergo a medical examination, the prudent employer will include in the individual's **contract of employment** a **clause** which obliges the employee to submit to a medical examination at the employer's discretion.

It is important to emphasise, however, that whenever a prospective or existing employee is requested to attend for a medical examination this should be carefully explained to the individual. The individual may not wish to undergo such an examination, in which case the employer needs to be clear as to their process and terms of confidentiality. It would be a usual process that the doctor will only confirm whether the employee is fit to work and will provide no details of any existing medical conditions that are not relevant to the employment.

Where the prospective or existing employee does have a relevant medical condition the employer needs to ensure that they are not unlawfully discriminating against the individual if they take any action.

Chapter Roundup

- Performance management is a recent approach which emphasises *both* defining the knowledge, skills, behaviours and standards required to produce the desired results *and* the appraisal and comparison of performance against objectives for the purposes of on-going performance improvement. It is a forward-looking, on-going and collaborative approach.
- Performance appraisal is the process whereby an individual's performance is reviewed against previously agreed goals, and where new goals are agreed which will develop the individual and improve performance over the forthcoming review period.
- Trends in appraisal include: the use of behavioural and results-oriented appraisal criteria; the use of multiple sources of feedback; and a problem-solving approach to interviewing.
- Sources of performance information can come from self-appraisal, peer appraisal, upward appraisal or 360-degree feedback.
- Appraisal systems are far from perfect and need to be approached with caution and carefully assessed to ensure that they are achieving the intended objectives and not treating any groups unfairly.
- Where performance is seriously falling short of management expectations it is sometimes necessary to invoke disciplinary action.
- There is a recognised approach to conducting disciplinary action that is outlined in the ACAS code.
- Employees who are dissatisfied with their workplace may chose to express this by failing to attend work regularly. Additionally, of course, employees can be genuinely ill, sometimes with very serious illnesses.
- Absence is normally identified as short-term versus long-term; authorised versus unauthorised.
- When managing absence, organisations need to ensure that they establish sickness procedures and where employees do not comply with these that they follow fair and legally compliant policies.

Quick Quiz

1. When considering the topic of performance management, what does MbO stand for:
   - Management by Operationalisation
   - Management by Observation
   - Management by Objectives
2. What are the four key performance management stages?
3. What are the purposes of appraisal?
4. What bases or criteria of assessment might an appraisal system use?
5. What kinds of criticism might be levelled at appraisal schemes by a manager who thought they were a waste of time?
6. Reflecting the idea of progressive discipline, should an employee be dismissed for their first minor offence?
7. According to the ACAS Code of Practice and Disciplinary and Grievance Procedures 2009, should an employee be allowed to appeal against a decision, even if they admit to the offence?
8. Identify three costs that employee absence can incur.

9 Which of the following is not considered an effective method for reducing short-term absence?

- Return-to-work interviews
- Trigger mechanisms to review absence
- Disciplinary procedures
- Increasing sick pay

10 Identify one of the typical methods that medical information is obtained about a prospective employee before they commence employment.

Answers to Quick Quiz

1 Management by Objectives (para 1.3)

2 Preparation of performance agreements or contracts, preparation of performance/development plans; on-going management of performance; performance reviews. (para 1.4)

3 Identifying performance levels, improvements needed and promotion prospects; deciding on rewards; assessing team work and encouraging communication between manager and employee. (para 2.1)

4 You should have chosen job, role or competence descriptions; department plans; individually negotiated goals but not organisational share price as this cannot be influenced by employees alone (para 3.1)

5 The manager may say that he or she has better things to do with his or her time, that appraisals have no relevance to the job and there is no reliable follow-up action, and that they involve too much paperwork. (para 4.1)

6 No, progressive discipline provides for increasing severity of the penalty with each repeated offence (para 6.2)

7 Yes (para 6.2)

8 You could have chosen from: hiring, and paying for, temporary replacement staff; missed deadlines due to a lack of trained, experienced employees; customer satisfaction levels – service levels drop due to insufficient personnel; low morale among colleagues expected to take on extra responsibilities; diminished reputation with customers and potential employees (para 7.2)

9 Increasing sick pay (para 7.4)

10 A self-completed questionnaire, or a brief examination by a doctor or nurse. (para 8.1)

Answers to Activities

Activity 1

Disadvantages to the individual of not having an appraisal system include the following. The individual is not aware of progress or shortcomings, is unable to judge whether s/he would be considered for promotion, is unable to identify or correct weaknesses by training, and there is a lack of communication with the manager.

Activity 2

Problems with upward appraisal include fear of reprisals or vindictiveness (or extra form-processing). Some bosses in strong positions might feel able to refuse to act on results, even if a consensus of staff suggested that they should change their ways.

Activity 3

The effects of appraisal on motivation are a tricky issue.

(a) Feedback on performance is regarded as vital in motivation, because it enables an employee to make calculations about the amount of effort required in future to achieve objectives and rewards. Even negative feedback can have this effect – and is more likely to spur the employee on to post-appraisal action.

(b) Agreement of challenging but attainable targets for performance or improvement also motivates employees by clarifying goals and the value (and 'cost' in terms of effort) of incentives offered.

(c) A positive approach to appraisal allows employees to solve their work problems and apply creative thinking to their jobs.

However, people rarely react well to criticism – especially at work, where they may feel that their reward or even job security is on the line. In addition, much depends on the self-esteem of the appraisee. If s(he) has a high self-image, (s)he may be impervious to criticism. If s(he) has a low self-image, (s)he may be depressed rather than motivated by criticism.

Activity 4

The purpose of this is to develop your evaluation skills of appraisal systems and forms. Also when you complete a form, you may see that the questions or design is ambiguous and not obtaining the information sought.

Activity 5

Reasons for disciplinary action might include:

(a) Breaking rules regarding rest periods and other time schedules, such as leaving work to go home early

(b) Improper personal appearance or dress

(c) Breaking safety rules, such as failing to observe fire regulations, failing to wear protective clothing and so on

(d) Other violations of rules, regulations and procedures, such as smoking in a non-smoking office, or abuse of expenses claims

(e) Open insubordination: refusal to carry out a legitimate order

(f) Fighting, sexual harassment, racial or religious abuse or other forms of unacceptable conduct towards others.

Activity 6

As the employee has been off sick with stress you should approach this matter with caution. However the individual was clearly told that they could not go on holiday and all the evidence points to them having decided to ignore the reply to their request to go on holiday and lied about being absent due to sickness. This is a clear case of disregarding a instruction and then lying to be able to go on holiday.

Depending upon the organisation's disciplinary policy, upon their return to the office Mr P should seen and interviewed regarding the circumstances of why they ignored a refusal of their holiday request and why they lied about being sick. Assuming that the matter constitutes gross misconduct the employee should be suspended with pay. They would then be invited to a formal disciplinary hearing, and informed in the invitation letter that a potential outcome of the hearing is their dismissal from employment. The disciplinary hearing will need to determine the outcome. The probable outcome is that they will be dismissed for lying and ignoring a direct instruction i.e. you cannot take holiday next week.

Chapter 10

Standing out from the crowd

Throughout this study text we have considered the importance of the relationship of the employee or worker with their employing organisation. We have considered what has been necessary to ensure that the employees are committed and engaged, what environments are most conducive to achieving this and the role of line managers.

In this chapter we will consider how the organisation as a whole can package itself to be attractive to potential employees and continue to confirm the value of the relationship during employment; we will focus on the concepts of 'employer of choice', 'employer branding' and 'employee branding'.

Employer branding is important as it can provide an organisation with the competitive advantage to attract the best candidates. This idea is then developed further through the idea of employee branding whereby the employees internalise the values of the organisation they work for such that they live the values and so in turn confirm the customer's brand expectations of the organisation. This brand reinforcement then goes to enhance the brand even further.

As often happens in matters relating to Human Resources the terms of employer branding and employee branding are interchanged and the same topics can all be covered under the one heading. Indeed if you input any of the terms into search engines you will be provided with choices that relate to each. However this study text has delineated between them.

TOPIC LIST		LEARNING OUTCOMES
1	Competitive advantage	8.2
2	Employer of choice	2.3, 8.1, 8.3
3	Employer branding	2.3, 8.1, 8.3
4	The psychological contract	
5	Employee branding	8.1, 8.3
6	Branding in Action	8.3
7	The business case for employer branding	8.3

1 Competitive advantage

For organisations to achieve their strategic objectives they need people. The human resources they require may already be within the organisation; however they need to replace leavers, recruit a new quality of employee or simply increase the size of the workforce. With so many employing organisations in the market the challenge is how to make the organisation be seen and be more attractive than the competition.

Being seen can be very simply achieved by advertising the job and raising awareness only as and when required. The use of extraordinarily high salaries could have the desired effect, but the impact on budgets, internal equity and the unpredictable response of competitors makes this unattractive. By limiting awareness to occasional recruiting it lacks credibility to be considered a strategy and does not enjoy any lasting impact or effect.

Organisations may wish for greater resources to meet their strategic needs, there may be a shortage of skills on the market and they have a high volume need, they may wish to be highly selective in who they employee and so need high volumes of suitable applicants, they may wish to change or upgrade the types of people they employ and so need to alter their perception in the market. To achieve any of these they cannot rely on high-profile job advertising alone.

Organisations may aspire to reach a position where their reputation alone ensures that they have an over-abundance of suitably qualified applicants. In the early 2000s Accenture enjoyed a position where two-thirds of all graduates in the UK applied for their graduate scheme. Amongst the highest levels of graduate pay in the market, high quality training, interesting assignments, working with reputable clients and the kudos of working for Accenture all contributed to the organisation being able to be highly selective in who it chose to recruit.

ACTIVITY 1 30 mins

Identify an organisation that you immediately think of as being a highly reputable employer. List the reasons that have influenced your decision. How do you know of this organisation? What information have you seen that informed you about them?

2 Employer of choice

Employer of choice is an organisation whose employment practices and HR management practices give it an edge over its competitors in recruiting and retaining appropriately skilled employees and optimising their productivity.

The term Employer of Choice has become less prevalent over recent years, possibly because Employer Branding is seen to be its superior successor, or possibly because Employer Branding captures the imagination more with the current interest in 'brands'. Or alternatively there is the argument that Employer of Choice is not a term to describe a body of effort, but simply a turn of phrase to describe an outcome '...so you are this applicant's employer of choice'. For the purposes of this section becoming an Employer of Choice will be treated as a discernable and conscious decision.

Employer of Choice has the same intention as Employer Branding, to be **attractive** to candidates and once those candidates become employees to **retain** them.

What is probably different between Employer of Choice and Employee Branding is that organisations who seek to be Employers of Choice are creating an attractive employment experience to applicants when they actively engage in the process of considering the organisation and what it has to offer ie the candidate has to be actively seeking employment and consciously evaluating potential employers. Employer Branding can be a more passive process with future applicants having an increasing awareness of an employer without being in the market of job hunting.

To engage in an Employer of Choice campaign the organisation will determine that it wishes to be more attractive than other organisations - typically the **direct competitors**. To start the process requires an assessment of the current **strengths** and **weaknesses** of the organisation and the competition. Some strengths may already exist and simply reflect the organisation's culture eg a willingness to allow employees to be flexible, some may be conscious strategies eg to pay above market median. Where the weaknesses are identified eg inferior benefits package, this may need the development of a business case to obtain the necessary funds to improve what is on offer. For example the reviewing organisation may find that it is paying below the market median. To move its position to market median will require funds and a multi-year strategy to achieve the desired position. The review of the employment package, the working environment, supervisory style are all reviewed to ensure that they are attractive, or, when they are not, at least the weakness is known.

A **communications campaign** may then inform existing employees of the positive position. Recruiting managers will also be briefed to ensure they are able to 'sell' the organisation to applicants. Such messages may be communicated externally, typically within job adverts or maybe a press release to inform the market as to changes in a benefits plan.

3 Employer branding

Employer Branding An organisation's image as seen through the eyes of its workforce and potential hires; it conveys the organisation's culture as an employer describing the value proposition in terms of values, employee-employer relationship, culture and shared goals.

3.1 Introduction

> 'Your employer brand can be a magical combination of what your business values, offers and rewards – marrying what your brand promises outside with what your experience demands inside; what your business believes in and how you fundamentally respect the people who deliver your brand' (Sartain and Schumann 2006)

It has long been the case that certain employers had a good reputation and they could expect high numbers of well-qualified applicants. The innovative change that employer branding brought is the deliberate action of creating the perception of the organisation as a desirable place to work in the minds of the external labour market.

To be differentiated in the market and perceived of as a good organisation to work for, organisations have to do more than rely simply on word of mouth, they need to **actively engage** prospective applicants. Just as commercial organisations use marketing techniques to build a brand perception, so too organisations develop a brand as an employer. Compared to Employer of Choice, Employer Branding is a more proactive process, whereby the employer is actively seeking to imbed preconceptions about the organisation in candidates' minds.

It is also argued that to attract the types of candidates the organisation desires as future employees, then employer needs to think in the same way as companies wishing to attract people to their product. They need to create a **'brand'**. The brand image needs to target the types of potential employees the organisation believe will contribute to their long-term success.

Employer Brand is often linked with the ideas of Talent Management. Through Talent Management the organisation has identified the types of behaviour and traits it is looking for. Through careful branding it can seek to attract that person to work for them.

Additionally it can be regarded as a method for reducing recruitment costs. As the organisation builds its Employer Brand awareness less has to be spent on eye-catching advertising, more speculative applications will be received, and agencies will have no problem in persuading candidates to put themselves forward for consideration.

As we will see later in this chapter it is also argues that not only can a successful brand attract suitable employees it can also work to retain them through continuing to reinforce perception of the organisation through ongoing internal and external messaging. These messages remind employees of the strengths of their organisation and promote a sense of pride in their organisation. As Taylor (2010) explains:

> 'The primary audience may be potential recruits but existing staff hear and see the same messages. If they are well-designed, consistently articulated, rooted in reality and genuinely serve to differentiate the lived employment experience, in a positive way, the organisation's reputation in the eyes of its own staff should be enhanced.'

Further to this the employees also enjoy the halo effect of their employer; as acquaintances and friends realise which organisation they work for, they engage in conversation and take an active interest about their employment. Such encounters only reinforce the positive feelings about working for the organisation.

Can you recall being at a social event where someone explained who they worked for and people took an immediate interest e.g. luxury brand, high profile car manufacturer?

Likewise can you recall whether you know people who go out of their way to not tell people who they work for e.g. a 'bailed out' bank.

The CIPD identify the following benefits of employer branding:

- Less expensive, more effective recruitment i.e. attracting applicants with the right behaviours and cultural fit
- Better retention
- More fully joined-up employee communications
- Higher levels of employee engagement.

3.2 The importance of brand

Employer Branding is where the worlds of marketing and Human Resources converge. Much of the thinking related to Employer Branding relates to the concepts of organisational or corporate branding. For a brand to be powerful it has to be noticeable, relevant and resonant, and unique. A brand is a **'promise'** between the organisation and the stakeholder.

Usually for most people their perception of a brand comes from the advertising, quality of the product and their interaction with the organisation's employees.

A strong organisational brand sends a powerful message to not only customers, clients and other external stakeholders, but also existing and potential employees. The brand is an explicit promise between the stakeholders and the organisation, and so it is important that the **brand promise** is kept at all times.

To clarify what the brand stands for organisations will often define it with vision, values and strap lines e.g. 'Never knowingly undersold' (John Lewis), 'the ultimate driving machine' (BMW).

ACTIVITY 2 — 20 mins

McDonalds, the restaurant chain: what are the brand promises that you associate with this fast food chain?

All organisations have an employer brand, whether they actively seek to create one or not. There will be a perception amongst potential recruits as to what kind of organisation it is to work for. Organisations may wish to reinforce their current brand or overcome it; either way they will wish to market what 'employment' is like with them.

Whilst it is accepted that all organisations will have some level of external perception, how far they go to reinforce or overcome this depends on what they wish to achieve.

3.3 Recruitment branding

For some organisations, employer branding goes little further than 'recruitment branding', which restricts itself to conveying messages during recruitment exercises and in conjunction with vacancy advertising.

Some organisations develop this concept further. They focus on promoting the culture and the employment experience within the organisation and do not mention specific vacancies. Organisations do this when they have many vacancies and wish to attract applicants or are starting on an employer branding exercise.

The information that will be conveyed would make reference to:

- Career development
- Reward and recognition
- Employee involvement
- Work content and skills development
- Work environment

To reinforce the message, attention is given to ensure that there is alignment across the recruitment process, and so similar images, messages and values will be portrayed in:

- Job adverts
- The selection process
- Offer letter and other new joiner materials
- Employee handbook
- Induction and employee benefits materials

Other organisations not only wish to use employer branding to recruit employees but also to engage them and retain them.

ACTIVITY 3 — 30 mins

Obtain a number of national newspapers and professional journals. Find three examples of Employer Branding in recruitment

3.4 Creating an employer brand

Creating an employer brand draws upon many marketing techniques, Mitchell (2002) developed the following on selling the brand internally using marketing principles

Choosing the moment	Capitalise on the critical receptive contexts for change, usually when a fundamental revisiting of the values, direction and structure of the organisation is taking place.
Linking internal and external marketing	Ensuring alignment in the messages internally and externally, enabling employees to deliver on the external message and ensuring that the external message is a credible one with employees
Bringing the brand alive for employees	Creating an emotional connection between employees and the brand by drawing on key values and attitudes of different segments of the labour force and extensive participation in the design and roll-out of the employer branding messages

The five communication messages for selling brands are:

a Don't preach but listen to employees and use their language
b Emphasis on beliefs rather than intentions, because beliefs capture the brand and are more inspiring to employees
c Make the medium part of the message, using surprising and innovative media rather than traditional presentations
d Design material fit for purpose and easy to use
e Have fun

It is imperative however that the messages align to the organisational strategy, and so the process flow can operate as follows:

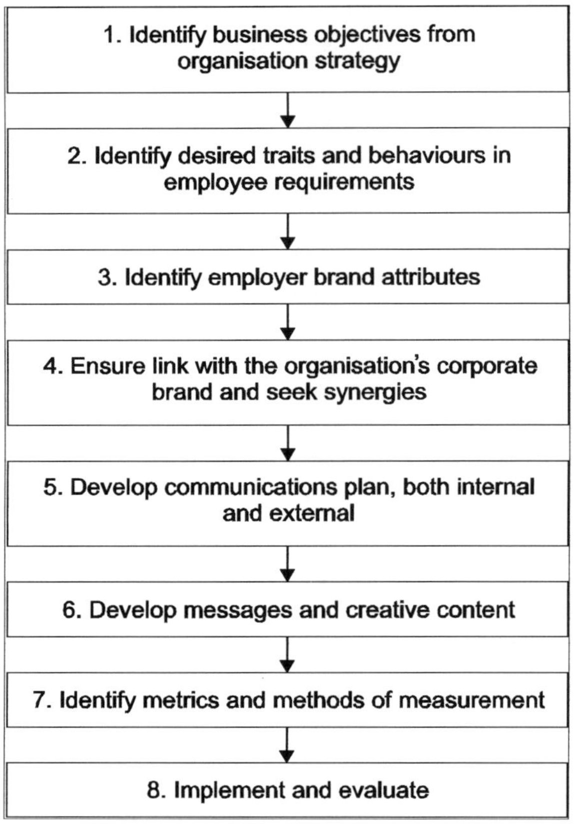

Figure 10.1 Recruitment Branding

Stage 3 is of particular importance, it is at this stage that the organisation discovers what is valued by the employees and how the organisation is different from the competition. This information can be discovered through workshops, employee surveys, focus groups and management interviews. Through this process the researcher tries to identify the symbolic meaning of what it means to work for that particular organisation. Lievens (2007) identifies five key sets of traits that are often discovered:

1 **Sincerity** (honest, sincere, friendly)
2 **Excitement** (trendy, spirited, innovative)
3 **Competence** (reliable, secure, successful)
4 **Sophisticated** (upper class, prestigious)
5 **Ruggedness** (masculine, tough)

For Stage 5, the CIPD identified the following potential communication channels.

External	Internal
• Website • Web-driving press advertising • Print-based advertising • HTML email • SMS text messaging • Online advertising on professional or special-interest sites • Presence on social networking websites • Digital TV • Webcasts and podcasts • Posters • Campus marketing • Classic PR • Guerrilla marketing • Employee referral programmes • Community-based initiatives and events	• Company intranet • Induction programme and materials • Online newsletter • Salary slip 'stuffers' • HTML email presentations and meetings • Awaydays and events • Welcome packs • Management conferences • Posters and displays • Team briefings • Teambuilding events • Appraisals and assessments

For Stage 7, the metrics suggested to measure the impact of the branding exercise:

- Number of job applications overall
- Number of speculative applications
- Number of applications in response to specific campaign
- Time it takes to fill vacancies
- Ratio of job offers to acceptance
- Number of employee referrals
- Staff retention levels
- Number of internal promotions

It is important to emphasise that an employer branding exercise cannot be launched in the simple belief that it will enhance the organisation. The brand has to deliver on the promise, consequently before claims are made it is important to ensure that these can be delivered in the workplace. These claims are easy if the employer already believes they have a good working environment and people simply need to be told about it. The challenge is far harder for an organisation trying to reinvent itself.

Work undertaken over last year to improve employer brand (%)	2011
Employee surveys	39
Developing online careers site	30
Introducing/extending flexible working/home working	24
Placement students	23
Graduate careers fairs	15
Working with charities	14
Corporate sponsorship	11
Introducing sabbaticals	3
Other	7
No action taken to improve employer brand	27

CIPD 2011

4 The psychological contract

4.1 Introduction

A **psychological contract** is the set of values that determines what an organisation expects of its employees, and what they expect of it, in the employment relationship.

It can be argued that the psychological contract is the **'promises'** between the employee and the employer. For the employee the promise includes such things as fair pay, fair and reasonable treatment, skills development and career development. For the employer it will be that the employee will apply their skills, they will not act against the interests of the organisation, they will develop and learn.

Sparrow and Cook (2003) identified four key aspects to psychological contracts:

1. They are subjective, unique and idiosyncratic:
   - They are based on the subjective expectations and perceptions of employees (and employers).
   - Every individual has their own interpretation of these expectations and perceptions.
   - They vary from one person and organisation to another.
2. They are **reciprocal**, they emerge in the context of a specific mutual employment relationship.
3. They are not objective 'facts', but based on **beliefs and expectations**. However because individuals may make decisions based on these beliefs and therefore are affected by the consequences of these decisions, they are 'real'.
4. They arise from beliefs and perceptions of **obligations** that, in the case of employees, are what they believe that they are entitled to as a consequence of **perceived promises** either explicit or implicit made by the employer.

The promises may arise in a number of ways, in written or spoken communications, for example mission statements, corporate social responsibility statement

EMPLOYER VALUES

Price Waterhouse Coopers has a statement called Doing the Right Thing - The PWC Way, within it is a section called Respecting Others:

- We treat our colleagues clients and others with whom we do business with respect, dignity, fairness and courtesy.
- We take pride in the diversity of our workforce and view it as a competitive advantage to be nurtured and expanded.
- We are committed to maintaining a work environment that is free from discrimination, harassment and retaliation.
- We try to balance work and private life, and help others to do the same.
- We invest in the ongoing enhancement of our skills and abilities.
- We provide a safe working environment for our people

Other 'promises' may come from how leaders act within the business; these are usually observed and maybe discussed between employees.

Can you think of a situation at a work place or education establishment where a leader in the organisation made a public statement (maybe unwittingly), and the audience perceived that as a 'promise' having been made?

Did the organisation keep to its 'promise'?

Whether the answer is yes or no, what were the longer-term consequences for the organisation?.

4.2 The 'old' and the 'new' psychological contract

During the 1990s, when globalisation was increasing and the economy was faltering, there was much discussion as to the demise of the 'old' psychological contract. The old contract was based on **hard work** and **loyalty** on the part of the employee and in return the employer would provide **job security** and **career prospects**. In its place came a more **transactional relationship**, one based on the employee expecting a good salary, skills development and interesting work. In return the employer would expect the employee to bring up-to-date skills and creativity; they would also not be burdened with managing employee expectations.

There is much debate as to whether the old contract really has declined. In this study text we have placed much emphasis on the value and importance of retaining skilled, talented and valued employees. Indeed in this chapter we are considering the value an organisation can gain through employing personnel who are aligned and 'living' their values, naturally they wish to retain such valued resources.

However as discussed in Chapters 2 and 4, many organisations have different types of workers within them and so some may have expectations of continuous service and career development, others may simply expect competitive pay for their skills. The growth in recent years of self–employed contractors and interim managers bears evidence that some people are choosing to work in a more fluid and mobile way.

4.3 The psychological contract and employer brand

There is an inevitable link between the psychological contract and an employer brand. The traditional thinking is that the psychological contract is developed over time as the employee is imbibed with the culture of an organisation. Their understanding of the culture will begin during the recruitment and selection processes and then will be developed further during employment. When engaging with employer branding, the organisation is making overt statements about what it is like to work in an organisation without the applicants having experienced this first hand. The brand 'promise' is still in effect, however in this situation the promise is held out to prospective employees, the organisation therefore has a lot to live up to. Many organisations observe a higher than average turnover in the first years of employment, what is sometimes referred to as the 'induction crisis'; breaking the brand promise should not be allowed to be a contributing factor.

The psychological contract is central to the employer branding process, in that the level to which organisations uphold the psychological contract influences employees' trust in their employers. **Trust** is highly important; where an organisation is unstructured and with few rules and policies, employees have to trust their employer. In other situations where there may be policies and procedures, employees have to trust their supervisor to do what they said they would do. The greater the level of trust between employee and employer, the stronger the relationship.

Even though the formation of the psychological contract is always an **individual process** and **unique** to each person, organisations can actively shape employee perceptions and so directly influence the development of how the psychological contract is built. However whilst employees have always developed preconceptions of an organisation through their recruitment and selection process, employer branding is more overt as to what the employee should expect. Therefore there is greater onus on the induction process and communications to ensure that the employee does not feel that their 'promise' has been broken. Just as we have seen how strong alignment can improve retention, the failure to meet expectations can have detrimental effects.

We looked in earlier chapters how the workforce is becoming increasingly diversified; an additional challenge is to provide an employer brand that will appeal to all.

5 Employee branding

Employee branding is the process by which employees internalise the desired brand image and are motivated to project the image to customers and other organizational constituents.
(Miles and Mangold 2004)

Employer branding is primarily focused on presenting an attractive proposition, primarily to the **recruitment market** but also to **internal employees**; and Employee Branding which is focused on **employees living the brand** and organisations truly differentiating themselves through the action of their employees. Discussions concerning internal branding are very similar to those relating to Employee Branding.

If a brand acts as a promise to the outside world, then to be effective it needs to be fully understood within the organisation. The employees have the ability to reinforce or break a brand through their actions. They are instrumental in both what is delivered and how it is delivered eg with a smile or a grimace. As customer satisfaction has been identified as one of the key drivers to organisation performance and profit (where applicable) it is imperative that employees provide and receive the best possible service to ensure that they in turn provide the best possible service to customers or clients. It is the employees who bring the brand to life. It is important therefore to ensure that there is **close alignment** between the employees and the brand values.

Some consultancy organisations talk about employers' 'signature' experiences that differentiate them from every other employer i.e. what the organisation does especially well; the odd or unique process that makes an organisation stand out in people's minds.

Discuss with your fellow students or friends any 'signature' experiences that you may have come across. How did it shape people's perception of the organisation?

There are two theories that can be considered in these circumstances.

Social identity theory (Ashford and Mael, 1989). This theory states that distinctive and compelling brand values act as a focal point to help employee identify with an organisation. Internal branding will help develop this identification.

Organisational identity theory suggests that employees who identify with an organisation will endeavour to accomplish the organisation's strategic interests. This can be developed further to suggest that employees feel more emotionally attached to an organisation if they accept the values.

ACTIVITY 4 — 15 mins

What are some of the risks that an Employee Branding strategy could encounter?

Organisations that wish to extract the maximum value from their Employer Branding expenditure look beyond simply conveying messages to the recruitment market. Organisations that are fully engaged in the process seek to not only ensure that the branding messages are **complementary internally** and **externally,** but also that employees have internalised the message and values and so 'live' them. For example, if one of the core values of the employer is excellent customer service, the HR process is not limited to ensuring customer-orientated people are recruited, all the HR processes must be aligned to supporting excellent service to its internal customers. Additionally all the internal messages about what is valued by the organisation are also aligned to the general organisational messages of excelling in customer service.

If a message is to be successfully transmitted internally the mission, values and brand image all have to be conveyed as well as the **behaviours** and **attitudes** that are expected from employees. Perhaps most importantly, the messages must be distributed **frequently** and **consistently** through all the communication channels available eg organisation newsletter, employee briefings, annual organisation review.

The Employee branding process enables the organisation to consistently deliver its desired brand image to customers, thereby solidifying a clear position in the minds of customers and employees alike.

Effective branding programmes have the potential to deliver several benefits.

1 They enable organisations and their products or services to be **effectively positioned** in the minds of customers and other organisational stakeholders.

2 **Increased employee satisfaction** and **reduced staff turnover,** as they feel highly aligned to organisation that reflects their values and are more likely to be emotionally and intellectually connected to it.

3 Higher levels of **customer satisfaction and loyalty**, and a favourable overall reputation because the desired brand image is being consistently reflected by employees.

In the 2010 Sunday Times Best Companies to Work for (Mid sized Companies) the top two organisations were not-for-profit. Why are not-for-profit organisations able to compete with commercial organisations in such surveys?.

The criteria used in the survey are reviewed in Chapter 8 section 9

If an organisation is to deliver its brand through its employees, this is greatly enhanced by the right type of employees being recruited in the first instance. This effectively takes us full circle to the importance of the Employer Brand in recruitment, and the first chapters of this study text regarding the importance of human resources planning. However it is also acknowledged that recruiting managers find it challenging to identify candidates whose values matched those of the organisation.

SUCCESSFUL EMPLOYEE BRANDING

Most notable among Nike employees are the Ekins (Ekin is Nike spelled backwards), most of them young men in their 20s, who travel the country advising retailers on technical matters. Donald Katz writes:

"Many of the Ekins wear a ritual tattoo shaped like a Nike Swoosh. The tattoos were mostly implanted during mass visits to tattoo parlors during the quadrennial Ekin gatherings held in various parts of the country. The Swoosh is usually applied to the calf, though some are drilled into skin near the groin, at the top of the leg." It shows when you are running in skimpy shorts.

The Swoosh, is, of course, the curved Nike symbol that is meant to invoke, onomatopoeically, the sound an Ekin (or any runner) makes when he passes someone.

Katz interviewed one Ekin named Duke Stump, who answered the common accusation that there is something too intense about a company that has its own tattoo: "It's a cult. But it's a great cult."

New York Times (1994)

Employee branding messages also serve to support the recruitment process. Where organisations have referral or 'bounty' schemes, such schemes rely upon employees to identify and recommend the organisation. This process is enhanced if the employees are able to articulate the brand values of the organisation to prospective employees and become advocates of what the organisation is trying to achieve.

If you are interested in the concept of 'employer brand', see:

CIPD 2009 Fact sheet on Employer Brand.

www.cipd.co.uk/subjects/corpstrtgy/empbrand

6 Branding in Action

It is widely recognised that Southwest Airlines has achieved the much sought-after position of their customer brand message being reinforced through their employees. Through a multi-faceted approach their employees have sufficiently internalised their brand image that they are motivated to project that image to customers and other stakeholders. Part of Southwest's success is that their 'corporate messages', for example excellent service, is ingrained within the employees. This in turn leads to employees seeing themselves the value in delivering excellent service, customers receiving it and so believe the brand promises of Southwest.

One of the key messages within Southwest is that customer service is highly valued. However rather than stating that the customer is the number one most important person, employees always come first, with customers a respected second. Southwest, however, expects its staff to extend customers the same level of warmth, respect, and responsiveness they themselves receive.

The centrality of customer service to the Southwest mission has motivated the company to identify key drivers of customer service and focus its operational efforts on those drivers. Thus, 'reliable, 'friendly, and 'low-priced' became the focus of Southwest's positioning strategy. Coining phrases to capture the spirit of what they are about is a key part of the strategy. However Southwest does not limit itself to coining phrases, it also describes how these would be delivered in terms of behaviours. This in turn leaves employees with no doubt as to what is expected.

Southwest's value system include fun, love (or 'luv' in Southwest's terminology), team spirit, and altruism (building warmth and respect among employees, customers, and the community). Supporting values that are deemed necessary to deliver Southwest's mission include profitability, cost-efficient operations, family, hard work, individuality, ownership, egalitarianism, commonsense, and simplicity.

Employees feel empowered to solve customer problems, and are extremely motivated to do what is in the best interest of customers, and know their efforts will be supported and rewarded. Their positive feelings and high levels of motivation, in turn, lead to operational efficiency.

Careful attention is paid to ensure the messages emanating from all organisational systems align with the company's mission, values, and desired brand image. The messages are issued almost daily with the emphasis on consistency. This alignment of messages across organisational message systems is a key success factor in Southwest's use of the employer branding process to position the organisation and its offerings in its customers' minds. The various message sources include:

- Messages from human resources and public relations clearly reinforce the organisation's commitment to its employees and to customer service. They also reinforce the values of fun, love, and teamwork. These themes are also clearly communicated in advertisements and other communications designed to attract employees to the organisation.
- If you are interested in the concept of 'employer brand', see: CIPD 2009 Fact sheet on Employer Brand. During recruitment, candidates are screened to ensure their attitudes and personal values are consistent with the organisation's values and desired brand image.
- The training and development programmes are designed to clarify and reinforce the behaviours and values sought. Southwest's own university enables employees to identify with the organisation, its culture, and its values, in addition to providing the basic knowledge and skills needed for the job. On-the-job training includes leadership, personal development, and the delivery of positively outrageous service.

- Compensation is also used; stock options and profit sharing create a sense of ownership in the company, as well as an incentive to excel within the organisation.
- The performance management system further reinforces the alignment between employee behaviours and organisational goals. Additionally attention is given to conveying the message that whilst it expects hard work and high levels of customer service, the company cares for them. The level of care is demonstrated by Southwest helping individual employees, financially or otherwise, in their times of need.
- Southwest also uses its public relations system to help employees internalise the company's mission and values. For example, Luv Lines (the company magazine) consistently reinforces corporate values. In one issue, it used the metaphor of geese migration to emphasise the importance of teamwork. In other instances, it relates stories that focus on how individual employees have performed heroic acts of customer service, or behaviours that are otherwise consistent with the company's values. The use of stories is a well-recognised technique in creating company culture.

Informal internal sources

Southwest recognises that the formation and reinforcement of appropriate employee behaviours is heavily influenced by organisational culture. The culture, in turn, influences and is influenced by the interactions that occur between co-workers. Clearly conscious of the risk of sub-cultures developing, Southwest organises and co-ordinates co-workers activities to ensure that the message is consistent with the company's mission and values.

The company's informal messages are, to some extent, formalised through its Culture Committees.

Culture Committees are established in each Southwest location, with the national committee made up of representatives from the local committees. They work to promote the Southwest culture and promote company values such as profitability, hardwork, low cost, love, and fun.

Informal messages are also communicated through the interactions of employees with their leaders. Great care is taken in selecting Southwest's first line supervisors, as they are key to the interaction between the company and the employee – Southwest's most important constituent. Supervisors are encouraged to make sure their communications consistently reflect the organisation's mission and values, as well as the underlying principles of integrity and caring for staff.

Southwest also operate an open door policy and invites employees to go to higher levels of management when they feel that the organisation's mission, values, and underlying principles are not being upheld by their immediate supervisors.

Formal external sources

Like most organisations, Southwest uses advertising to attract customers. However, it also uses advertising to communicate its mission and values to employees, and to demonstrate consistency between the messages delivered to customers and those delivered to staff. Southwest has been particularly successful at delivering parallel messages, which carry the same theme, regardless of the intended audience.

Informal external sources

Informal external messages often come in the form of customer feedback and word-of-mouth communications. At Southwest, word-of-mouth communication is widely understood, and is even addressed in the company's internal communications. Customer letters, both good and bad, are also widely shared with employees. When bad service events occur and are reported, the employee or employees involved are contacted for their insights into the cause of the problem, and possible solutions to prevent such a recurrence.

The psychological contract

The term 'covenant' is used frequently at Southwest, and is fairly synonymous with the term 'psychological contract'. Southwest's psychological contracts (i.e., covenant relationships) provide guidelines for employees regarding both what is expected from them and what they can expect in return.

This fulfilment of employees' psychological contracts has enabled the company to enjoy an enormous amount of trust on the part of its staff. It has also contributed to highly motivated workers who have strong drives to deliver the desired brand image to those with whom they come into contact.

The extent to which the psychological contracts of new Southwest employees have been upheld is assessed through a process that is, to some extent, formalised. Staff members who have been with the company nine months or less are randomly selected and invited to have lunch with senior Southwest executives.

The informal conversations surrounding these luncheons are intended to provide insight into just how well the new employees' expectations have been met (i.e., their psychological contracts have been upheld). Information is also sought regarding where the company may be going wrong and ways in which the recruitment, selection, training, and orientation processes may be improved.

Upholding employees' psychological contracts is crucial in obtaining a positive emotional connection that will motivate them to internalise and deliver on the desired brand image. Thus, developing employees' knowledge and understanding of the desired brand image while shaping and upholding their psychological contracts is key in the use of the employee branding process to position Southwest and its offerings in the minds of its customers.

Employee brand image

The employee brand image refers to the image employees project to those around them. The employee brand image is likely to be aligned with the desired company brand image when employees know and understand the desired brand image, and are sufficiently motivated to project it to others.

As discussed previously, Southwest takes a two-pronged approach to managing the employee brand image.

First, it develops employees' knowledge and understanding of the desired brand image by sending frequent and consistent messages. These messages communicate what behaviours are appropriate and what responses are suitable for a given situation.

Second, Southwest motivates its employees to deliver the desired brand image by ensuring their psychological contracts are upheld. The upholding of psychological contracts is rooted in the practice of consistently basing all organisational messages on the company's mission, values, and desired brand image.

Southwest's consistent message-sending (formal and informal, internal and external) aligns the employee brand image with the desired brand image, and effectively positions the organisation and its service offerings in the minds of its customers. This use of consistent messages to effectively manage the employee brand image is a key to Southwest's employee branding success.

Outcomes

Southwest enjoys the lowest employee turnover rate and the highest level of employee satisfaction in the industry. Their effective use of employee branding has also contributed to high levels of customer satisfaction.

The continuous monitoring of outcomes pertaining to such variables as employee satisfaction and turnover, customer satisfaction and loyalty, its reputation in the business community, and its internal performance metrics has enabled Southwest to build on its employee branding strengths and to identify and address employee branding problems while they are in their early stages. Thus, the continuous monitoring of outcomes is another key success factor in Southwest's use of the employee branding process to position the organization and its offerings in its customers' minds.

Miles and Mangold Business Horizons 2005

This study text has identified employer of choice, employer branding and employee branding as subtly different concepts; are there really distinguishable differences between them or could the subject be managed under one heading?.

7 The business case for employer branding

In this section we will consider the practice of creating a business case, and how this can be applied in a situation such as launching an Employer Brand. However developing a business case can be applied to any number of different situations, the approach is the same, the details of course will be different.

In this example we will assume that the Employer Branding initiative is going to be a relatively modest. It will include appointing a consultancy to identify and develop what makes the organisation unique. The consultancy will develop some messages and art work to convey the information both internally and externally. It will develop an internal campaign to convey to employees the organisation's people values and what they enjoy about working for the organisation. The consultancy will also review and amend all the information that goes to recruitment candidates to ensure that they receive coherent and congruent messages about the organisation and what they can expect from an employee.

7.1 Business case development

A **business case** is a justification for a project or particular course of action (such as an investment) to be undertaken.

General framework

A business case aims to convince decision makers within an organisation that an investment is justified. The case should provide a clear understanding of the implications of proceeding with the proposed investment.

Many organisations have a general framework under which all competing business cases are submitted. Using a standard framework enables comparisons to be made between different types of investments to be made more easily.

The **general** framework for business case development has three stages:

1	Where we are	W^2R	(the present)
2	Where we want to be	W^32B	(the future)
3	Going to get there	$(GT)^2$	(the plan)

Other material such as **justification** may also be included.

The syllabus includes a generic framework for business case development with three basic stages. We look at each of these stages in the table below – in the context of an investment in an Employer Brand initiative.

Stage		Comment
1	W^2R *(Where we are)* **The present**	A business case starts by establishing **what the current position is**. The person (or people) responsible for authorising the investment will use this information to develop an understanding as to why an Employer Brand initiative is being proposed. Documenting the current situation may involve analysis techniques such as interviews, observations, comparative market data and benchmarking against the competition. As the aim is to justify the investment in the context of the organisation's overall operations and strategy, an environmental analysis should also be undertaken (eg SWOT, PESTEL). The information compiled during this stage should provide a clear picture of where the organisation is at present.
2	$W^3 2B$ *(Where we want to be)* **The future**	This stage involves devising a statement of where the organisation would like to be (**the desired position**), and a justification (maybe a cost-benefit analysis) showing why the position described is desirable. The statement may be broken down into more detailed objectives for the investment. These objectives are in effect what the investment hopes to achieve (the benefits) – decision-makers can compare these against the cost when assessing the investment.
3	$(GT)^2$ *(Going to get there)* **The plan**	This stage focuses on the actual work that needs to be undertaken to move from W^2R to $W^3 2B$. A clear plan of exactly **what is involved in the project** should be developed.

7.2 Business case justification

Cost-benefit analysis is a key part of a business case justification. Cost-benefit analysis of an Employer Branding initiative is complicated by the fact that many of the cost elements are defined in terms of employee time and that benefits are **subjective** in nature e.g. 'organisation is more attractive to future applicants'.

All **costs** and **benefits** (financial, commercial, strategic etc.) should be considered. For example, the initiative may look expensive as a Human Resources only project and is not cost-effective when viewed in isolation. However the marketing department may believe that synergies can be gained in terms of raising overall brand awareness and so contribute to the benefits case. Alternatively the organisation may believe that the competition is gaining too much advantage when recruiting talent and so some action needs to be taken, so the question is 'what' action to take, rather than 'should' action be taken.

The most common method for evaluating the **financial viability** of a human resources project is the payback period.

> Payback period is the length of time a project will take to recoup the initial investment; in other words how long a project will take to pay for itself. The method is based on **cash flows** i.e. how much money will be absorbed from the organisation to fund the activity and how quickly will it be available again for alternate usage

An added complication is that the benefits or returns are not certain – there is a **risk** that the benefit will not eventuate. Probabilities can be assigned to different levels of return and an **expected value** of the return established.

7.3 The costs of the initiative

The costs of a new system will include costs in a number of different categories.

Cost	Example
Consultancy costs	This is the time cost for the consultants to conduct the interviews and focus groups, compile their report and the key findings regarding what makes the organisation unique
Art work and copy development costs	These include costs of the art work and copy to convert the finding into attractive and attention-grabbing pictures and words
Personnel costs	• Time of managers to be interviewed • Time of employees in focus groups
Operating costs	• Consumable materials, printing brochures, posters and other collateral to support initiative • Updating website • Briefing recruitment managers • Briefing recruitment agencies
Intangible costs	Some costs are harder to quantify. • 'Learning curve' – time of recruiting managers and HR to become familiar with the Employer Brand • Staff morale may suffer from changes seen as unnecessary • Investment opportunities forsaken – the opportunity cost

7.4 The benefits of the Employer Brand initiative

The benefits from a proposed initiative must also be evaluated. These consist of direct and indirect or intangible benefits.

Direct benefits

(a) Savings because no creative work is required for subsequent advertisements, it will now all be taken from the template created.

(b) Recruiting managers now have a template of how to communicate the benefits of working for the organisation, and so deliver a coherent and compelling message and improve conversion rate of interviewees to accepted offers.

(c) Less attrition as employees are more inclined to remain with organisation that values its employees. Less attrition in turn leads to less recruitment.

Intangible benefits

Many of the benefits are **intangible**, or impossible to give a money value to.

(a) Greater attraction of high quality applicants and those who 'buy-in' to the organisation's values

(b) Improved long-term retention of new employees who are aligned with organisation's values

(c) Improved employee engagement as a result of working in an employee-valuing environment

(d) Recruitment agencies and industry recognise organisation is serious about employee attraction and retention

(e) More cohesive and co-ordinated approach to advertising vacancies, as now all have to fall within design parameters

The fact that so many of the benefits the Employer Brand provides are intangible means that it is difficult to construct a meaningful cost-benefit analysis. There are three possible approaches to dealing with this problem.

Approach	Comment
Calculate a value for the benefits	Estimate the worth of each of the intangible benefits and allocate an appropriate cash value. The problem with this approach is that realistically it is nothing more than guesswork.
Ignore the 'too intangible' benefits	Allocate a value to those intangible benefits that it is possible to estimate a realistic value for. Ignore the other intangible benefits. This approach will significantly undervalue the proposal.
Adopt a qualitative approach	Find a reasonable non-financial way of stating intangible benefits. For example employee engagement could be established through questionnaires – as could improved recruitment outcomes, and recruitment agency perception. The problems with this approach are: • Much of the information would only be available after the Employer Brand had been launched • Determining appropriate measures • Isolating the effect of the Employer Brand system from other factors e.g. employment market

7.5 Business case report

The business case should be presented to the decision makers in report format. The report should **summarise** the findings of the activities carried out under the stages of the general framework. If detailed analyses are included they should be added to the report as appendices.

The report should contain:

- An introduction stating the terms of reference
- An outline of the current position highlighting problem areas
- The relevant objectives from the organisation's People Plan
- A gap analysis of the current situation and where the organisation aspires to be
- Different options explored and a summary of the cost-benefit analyses
- A conclusion, and a recommended course of action.

Many initiatives that relate to People have many intangible benefits; what techniques or methods have you seen that have helped overcome this common problem?

7.6 Business cases for other Planning and Resourcing scenarios

The business cases discussed in the example above related to creating a case for Employer Branding, however the same approach can be taken for building a business case for any number of planning or resourcing situations for example:

- The purchase of a web based recruitment system so that applicants can apply directly online to the employer
- Outsourcing responsibility for recruitment to an agency
- The consolidation and centralisation of different recruitment activities within an organisation
- The appointment of a consultant to undertake a specialist piece of work.

In all such cases the approach will need to be the same, however in certain cases a strong financial case may be possible. For example the purchase of a web based recruitment system may produce a number of clear benefits:

- As applicants can apply directly there will be less reliance on using recruitment agencies, this could reduce fees paid per year by 40%.
- After a period of time the organisation will have built its own database of applicants. These applicants could be contacted directly when suitable vacancies arise in the future, reducing the recruitment period by two weeks.
- As applicants will be communicating directly with the employer, rather than through a third party, the applicant experience will be enhanced and so improve the employer brand within the market, leading to a 5% increase in future applicants.

Such benefits may make it easier to develop a more compelling case. The costs will of course be different and in such an example these would include:

- Purchasing the licence to use the system
- The maintenance contract for the system
- The time the IT department will need to spend understanding the system and the internet requirements and any implications it may have on the organisations other systems
- The time spent training the expert users on the system
- The time spend training the casual users on the system
- The time spent publicising and educating the internal stakeholders and external stakeholders as to how applicants will now apply to the organisation.

Each business case will be different and will need to be refined to suit the organisation and the challenges being faced. As many stakeholder should be consulted as possible. Consultation and detailed preparation are always prerequisites.

Chapter Roundup

- When there are multiple employers seeking to employ from a limited pool of applicants, employers need to take action to differentiate themselves, they need competitive advantage.
- Employer of Choice has evolved as a term describing an outcome rather than a bundle of activities to differentiate an employer. However to become an Employer of Choice the employer will usually engage in activities that stand out when compared to immediate peer group.
- Employer branding is the application of marketing techniques to human resources practices. The intent is to develop a positive association in the minds of potential applicants and current employees that the employer is a good place to work – an Employer of Choice.
- Successful Employer Branding is not only seen as beneficial in attracting and retaining employees but it can also be more cost-effective than multiple recruitment campaigns.
- The psychological contract is a non-written contract between the employee and employer. It expresses the expectations that both parties have of one another. It is argued that the contract has evolved with the changing economic periods, however employees often remain for long periods of their career and employers value long-serving employees.
- Employee Branding is the process whereby the employees 'live the brand' and project the brand through their actions and customer interactions.

Quick Quiz

1. Define Employer of Choice.
2. According to Taylor who is the primary audience for Employer Branding?
3. Which of the following is **not** a benefit of Employer Branding
    - Less expensive, more effective recruitment
    - Better retention
    - More fully joined-up employee communications
    - Less time spent managing employees
    - Higher levels of employee engagement
4. What is a brand?
5. What is the fourth step in the process of creating an Employer Brand?
6. How many traits to describe an organisation does Lievens identify?

    (a) 3
    (b) 4
    (c) 5
    (d) 6
7. According to the CIPD which is the least popular action taken (where action is taken) to improve employer brand?
8. During the 1990s how was the psychological contract perceived to change?
9. What does organisational identity theory suggest?
10. Identify two of the benefits of Employee Branding

Answers to Quick Quiz

1 An organisation whose employment practices and HR management practices give it an edge over its competitors in recruiting and retaining appropriately skilled employees and optimising their productivity (para 2)

2 Potential recruits (para 3.1)

3 Less time spent managing employees (para 3.1)

4 A brand is a 'promise' between the organisation and the customers, clients, employees and other stakeholders. (para 3.2)

5 Ensure link with organisation's corporate brand and seek synergies (para 3.4)

6 Five: Sincerity; Excitement; Competence; Sophisticated; Ruggedness (para 3.4)

7 Introducing Sabbaticals 3% (para 3.4)

8 Away from one in which the employee expected in return for hard work and loyalty, job security and career prospects to a more transactional relationship one based on the employee expecting a good salary, skills development and interesting work (para 4.2)

9 Organisational identity theory suggests that employees who identify with an organisation will endeavour to accomplish the organisation's strategic interests (para 5)

10 You could have identified:

- Enables organisations to be effectively positioned in the minds of customers
- Increased employee satisfaction and reduced staff turnover
- Higher levels of customer satisfaction and loyalty (para 5)

Answers to Activities

Activity 1

Example answer.

Sky Television, they sponsor a sport/activity that I am personally involved in. They perform well in the sport which is shown extensively on television, which indicates that they invest heavily and take the matter seriously.

I also notice in their advertising that they sponsor animal welfare projects, which demonstrates that they are environmentally conscious, which I approve of.

Their customer service vans are eye-catching, smart and visually appealing, I interpret this level of attention to detail and imagination being applied to all their work and activities.

I know someone who works for Sky and talking to them I know that they seek to implement current 'best practice' in their professional activities. They also have interesting and imaginative employee benefits. I interpret this as them being a leading-edge employer and one that is keen to invest in their employees and so their business.

Their television service is the market leader and the technology they employ and seek to innovate indicates that they are at the forefront of their industry.

I know from seeing the news that Murdoch wanted to acquire them as they are profitable and cash rich. High profits and plenty of cash indicates that they are successful.

Activity 2

The most universally recognised brand promise of McDonalds is that anywhere in the world you can order one of the standard food items e.g. Big Mac, and it will be prepared and taste exactly the same. You can also be confident the price will be reasonable, relative to the local market.

However upon investigation of their website you will see:

- They source food from the local country, they follow the codes of animal welfare and sustainability.
- They endeavour to support the local country economy.
- They work to be environmentally conscious as possible.
- They contribute to their local community through litter collection, investment in sports and charitable actions e.g. Ronald McDonald House Charities.

Activity 3

This activity is for your own development and information. Hopefully you found information and examples with:

- Inclusion of awards logos to demonstrate professional excellence or industry recognition
- Descriptions of what it is like to work for the organisation rather than the job itself
- Descriptions of the organisation's strategy, mission or values, with almost only a cursory mention of the positions that are being recruited for.

Activity 4

In Chapter 4 we discussed the merits of having a diverse workforce; the risk for an Employee Branding strategy is that through the search to find the person who fits the 'employee template' is of a certain type and consequently diversity is dispensed with. Additionally this type of person may be a typical gender, age, race etc and consequently may risk also being unlawful.

A second risk is that the organisation recruits a certain type of person aligned to the brand values; if the organisation changes strategy its workforce will not necessarily be predisposed to those brand values.

Finally it is very difficult to recruit people according to their predisposition to values, and the organisation could invest large amounts of time and money not fully certain it knows how to identify the competences and values sought.

Bibliography

Armstrong, M (2003), *A Handbook of Human Resource Management Practice* (9th edition). London: Kogan Page

Armstrong, M (2009) *Armstrong's Handbook of Human Resource Management Practice* (11th edition). London: Kogan Page

Atkinson, J (1984) 'Manpower strategies for flexible organisations' in *Personnel Management,* August

Barker, M., and Shepherd, S (2007) 'Case Study: Royal Mail Group' in *InsideKnowledge*, January

Bratton, J. and Gold, J (2007) *Human Resource Management: Theory and Practice* (4th ed). Basingstoke: Palgrave Macmillan

Bridges, W (1995) *Jobshift: How to Prosper in a Workplace Without Jobs*. London: Nicholas Brealey Publishing

Connock, S (1991) *HR Vision: Managing a Quality Workforce*. London: Institute of Personnel Management

Cuming, M. W (1993) *The Theory and Practice of Personnel Management*. Oxford: Butterworth-Heinemann

Gennard, J. and Judge, G (2005) *Employee Relations* (4th ed). London: CIPD

Graham, H. and Bennett, R (1998) *Human Resources Management* (9th edition). Harlow: Pearson Education

Hargreaves, P. and Jarvis, P (2000) *Human Resource Development Handbook.* London: Kogan Page

Hofstede, G (1910) *Cultures & Organisations.* London: McGraw Hill

Hofstede, G (1984) *Culture's Consequences*. Beverly Hills: Sage

Kane, R. and Stanton, S (1994) 'Human Resource Planning in a Changing Environment.' In A. Nankervis and R. Compton (eds) *Readings in Strategic Human Resource Management*. Melbourne: Thomas Nelson

Liff, S (2000) 'Manpower or human resource planning: what's in a name?' In S. Bach and K. Sisson (eds) *Personnel Management: A Comprehensive Guide to Personnel Management* (3rd ed). Oxford: Blackwell

Livy, Bryan (1988) *Corporate Personnel Management*. London: Pitman

Lockett, J (1992) *Effective Performance Management*. London: Kogan Page

Maier, N (1958) *The appraisal interview*. New York: Wiley

Marchington, M. J., Goodman, J., Wilkinson A., and Ackers P (1992) 'New Developments in Employee Involvement', Employment Department Research Paper No. 2

Marchington, M. and Wilkinson, A (2008) *Human Resource Management at Work: People Management and Development*. London: CIPD

Marchington, M., Wilkinson, A., Ackers, P., and Dundon, T (2001) *Management Choice and Employee Voice.* London: CIPD

Munro-Fraser, J (1971) *Psychology: General, Industrial, Social*. London: Pitman

Pedler, M. et al (1991) *The Learning Company. A strategy for sustainable development*. London: McGraw-Hill

Plumbley, P (1991) *Recruitment and Selection*. Worcester: Billing and Sons

Rhodes, S. and Steers, R.M (1990) *Managing Employee Absenteeism*. New York: Addison- Wesley Publishing Company

Rodger, A (1970) *The Seven Point Plan*. London: National Institute for Industrial Psychology

Sartain, L. and Schumann, M (2006) *Brand From the Inside: Eight Essentials to Emotionally Connect Your Employees to Your Business.* San Francisco: John Wiley and Sons

Taylor, S (2010) *Resourcing and Talent Management* (5th ed). London: CIPD

Torrington, D, Hall, L. and Taylor, S (2002) *Human Resource Management* (5th ed). London: Pearson Education

Torrington, D., Taylor, S., Hall, L. and Atkinson, C (2011) *Human Resource Management*. Harlow: Financial Times/Prentice Hall

Whetten, D. and Cameron, K (2002) *Developing Management Skills* (5th ed). New Jersey: Prentice Hall

Index